Managing and Caring for Your Heavenly Tribe

"You need to fulfill the mission of the second creator who can multiply God's Word. In other words, you need to become multipliers of the Word, multipliers of life, and multipliers of substance. Only when you can do so and unite as one centering on love, will you be able to attend God eternally."

[*Sermons of the Rev. Sun Myung Moon*, 3-329]

Heavenly Tribal Messiah Collection 4

| MANAGEMENT · CARE |

Managing and Caring for Your Heavenly Tribe

Heavenly Tribal Messiah Academy

PREFACE

Every person is a microcosm of the universe. That means each of us is a mini-universe who stands in front of the great universe. We get the elements and strength we need to grow and develop from a pipeline that connects us to the great universe. Thus, we have a relationship of object partner to the great universe. There are universal rules and principles that govern our life and our relation to the universe.

The sun rotates, and the earth and the other planets also rotate as they revolve around the sun. Just as the universe is kept in balance by the rotation and orbits of the heavenly bodies, the animals and plants, and even people, need to keep balance through the rotation and orbits of their relationships with each other.

In the human world, rotation means controlling ourselves well. This means being able to move the body freely, while we live with the conscientious mind that controls the actions of the body. And a life of revolving means giving and receiving with our counterparts while rotating in the proper direction. The energy that we get from revolving creates the power to rotate.

In a similar fashion, our work as a heavenly tribal messiah is interconnected with the story of our life, and they rotate together. While the sun rotates, it also keeps the entire galaxy in order through its interaction with all the planets. And you, as a heavenly tribal messiah, must bring order and organization to everyone in your tribe. Each organization with Heavenly Parent at the center strives continuously to maintain the connection of its relationships. Through the energy gathered from the revolution in those relationships comes the power to rotate and then, from the energy gained by rotation, comes the power for revolution.

In this book we have sought to summarize True Parents' words on how heavenly tribal messiahs can organize their tribes, and facilitate rotation and revolution according to the order of creation.

To briefly introduce the contents of the book, Chapter 1 explains how to use the trinity structure to bring victory as a heavenly tribal messiah. If we examine the heavenly tribal messiahs who already have been victorious, we can see that they made good use of the trinity structure. This is the same pattern True Parents have used along their path. The book also explains the procedure for daily hyojeong reporting, which each family should practice. Next, in order to become a heavenly tribal messiah, we need to purify ourselves and our families so that we can move toward achieving perfection, and we must share home group (three-cycle) activities with our neighbors and all our tribe members.

Chapter 2 tells how to operate a home group. It introduces the three-cycle process that should be focused on in the home group. These cycles are building relationships with neighbors and the members of the tribe with jeongseong at the core, inviting them to attend the Blessing and live their lives as citizens of Cheon Il Guk: living lives of multiplication by becoming blessed families and heavenly tribal messiahs. This chapter also includes a more specific 16-week program.

Chapter 3 focuses on the role of a trinity of blessed families in supporting a heavenly tribal messiah, and how to multiply and organize a tribe. The role of Cheon Il Guk coaches in supporting this process also is explained.

Chapter 4 emphasizes the importance of preparing the soil in order to bring a fruitful harvest. In order to successfully gather a tribe, the first step is to organize trinity home group teams. Next comes the process of creating a tribal vision and mission statement that can be shared by the members of all the teams, so that they will be working together toward a shared goal. There is also a discussion of the importance of educational programs for tribe members, so that they can invest in supporting the heavenly tribal messiah victory.

Chapter 5 explains the significance of the HTM Leader School program for home group members. The HTM Leader School workshops teach about the importance of hyojeong and educate home group members with skills they need to become leaders. In order to work strategically to build Cheon Il Guk, it is important for everyone in the trinity to complete their individual and family four-position foundations. The workshops also teach about the strategy of creating a trinity for heavenly tribal messiah victory and the core vision of the three great blessings that should be shared by all the families in the trinity.

We describe the process of building a tribe based on trinities as the 3·3·3 strategy. It is our sincere hope that this book will assist you in achieving heavenly tribal messiah victory using the 3·3·3 strategy. The appendixes contain information on how this process has been used to bring victory in various countries.

We hope this book will be a valuable resource for blessed families as they strive to make one world of humankind centered on Heavenly Parent and True Parents as heavenly tribal messiahs.

February 1, 2018
Family Federation for World Peace and Unification
International Headquarters

CONTENTS

PREFACE 4

Introduction

Case 1: Coaching Interview by Professor Gil Young-hwan with Hajime Saito, Cheon Il Guk special emissary to Cambodia 17

Case 2: Coaching Interview by Professor Gil Young-hwan with FFWPU-Malaysia Vice President Lei Peng Kong 25

Chapter 1 How Do You Become a Heavenly Tribal Messiah?

1. Forming a Trinity 41
2. The Work of Large Group Family Federation Centers and Local Hoondok Family Groups 80
3. Family and Home Group Report Programs 91
4. Hyojeong Home Group Report Process 119

Chapter 2 How to Conduct Home Group Report Meetings

1. Understanding Home Group Report Meetings 161
2. Jeongseong Report Meetings—Understanding and Practice 174
3. The Relationship-Building Report Meeting— Understanding and Practice 186

4. The Invitation Report Meeting—Understanding and Practice ... 200
5. Multiplication Report Meeting—Understanding and Practice ... 210
6. Home Group 16-Week Program Week 222

Chapter 3   HTM Organization Management through Multiplication of Home Groups

1. What is a Hyojeong Home Group? 259
2. The Process of HTM Organization Management through Multiplication of Trinities 281
3. Organizational management relationship with HTM groups through large groups and home groups 290

Chapter 4   Building a Foundation for the Success of a Trinity

1. Promoting a Vision and Mission 299
2. Establishing a Vision and Mission 302

Chapter 5   The Trinity Home Group and HTM Leader School

1. Is It Good Enough Only with Home Groups? 329
2. Two Types of Leader School 333
3. The Three-Step Value Realization Process of HTM Leader School   337

Appendix

Appendix 1	Implementing Happy Day	351
Appendix 2	DISC Assessment: Getting to Know Each Other—A Tool for Healthy Home Groups	357
Appendix 3	Blueprint for HTM Leader School	364
Appendix 4	Roadmap for Multiplying a Home Group into a Hoondok Family Center	365
Appendix 5	The Six-Base System for Management of Member Growth	366
Appendix 6	Heavenly Tribal Messiah Practice Balance Coaching	368
Appendix 7	Education Testimony Report	370

Bibliography 389

A GLOSSARY OF KEY TERMS 392

Introduction

After witnessing what is going on in the mission field in Asia and Africa, which are truly on fire with blessings and grace, thirst and yearning, it is clear that a new culture has started blooming after Foundation Day. The amazing growth taking place in Asia and Africa is the expansion of the revolutionary hyojeong culture, which is burning brightly like a fire. Those who are waiting for the Blessing with the hope to become true families almost seem people who already have been blessed by Heaven. In particular, the active support for True Parents and cooperation with the Family Federation coming from highly placed government and state officials and enlightened local leaders bear witness to the presence of the pure hyojeong culture in the new world after Foundation Day.

Like hungry people waiting for food, people are yearning to meet True Parents, and they are filled with the thirst for the truth that FFWPU is teaching, and for the Blessing, pure love and hyojeong. They wish to hear more, to read more, and start to practice what they have learned. In light of this fact, the International Mission Headquarters has decided to support the tribal messiahs in the field and their new tribe members by producing books on the organization and management of the heavenly tribal messiah mission. Therefore, the book that you are holding is not a theoretical book but a practical one.

True Parents said that, in order to fulfill the mission of tribal messiah, we need to restore the Cain tribe as well as our own blood relatives, the Abel tribe. [*Cheon Seong Gyeong*, 9.2.2:3] When all is said and done, this means following the path walked by True Parents. This book is a practical book that will help us find that path.

First, this book is organized in a way intended to be suitable for heavenly messiah tribes in Asia and Africa, where more and more blessed families are sprouting up. It will help in organizing newly blessed tribe members and educating them to become regular members, while at the same time training and encouraging them to go on and become heavenly tribal messiahs in their own right.

Second, for members in such countries as Korea, Japan and the United States, where members are already settled in large groups, this book contains contents that will aid them in walking the path of heavenly tribal messiah, starting with the basic construction of the trinity all the way to practices for purification and growth toward perfection through the heart of hyojeong. Despite everything, there are many places where it is difficult even to get a group of three persons to grow and become twelve. People in such places should be coached constantly to form trinities. They will have to form home groups as trinities and heal and restore themselves first, after which they will be able to take the next step toward growth. To that end, they need to go through the process of holding hoondokhae and offering jeongseong (supreme loving devotion in both thought and action) and creating trinity home groups in their families and home groups. However, there are limitations in proposing consistent measures to be followed in all the mission countries around the world, due to the different environmental and cultural characteristics of each locality. Therefore, you should know in advance that you may need to adapt parts of the contents of this book to suit the local situations of different nations.

Here is one last word of advice from Rick Warren, the founder and senior pastor of the Saddleback Church in the United States and an authority on global church growth. People from all over the world come to study the strategies by which that church achieved its amazing growth. However, many groups fail to duplicate its success. Rick Warren responds simply that there are things that can be passed on and things that cannot be. First, the church's environment cannot be passed on. Second, its workers cannot be passed on. Third, other people cannot become Rick Warren. There is one thing that can be passed on: the principle of Saddleback.

What do you think? What could our readers take from this book? It contains examples and methods from various nations, but they may be completely different from the cultures and situations you are in. What will you do? Will you give up if this book does not match your situation and environment? Or will you study the contents until you understand the principle for multiplication and apply it to your own environment and culture?

This book will start out by introducing stories from the active mission field to help you better understand what the book is seeking to teach. It would be good to read what those stories tell us and take some time to think about them together. What follows are portions of coaching interviews held in Cambodia and Malaysia by Professor Gil Young-hwan during a tour he made of six strategic nations as the director of the Heavenly Tribal Messiah Academy. Professor Gil has been entrusted with the mission of educational itinerary worker for the Asia Pacific region.

The example from Cambodia illustrates how blessed families multiplied trinity home groups most remarkably in Battambang Province. The example from Malaysia is an instance of how the heavenly tribal messiah region was gradually expanded, centering on home groups in a large group center located in the capital, Kuala Lumpur.

Case 1: Coaching Interview by Professor Gil Young-hwan with Hajime Saito, Cheon Il Guk special emissary to Cambodia

Professor Gil: Cambodia seems to be one of the countries in Asia where heavenly tribal messiahs are most successful. What do you think is the reason for that?

Emissary Saito: According to Asian Regional President Yong Chung-Sik, the first thing to be done in pioneering a new region is to find John the Baptist figures. That is why, through the Asian Leadership Conferences (ALC) held once a month in Bangkok, I have been educating the governor, vice governor, mayors and magistrates of Battambang Province on the Divine Principle, True Parents' life course, and life of faith. This has motivated them. After the vice governor, mayors and magistrates attended the ALC workshops as VIPs, I continued develop relationships with them and finally succeeded in making them regular FFWPU members. This process was made possible through home groups and leadership workshops.

Professor Gil: Can you explain that in more detail?

Emissary Saito: When people listen to True Parents' words or the Divine Principle, they begin to develop a vision. The fastest and most straightforward method of implanting this vision in the hearts of VIPs was by forming relationships with them in small groups, that is, in home groups. While inspiring them with the vision, I also gave them the practical mission of concretely realizing that vision. Through home group activities, VIPs came to realize on their own accord that they need to form trinities with others who hold the same set of values as they do (becoming a true parent, true teacher and true owner).

The vice governor, mayors and magistrates earnestly yearn to become "true owners," because they are politicians, but even people who work for the government do not really know the way to become true owners. While holding home groups and HTM Leader School workshops in Cambodia, they began to see the process by which they could concretely realize their vision through Asian Leadership Conferences. We were able to develop this into a framework through which leaders of the society can be made into regular FFWPU members by forming trinities, that is, home groups, in which the vice governor, mayors and magistrates can form relationships easily and learn along with others in the same group.

Professor Gil: That is very persuasive. The fact is that knowing the contents is not enough. What was the driving force that enabled you to help them put into practice what they had learned?

Emissary Saito: That's a good question. After studying about home groups, I supported these leaders with the hope that their home groups would be not merely sustaining home groups but multiplying home groups. To drive them to become multiplying home groups, I toured the region earnestly to check up on and coach them. In particular, I placed the greatest emphasis on the use of the trinity structure in the home groups.

In Battambang Center, there is a trinity of three regular members who are mayors. There is also a mayor from a district next to Battambang. What they all have in common is that, after they formed their trinities, they took the initiative to create 13 strategic trinities under their trinity and continued expanding, to complete 430 couples as heavenly tribal messiahs.

Strategic trinities refer to multiplying home groups. While leading this kind of home group, those mayors automatically became regular members. Of course, there are other mayors who are not regular members but who still are connected to us. However, trinities that are sustaining home groups, only active enough to maintain themselves, that is, home groups that only hold meetings, cannot develop, and though they may create regular members and semi-members, there is a limitation in making those members into regular members.

From the standpoint of the Family Federation, sustaining a home group, even getting the members to participate in home group events and attend HTM Leader School, requires a great deal of patience and persistence from the center leader and group leader. If they have not experienced the vision and power of actively multiplying home groups, it is very difficult to guide them to grow.

The old concept of witnessing and education is another hindrance. In leading home groups, there must also be a John the Baptist home group, which must be a multiplying home group. Since the mayors were part of a multiplying home group, those mayors automatically became regular members, and the home groups under them were also able to give birth to regular members.

We are human beings with fallen nature, and so, though home groups can be maintained for a year, in order for them to continue to develop even after three years, their members need to undergo the experience of personally meeting God Himself. To be able to meet God, there must be spirit and truth within the home groups, and for the group members to be able to feel that spirit and truth, home groups must actively work with spirit and truth. My experience has taught me that home groups that bring spirit and truth can be created only when home groups and the HTM Leader School work together.

Professor Gil: You obviously have a clear goal and a strong will to pursue and fulfill it. As a result, you gathered a solid and sturdy trinity of mayors. You also chose a trinity to stand in the position of John the Baptist. In short, you have created a model trinity. Can you give any additional explanation on your experience with leadership education, and how it helped you achieve your purpose?

Emissary Saito: Home groups and the HTM Leader School are an integrated educational system. Particularly for heavenly tribal messiahs, if they wish to be successful, I believe they need to have a clear understanding of this system and be able to put it into practice.

The first level of leadership education is where the truth—True Parents' words and the Divine Principle—are taught. In the past, we thought that this was the entire goal of witnessing. With HTM Leader School, the element of participating in home groups while learning the Divine Principle is added, which gives the opportunity to experience spirit as well, so you encounter spirit and truth at the same time.

The second level of leadership education (HTM Leader School II) is where, through a home group, you can become an owner by engaging in the heavenly tribal messiah mission in earnest. When people reach this stage, they start to yearn to multiply. In a heavenly tribal messiah region, not only previously married couples but also unmarried candidates for the Blessing start to appear.

The center in Battambang is only four years old. All forty of the full-time CARP members currently working in Battambang come from heavenly tribal messiah home group regions. This was made possible thanks to the connection among the three levels of leadership training (HTM Leader School I, II, III). Having an educational system is similar to having a spiritual system. When there is multiplication, you can feel the spirit, and when you study the Word, you can feel the truth. In heavenly tribal messiah regions, small groups attend the HTM Leader School and are educated about developing into midsize groups through more intense workshops like the three-day, seven-day and 21-day workshops.

Professor Gil: That is wonderful conviction. If you have any tasks to be carried out in the future, what would they be? What are your thoughts on tackling those tasks?

Emissary Saito: I will take Battambang Province, where things are working out very well, as an example. The home groups and HTM Leader School are already well underway, and I am happy to say that we have lecturers who can teach the material. However, I believe that a unified curriculum should be developed so that unified content can be taught in all of the leadership courses. At present, Battambang Province is using the teaching materials used in the Bangkok Asian Leadership Conference, but the drawback is that the content developed for VIPs is difficult for people from rural areas

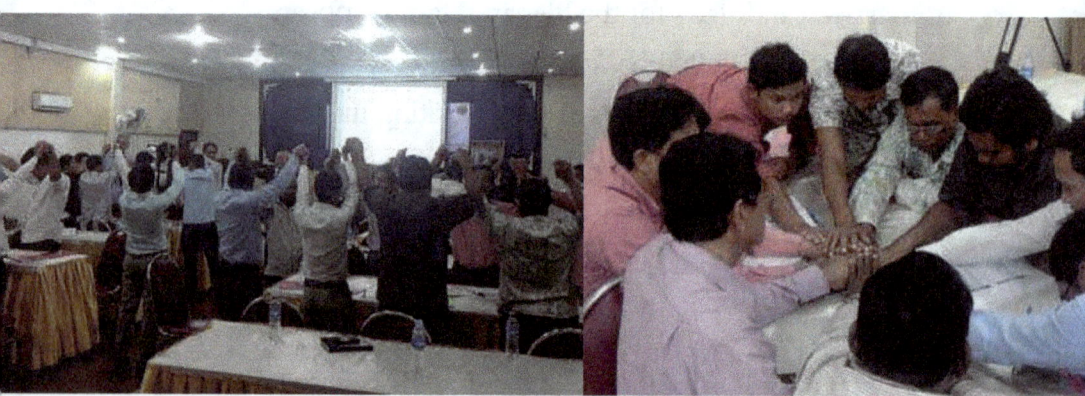

◣ Scenes from home groups and leader school workshops in Cambodia

who have never even attended school. There is a need to develop heavenly tribal messiah teaching materials that everyone can understand. Right now, our leadership trainers are giving Divine Principle lectures, because there has been an urgent need for them, but we still need a system in which the lecturers can check each other's content and quality, and we need a teacher training center where they can learn to teach properly. The 16-week curriculum used in home groups also contains elements that people who do not have a Christian background find difficult to understand, so there is a need to develop the curriculum further and make it more universal. Once all of this has been developed, we will need a large group FFWPU center. We also need to research leadership programs run by the large group centers. We have small, midsize and large groups, but a stronger connection, like that between the small to midsize groups, is needed; the large group system in Battambang is still rather weak. We need to develop the format of midsize group meetings and make efforts to put everything we have talked about

into operation in the heavenly tribal messiah regions.

Professor Gil: Thank you. To sum up your suggestions, it sounds like we need easier and more integrated teaching material for the HTM Leader Schools, an educational system for lecturers who teach there, and an operating model for large groups, which can function as the models for the home groups. Thank you so much for today's coaching interview. I could see True Parents reflected in your clear goal aimed at achieving your vision, and your hard work in the field, where it looked almost as if you were everywhere at once. Thank you.

Hajime Saito, Cheon Il Guk special emissary to Cambodia, has a dream. He wants to pioneer in Vietnam, which is still an untapped territory in terms of mission work. In the meantime, as his work in the field in Battambang Province, Cambodia, continues, that area is growing into an example of success in the heavenly tribal messiah mission. This is helping the divine fire of heavenly tribal messiahs to spread across the entire world. The HTM Academy at International Headquarters will address the concerns in his coaching interview with the aim that easier teaching materials for the leader schools centered on home groups will be published and distributed to all parts of the world as soon as possible.

Case 2: Coaching Interview by Professor Gil Young-hwan with FFWPU-Malaysia Vice President Lei Peng Kong

After HTM Leader School workshops were held three times in Malaysia, along with the fourth one, Professor Gil held a follow-up coaching workshop to see if those in Malaysia were implementing what they had been taught. The home groups in the country are still in the process of growing, centering on the capital, Kuala Lumpur. A characteristic of this place is that all home group leaders are practicing to the letter what they have learned through the workshop. The situation in Malaysia is a good reference for urban regions in locations like Korea, Japan, the United States and Europe, where active large group centers are already in place.

Professor Gil: What home groups have been most successful at witnessing in Malaysia, and what are their characteristics?

Vice President Lei: I will use the passion home groups of Kuala Lumpur, the capital of Malaysia, as an example. Members of those home groups are overflowing with the desire to witness to others after attending home group meetings. In the case of one housewife, she is quite busy taking her children to school and picking them up from school every day. However, she is delighted that this provides an opportunity for her to reach out to and invite others to events and meetings. Now she is reaching out excitedly to other parents at the school and is also beginning to reach out to others on Google.

In the past, when members witnessed to others, they brought their guests to the center right away. However, to be perfectly honest, statistics show that almost none of those guests remained after listening to the Word, the Divine Principle, at the center. The more people we brought to the center, the more people left, so our task of saving people was not successful. That is why I now tell the members not to bring their guests to the center right away, but rather to connect them to home groups first.

We have happy-day programs in our home groups, in which invited guests can cook or attend health seminars together and form friendships with one another. We set up this program to spend time with our invited guests and form stronger relationships with them before sending them to Divine Principle workshops, and we had amazing results. The guests who first had been cared for in home groups accepted what they learned at the workshop more easily, and some of them were even brought to tears at hearing the words of the

Divine Principle, which truly amazed and delighted me. I repented with all my heart as a leader, thinking to myself that perhaps the reason I had been unable to save many people was that I did not know of this process. If I had tried it, perhaps I could have saved them all. The fact is that, in the past, the center had many difficulties in bringing guests to accept the Divine Principle right away. After experiencing how this system was working, I began to advise members never to bring their guests to the center right away. It is similar to the way, when you are raising a child, you do not send the child to school right away, but nurture the child at home first. We experienced failures because we sent the guests to school right away and they found it too difficult.

These passion home groups are guiding many candidates through the home group program in a systematic manner. Though those guests have yet to join the Family Federation, I am aware that they

◤ Poster for a one-day "Happiness, Victory, Blessing" leadership course

are forming relationships of trust and good faith with those guests. What I saw is that what the Family Federation center ideally should be doing is being done even better within the home groups. Once I realized that home groups are, after all, small groups, I began to have more faith in them. Now I am confident that those home groups will grow even more when their members begin learning about the Divine Principle and True Parents' words through the Family Federation and right there in the home groups.

Professor Gil: Wow! Passion home groups sound exciting! It is really true that passion home groups are the same as small communities. What other things do you think are necessary for those home groups to continue having vibrant success?

Vice President Lei: We need to think about how we can lay the foundation upon which we can meet even more people. I am also wondering whether home group members should be educated more, so that they can give lectures and coach their guests better.

Professor Gil: Oh, really? So your first concern is for ways to meet more people, and the second point is that the capabilities of the members need to be enhanced. Is there anything else that needs to be done?

Vice President Lei: I met a massage master in order to be able to meet more people. That person helps our home groups by giving free classes on massage to home group members. Through him, we were able to bring together twenty to thirty guests. However, those

Peace Blessing Family Festival in Malaysia (December 17, 2017)

guests at present are only coming to receive massages, so I am thinking about how I can move them one step further by connecting them to the education programs in the home groups.

Professor Gil: Oh, I see. Do you have a plan to make them into healthy home group members?

Vice President Lei: Yes. I think that we need to offer even more jeongseong (devotion) for them and develop deeper relationships with them in order to create healthy home groups. That is what is needed most, and I believe that if we can do that, everything will turn out as we hope. We need to offer more in-depth jeongseong, with tears and longing.

Professor Gil: Oh, is that so? Though Malaysia may be a little slow in its growth, I do not think that is a negative thing, because it is my opinion that that time is being utilized to develop the capacity of home groups in Malaysia. Muscles grow stronger and bigger through training. If you try to develop your muscles all at once, problems will arise. Once their capacity is enhanced with time, I believe those home groups will go through another period of explosive growth. Thank you. [October 12, 2017]

After this coaching interview, a series of Blessing ceremonies were held in Kuala Lumpur home groups, including the passion groups. Though they were small-scale Blessing ceremonies, they will serve as a good example for raising 430 couples through home groups. Influenced by those home groups, there have been cases in which people from other Christian denominations, composed of Myanmar tribes residing in Malaysia, also received the Blessing with great joy. Once those people are taught about the home groups, truly amazing things will take place.

The contents within this book include methods that have been tried out and applied for more than 15 years in Korea, Japan, Russia, Asia and Africa. The book also describes actual situations—for instance, the example of 12 young Chinese couples who participated in the home group process while Professor Gil was teaching at Sun Moon University, as well as the methods he applied in the successful Blessing of 430 couples in Surin Province, Thailand, while he traveled throughout the Asia Pacific region. There are also examples from various other nations. In this book, only a small part of the home group development has been introduced. More detailed and concrete contents will be added later. The contents in this book correspond to the leadership training material taught in HTM Leader Schools I, II and III.

Chapter 1

How Do You Become a Heavenly Tribal Messiah?

Walking the Path Trodden by True Parents

To become a heavenly tribal messiah, we need to be standing on the path of individual perfection on which we can have true dominion over ourselves. We also need to have received the Blessing, formed a good family-level four-position foundation with Heavenly Parent, and then form a trinity centering on our family and build an unbreakable unity within that trinity. Then we must win to our side 12 persons who will give us a base of 12 families and then expand to 36, 72, 120, 430 or more families. This is the path to being a successful heavenly tribal messiah.

To state it very simply, a heavenly tribal messiah is a person who follows True Parents' method of strategically expanding the Blessing, starting from a central trinity. True Parents organized trinities to promote the multiplication of blessed families and at

[Figure 1-1] Strategy for Expanding Heavenly Parent's Cheon Il Guk

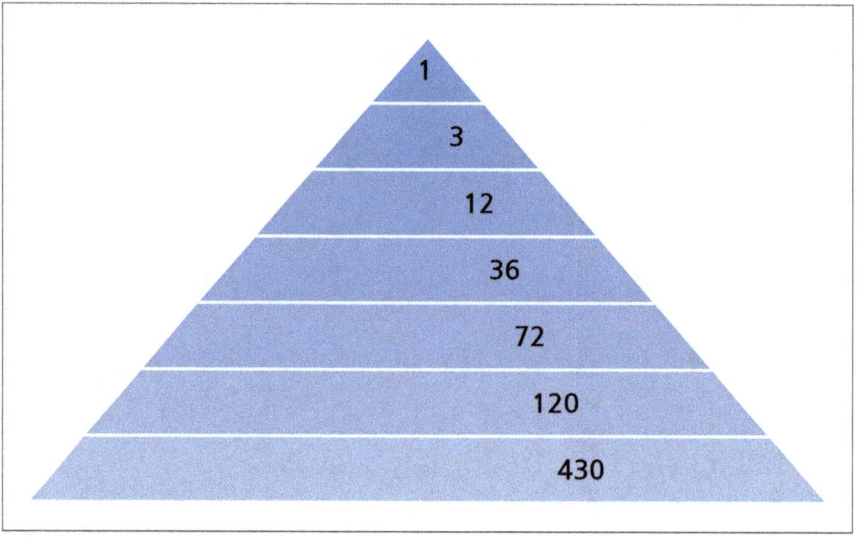

the same time educated and nurtured members through all kinds of workshops to build the leadership of the group. True Father spoke about this process, saying: "You need to organize a new Israel centering on your spiritual sons and daughters. Just as I found and established 36 couples, 72 couples and 120 couples centering on 12 couples, you must follow the exact same path." [CSG, 9.2.2:15]

True Father also said that, to achieve this, we need three spiritual children: "In order for you to stand in my stead based on the Principle, you need to create three spiritual sons and daughters, and expand them to become 12 sons and daughters." [CSG, 9.2.2:13]

In short, the most basic way to become a heavenly tribal messiah is to begin with three spiritual sons and daughters and multiply them to become 12. The fundamental basis of all of this is the trinity. From now on, a trinity will be referred to as a home group. A home group is defined as a small group in which a trinity has been organized and whose root is the hyojeong-filled heart of an individual or family. A trinity is a home group, and a home group is a trinity.

A Blueprint for Organizational Management by Heavenly Tribal Messiahs

To become a heavenly tribal messiah, we must be able to clearly see the blueprint that leads us toward our goal. It is similar to the bull's-eye on the target at which an archer aims when shooting an arrow. The heavenly tribal messiah archer must be able to clearly see his or her target, aim at it, and pull the bowstring accurately. Just as an archer's target identifies the goal, something that helps us to identify the path we need to follow, such as a photograph or a diagram, can be called a blueprint. This book presents the process by which a hoondok family group is created through trinity home groups, and that is the blueprint by which we can organize and manage the members of our tribe in order to become a successful heavenly tribal messiah.

The core of a heavenly tribal messiah's organizational management is the three-cycle report meeting in which members of the trinity or family come together to give reports. The three-cycle report meeting is a meeting held weekly or on another regular schedule in which members of the home group come together and give reports and offer jeongseong (supreme loving devotion in both thought and action). It is also where relationships develop among people, and where new guests are invited to participate, giving the group a way to bear fruit and multiply. The final element in operating a trinity or home group is the practical report meeting attended by all teams of the home group. When those report meetings are held regularly, new members can be born and nurtured. This is similar to the way a spiritual parent continuously nurtures and guides his or her spiritual children, with a clear purpose and plan.

Basically, this trinity group faithfully works to fulfill the three great blessings through the Word, and when their bodies and minds are united and the trinity is united, their light of hyojeong will shine forth brightly. Until the group can develop into a hoondok family group of 12 members, it continues to invite new guests through happy-day events or other invitational programs. Members form relationships with the guests and invite them again, thus bearing fruit that can be harvested. Learning about this organizational method and carrying it out correctly is the core of a heavenly tribal messiah's management of the tribe. To be able to do it correctly, we will need the support of Cheon Il Guk coaches.

When the above activities have been carried out for a while, members will be ready to attend leadership training, such as that offered in the three courses at the HTM Leader School. This step requires an HTM Leader School or another educational system operating within a nearby large group. What happens next to develop the tribe follows the steps in the diagram below. The development strategy in the blueprint below shows a strategy for starting with 12 members, and then multiplying them into further groups, so the tribe will continue to grow and we will be in sight of the path that leads to success as a heavenly tribal messiah. These ongoing activities are multiplied when the twelve members form their own trinities and begin their own work, and they all begin to multiply simultaneously, similar to how cells multiply in the body. If the home groups in the tribe are not multiplying, it means some part of this process is not being carried out correctly. Then the coach needs to step in and guide the process to ensure that management of the organization is carried out properly.

The diagram below shows the process by which a heavenly tribal messiah aspirant forms a trinity and multiplies it. It shows the home group expanding into a midsize group, and midsize groups coming together to grow into a large group. Once that takes place, one can become a successful heavenly tribal messiah.

This process can be explained as two tracks.

The first track covers the process from the formation of a trinity to the formation of a heavenly tribal messiah's large group. This is the basic method by which a heavenly tribal messiah first brings together three members and forms a home group, which then multiplies to become a midsize group and finally a large group.

The second track is an organizational management process by

[Figure 1-2] Roadmap for a Successful Heavenly Tribal Messiah

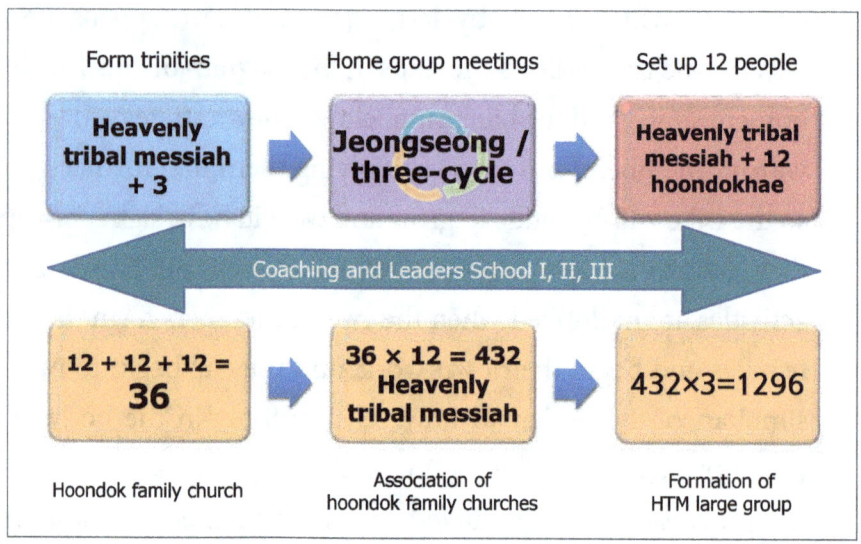

which members who have completed their course as a heavenly tribal messiah by gathering members and forming a large group can newly organize and educate the 430 or more blessed couples in the home groups who are not yet fully prepared. In this process, the successful heavenly tribal messiah chooses three couples, 12 couples and 36 couples from among the 430 or more couples who already have received the Blessing. The chosen 36 couples shoulder the responsibility of leading 12 couples each. The fact that coaching and HTM Leader Schools I, II and III have been placed in the middle of these two tracks shows that the educational process of nurturing home groups and leaders is integrated. From now on, this textbook will explain that process centering on these two tracks.

Forming a Trinity

There are many methods for organizing a hoondok family group of 12 people, using trinities. We can divide them into groups according to our experience or ideas about what will work well. Or we can set our goals and vision first and construct the teams in a way that is related to our goals. Moreover, another method is following True Parents' paths.

① General method of forming a team

With this method a witnessing leader organizes one team by choosing three persons from the existing large group who have similar attitudes and approaches to the mission. This method aims to gather people who will offer jeongseong to make a base for witnessing without any particular attention to position or organizational concerns. This can be the easiest way to organize a team. However, it often happens that the first two persons are easy to find, but finding the last person is sometimes difficult, since it may be difficult to unite the mindsets of three persons.

Here, the problem often turns out to be that the three persons chosen are already busy with responsibilities in the large group or have little time available due to other individual commitments, so it can be difficult to schedule meetings. Also, when somebody who is already responsible for important tasks engages with heavenly tribal messiah work, it is often difficult to find time to concentrate on it. In such cases, the heavenly tribal messiah activities suffer. In order to successfully conduct meetings, it is very important to develop a personal passion for the mission, take time to offer prayers, and make good true-love relationships with the witnessing guests. If you have three persons to start with, the rest of the 12 persons can be recruited from friends or relatives, or through street witnessing. Although this method is workable to grow from three to 12 persons, there is a limit to the extent it can support the greater multiplication of the tribe, because generally people practice witnessing activities based on the experiences they had when they were witnessed to. Generally, this gives only a limited selection of witnessing methods, which have been widely used by many of our members.

② Forming a team based on an organized system

This is a method to organize a team for witnessing and attracting new members through a specific witnessing system. What happens if a new member enters through an organized systematic witnessing method? The members who have experienced the system can bring more members by applying the same system that they are familiar with because of their own experience. This is called systematic witnessing. However, the drawback is that using this method may become habitual or mechanical. It often feels like a fresh method at first, but it ceases to be stimulating to the witnessing team as it is repeated many times. Using a systematic method is a proven way of growing an organization; however, the system must be backed up with spirituality and jeongseong.

③ Creating a trinity using True Parents' method

True Parents' method of organizing teams is based on the Principle of Creation. It is conducted according to a creative principle. True Parents illustrate it by using the human body as an example: "All organizations should resemble cells of the human body." They do not move or multiply in a disorganized manner. They can multiply according to the Principle of Creation, according to the natural laws created by Heavenly Parent. A heavenly tribal messiah also can successfully multiply spiritual children according to the Principle of Creation. This is the method that True Parents initially practiced, following natural principles. This trinity system principle for multiplying cells has been designated by True Parents as the organized system for the expansion of Cheon Il Guk.

Human cellular tissues are influenced by the original mind, which is in the subject position. The original mind—the source of hyojeong, and also of true love which allows one to care for others even while facing death—is structurally connected with the life of a true family. Organizations can grow without limit only if their structure has the DNA of True Parents.

A close examination of the strategy of True Parents shows that there is a trinity principle that is used for multiplication. This method has been systematized and organized and is being used in various places in Asia, including Korea and Japan. This method was applied successfully in Japan. The member who used it won an award for witnessing and was chosen to give a testimony at Cheong-Pyeong about how it was possible to expand the membership of their group. In Korea this method has been introduced as a program for empowering pastors, since 2015, and some groups that placed first in bringing people to the Blessing used this method. In Africa, home-group witnessing started after a home-group lecture tour was held for 20 days, starting from August 6, 2010. In Asia, heavenly tribal messiah work has been putting down roots and multiplying under the guidance of Regional President Yong Chung-sik, who has been teaching members to use a home-group system along with HTM Leader School education programs. The number of regular FFWPU members has dramatically increased through these processes. Let us look at some cases in which the trinity is established using this system.

1. Establishing Trinity Home Groups

(1) Establishing trinities based on True Parents' words

The Blessing tradition of True Parents includes organizing the blessed couples into trinities. Unfortunately, for many years now a lot of blessed families have lived their lives without knowing about the trinity system. As we go forward from here, all heavenly tribal messiahs who accomplish 430 couples should make the effort to organize them into trinities.

If you have not been organizing the members of your tribe in trinities so far, it may work best to set up trinity home groups. In the process, the most important task is to establish the trinities. However, members who have experienced home-group training in Korea and Japan during the past 12 years recognize that the most challenging thing was to unite three persons. Let's look at the words of True Parents, to support the reasons for establishing trinities. Many families understand the reason for unification, while they often ask about how to achieve it. The methodology of forming trinities has no fixed solution. It is up to us to find it.

① Establishment of trinities is "training for unity."

True Parents have spoken many times about the establishment of trinities. In particular, they earnestly requested leaders of large groups and home groups to establish trinities. In one crucial sermon, which True Father gave while he was working on forming trinities of blessed couples, he said:

> "The members of the trinity should be strongly united, so all the members can have a solid horizontal base of support as they pursue their life of faith. If they share their small victories and inspirations with each other, this will give all of them a base to work more strongly and successfully." [Sermons, 40-100]

The reason that True Parents have made this kind of effort to establish trinities is that their goal is to train people to be citizens of Cheon Il Guk. It is more difficult to unite three families than to match couples for the Blessing. Nevertheless, we must find a way to do it.

> "Is it possible to unite three families, when it is already difficult to get one husband and one wife to unite? Can three families live in one house together, where there are many matrimonial disputes even between husband and wife? (Never!) It will be impossible for them to live together. Since they do not know how to unite, we need to train them how to unite and live together." [Sermons, 44-153]

It is clear that the most important objective which all blessed families should achieve during their earthly life is to establish the trinity through which they can be trained in how to unite as human beings.

[Figure 1-3] Home Group - 3

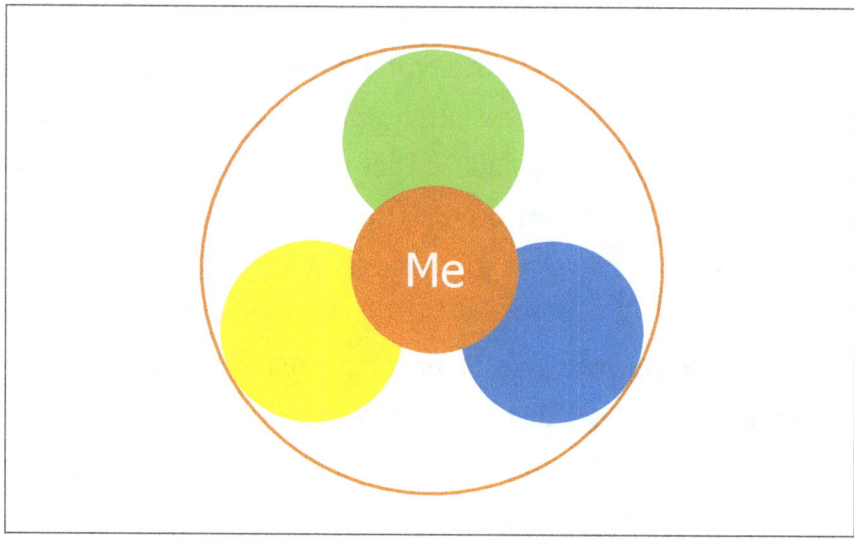

② A trinity is a combination of substance and function.

A question most often raised in training is "What is the best way to organize trinities?" Before answering the question, we should consider what kind of trinities we are discussing. The trinities that were organized when members were blessed are already substantially established. They were made at the same time the couples were blessed and are already relationships like siblings, so they cannot be changed.

On the other hand, trinities organized when the home groups begin are functional ones. In other words, they are strategically established for effective activities of the home group and for the success of the heavenly tribal messiah activities. While True Parents mentioned trinities when they blessed our members in the 1960s, they also mentioned trinities for tribal messiah activities. In the end, as members actively pursue heavenly tribal messiah activities, the substantial and functional trinities ultimately will become intertwined.

③ The trinity is an organizational unit for the strategic expansion of Cheon Il Guk.

"Today, January 3, I want you to make a strong determination, taking this principle into consideration. When your trinities are changed once every three months, you should be prepared to unite with whoever you meet. You should regard these meetings as historical destiny connecting you with the others in each new trinity. As you meet them, ask yourself, 'What ties from the 6,000 years of providential history have brought me to meet you?' In this way, three people, then ten, then 36 or 72 people can be united. An organization such as this cannot exist outside of the rules of the Principle, and the Principle cannot exist with this kind of organization. This is the essence of the life of an organization. Likewise, the center of the universe and the center of my mind must circulate as one along with the frequency of the universe, and the self also should circulate in accordance with operating principles of the world of all things." [Sermons, 3-246, 1958.01.03]

"You need like-minded persons. That is why I speak about trinities. You need to work together establishing trinities. God does not encourage to us to work alone, since we are likely to fail when working alone. This means you should make a plan to work together. Accordingly, I plan to develop an all-out campaign to move forward by organizing trinities, within this year." [*Sermons*, 19-148]

"Home church work should not be conducted alone, but led by a trinity, from beginning to end. Overall problems should be resolved by three people together. When three families are gathered, each one should fulfill its own obligation, while joint management is required for achieving common goals. If this practice is developed, you can set a record in home church, and you can make more trinities, so they can be raised up by Heavenly Parent. Thirty trinities can be created by Heavenly Parent. Therefore, as the number of trinities increases to 30, 300, 3,000 and 30,000 ... (a) hierarchy is created, once Heavenly Parent has accepted your victory." [*Sermons*, 102-128]

We can see above the reasons that the Family Federation forms trinities and uses strategies to multiply them, creating a modular structure. As the Blessing also is initiated primarily by the trinity, the number of members in trinities is increased to 3, 12, 36, and 72. The home groups constituting the hoondok family groups are also developed using the multiplication of trinities. Home groups can be smoothly prepared, once trinities are established.

④ **Working in trinities is a training course for perfecting one's personality.**

According to True Parents' words, trinities should not be organized only by like-minded persons. Each person should make a serious determination, with the aim of paving the way to completing his or her personality.

> "The trinity is not a group of persons with similar characters. Each person has his own personality. This is a way of encouraging different people to be united. The trinity organization is prepared for them as a course for unification." [Sermons, 33-141]

As shown above, a trinity is not necessarily composed of like-minded people, but of different members who have historical responsibility for and are willing to devote themselves to the goals of the organization during their secular lives and have determined to make efforts to find unity. Therefore, they should behave as people who are unfamiliar with each other but fight and die together when they have the same objective, like victory on the battlefield, until the objective of the heavenly tribal messiah mission is achieved.

The trinity should be established with a mind of ascetic practices toward completing one's personality. In relating to the people in the trinity, we should do our best to resolve common problems by withholding private concerns. Joint problem-solving must be used for all tasks necessary for the success of the heavenly tribal messiah mission. The trinity must be united to complete those tasks and be prepared to adapt to changes for the sake of growth and development. However, it is crucial that the direction of the trinity be set not for individual reasons but for the purpose of building the trinity's home group team.

⑤ The trinity is the place where Heavenly Parent dwells.

Surprisingly, trinities are the place where Heavenly Parent can move. True Parents have said that they created the trinity as a place in which Heavenly Parent can dwell. The Bible also shows that Heavenly Parent will be with you if two or three persons are gathered in His name. [Matthew 18:20].

> "When two or three people pray in one accord, God can move. Therefore, the trinity is created when your minds are united on God's Will. The problem is the extent to which your minds are united and harmonized around the trinity." [Sermons, 3-227]

We can feel that Heaven Parent lives in the trinity because we can experience Him through the trinity. He also reveals the answers to the questions we are looking for through the trinity. Although one of three persons makes a mistake, Heavenly Parent still can speak to that person through the trinity, if the other two have not repeated the mistake.

⑥ The trinity is a united foundation of faith and substance.

"It is impossible to pass the road of faith alone. You need faithful comrades. More than three people should be united, so a trinity is required. Heavenly Parent cannot directly help human beings vertically, because of the Fall. However, if three people are united and one of them makes a mistake, it is possible for Heavenly Parent to teach him about the mistake horizontally through the other two people. Even in the case of mountain prayer, grace can be received more quickly if more than three people offer prayers together. After the prayer, they should discuss it with each other. However, if they discuss with others who are not of their trinity, it gives Satan the opportunity to invade." [Sermons, 18-43]

The trinity is the fundamental unit of organizational expansion projected and practiced by True Parents to achieve the ideal of Cheon Il Guk. In 1960, True Parents initially organized a trinity between the first three blessed couples and explained what trinities are. Hence, the Family Federation began through the providence of multiplying trinities of blessed families.

True Parents said that the primary reason that Christianity has not achieved its end is because three disciples could not unite with Jesus. The main objective of Jesus' coming was to rescue and restore the fallen family of Adam. True Parents also taught us that Jesus' three closest disciples—Peter, John and James—were in the positions of Cain, Abel and Seth. Since the first trinity consisting of those three disciples could not achieve its objective of restoring the eight members of Adam's family, Jesus ended up being crucified. [*Sermons*, 3-240]. Hence, the trinity must be united, because it serves as the foundation on which Heavenly Parent can work.

> "Therefore, if the three people in a trinity do not unite, they can easily be destroyed. In particular, a trinity of three men should be united. They have to be spiritually and physically united, to determine whether they live or die. So, it is necessary to develop a kind of unity that transcends time, not a foundation that is confined within a temporal limit. If three people are united and they can establish a principled motivation that can replace their individual motivations—in other words, they create a trinity with the resolution that they will not change their goal, even though the heavens are transformed—Heavenly Parent will achieve His goal on that foundation." [*Sermons*, 3-240]

Becoming a heavenly tribal messiah means organizing and achieving a tribal realm. When a tribal realm cannot be secured, no matter hard we try, the primary reason is that we have not created unity within a trinity. We can enter the tribal realm only if our trinity is united.

> "God's intention to restore what was lost in Adam's family can be achieved if the trinity is united. God carried out His providential Will 2,000 years ago during Jacob's time by searching for 12

brothers. Likewise, if you find and are united with 12 disciples based on the number three, you can attend your parents and, furthermore, you can enter the tribal realm, rather than being a branch tribe. You have to be aware of this truth." [Sermons, 5-118]

⑦ The trinity is the foundation of a hyojeong family.

In the world, even one dutiful son or daughter is valuable. However, blessed families that intend to create Cheon Il Guk cannot be true hyojeong families until not only one dutiful son or daughter but all of the sons and daughters are united around the trinity. This is different from the general concept of a dutiful child. If a child becomes dutiful alone, he may he may bring pain to his parents' hearts, in a sense. When all the family members are united with the trinity, the family can be a true hyojeong family, which will bring true joy to the parents.

> "You should be dutiful children before God. You cannot be dutiful sons or daughters alone. You can be dutiful sons or daughters only if three brothers and sisters are united centering on the trinity."
> [Sermons, 30-220]

The trinity can be established through conferences and plans by leaders of the large group or a home group, or it can be formed by gathering members who share common goals. The direction that the trinity adopts should correspond to "the common objective of the organization." On the basis of the experiences and True Parents' words above, let's review some points about the establishment of trinities.

- » The trinity is a process in which one finds and unites with like-minded persons through a confession of faith.
- » The trinity is the unit of team structure in which one and one's team are trained.
- » The trinity should form a structure in which tribes are united centering on the family.
- » The trinity can be reorganized to achieve its objective.

(2) How to set up trinities

Now, let's discuss how to organize the trinity based on True Parents' words. The simplest and easiest way is to find like-minded persons from among the large group.

① Organize trinities by finding like-minded persons from the large group.

If this method is used, each member who begins heavenly tribal messiah work will find three persons from the large group who can relate well to each other and are committed to being in the trinity, and then he or she will report to the large group.

② The pastor of the large group determines the trinity administratively.

In this method the large group educates members through home group vision seminars and workshops about heavenly tribal messiah activities, and then the pastor sets up trinities from among those participating. The trinities may be organized from among the large group based on the localities where they live, or their place of work or other means. This is a method that works well for members who have the mindset of following what is asked of them in the organization. The members can follow the vertical guidance of the pastor, rather than run the risk of following their own individual direction. However, it can also lead to difficulties if members without a common base are put together and have difficulty creating unity.

③ Organize trinities in families or tribes.

If there are families, relatives and tribes in the large group, a trinity composed of members of the same family can be established. Then, if the number of members increases to 36, there will be a very good foundation for continuing success. Some problems related to meeting locations and meals for the trinity can be solved easily if they are in the same family. There are advantages that make this method work smoothly, as the members of a family or tribe often can work well together, befitting the name "tribal messiah."

(3) Field case of a trinity of sisters in Malaysia

Recently home groups have been having good success in Kuala Lumpur, the capital of Malaysia. Here is a story from the passion home group, one of the home groups in Kuala Lumpur, which was created by a trinity of blessed members who are sisters from the same family.

"We began our home group one year ago. We decided to begin a home group after attending a workshop by Professor Gil Young-hwan. We started by attempting to practice what we had learned in the workshop. We formed a trinity of sisters. After five months, Professor Gil came again and coached us. We reflected deeply on the state of our home group. We were aware that we should still make much effort to achieve purification, offer jeongseong and seek for unity as a trinity. We conducted a SWOT (strengths, weaknesses, opportunities, and threats) analysis and uncovered our weaknesses. We worked to match the necessary standard for purification and jeongseong by making a new resolution, and we invested time in loving our VIPs (our witnessing guests). After five months, we felt that the home group had become stabilized, and we established a great spiritual foundation.
We trust, take care of and help each other. When we face difficulties and challenges, we overcome them through prayers, purification and jeongseong. Since that time we have experienced a lot of spiritual phenomena in our home group. In meetings with VIPs, good spirits who are supporting us helped us to win the battle between the good mind and the evil mind. Other members became inspired to care for the VIPs. The members gained substantial inspiration from the home group meetings, and their faith was enhanced and refreshed. They were able to substantially

feel the love of Heavenly Parent and His spiritual power. Heavenly Parent has prepared many people for our home group. We have successfully invited 16 people to visit our home group. Now we have a new list of VIPs, and we are preparing to multiply two home groups in early 2018. As a home group leader, I am deeply grateful to Heavenly Parent for guiding us through the home group system and for the home group education of Professor Gil."

This passion home group has become a good model, bringing members who finish the regular course through the home group to participate in the Blessing ceremony hosted by the Malaysian Family Federation.

(4) The case of activities by trinities in Surin, Thailand

This is the case of the author: We conducted Blessing activities by organizing trinities of members and social VIPs.

"At first, 12 persons were active in the trinity home group of a hyojeong coaching center (CARP Center) in Bangkok. In order to multiply the center, I also pioneered the Surin area by selecting trinity members who were born in Surin Province, so that we could carry out activities in Surin in addition to activities in Bangkok. I organized the home group trinity by recruiting three natives of Surin, and they returned to their hometown to do heavenly tribal messiah work. As they continued, three trinities comprising the existing members, youth and VIPs who had been witnessed to were established in the Surin Coaching Center. This gave us the opportunity to promote the heavenly tribal messiah Blessing.

The strategy for planning the heavenly tribal messiah Blessing was decided. A workshop for 30 school principals was held with the assistance of the local Surin ministry of education. Among them, three principals agreed with this objective, so a trinity was formed naturally. Surprisingly, they were naturally united in participating in the Family Federation, and I did not have to push them to create the trinity artificially. This was the amazing work of Heavenly Parent. A former local senior principal recently was elected as the president of the Family Federation. Around him, the other principals in the trinity are actively engaged in Blessing activities, in spite of their busy school schedules.

We created hyojeong coaching clubs in three schools to first teach students about purity and home groups. Then during a workshop we recruited 12 teachers and parents from each school and their spouses through applications to guide these students. In other words, the principals from each school hosted two-day workshops on true families and the Blessing at their schools. These principals then recommended 12 Blessing candidates. In September 2017, we held two workshops at their school in which a total of 72 people participated. Out of that, 36 couples received the Blessing. Now, the 12 couples from each school gather for home groups each week centering on the school's principal.

In the process, the core trinities in the Surin Family Federation and the hyojeong coaching center have educated them and developed the home groups at three schools. The home groups plan to create 36 family groups of blessed members with each family including 12 persons. If this plan is achieved, 432 members will have been recruited. In the process, the most amazing thing was how incredible and wonderful the power of the trinity was. I truly felt it must have been a trinity prepared by Heavenly Parent. With such power, we are working to multiply blessed families from each school and we have a vision to turn parents from all schools into blessed families through this trinity. We also dream of extending the Blessing movement into 88 junior and senior high schools in the heavenly tribal messiah areas in Surin."

2. Recruiting 12 Persons—Creating a Hoondok Family Group

If one wants to be a heavenly tribal messiah, one should gather 12 spiritual children. To accomplish this, it is first necessary to establish trinities. First, the existing members, including those who are preparing to be heavenly tribal messiahs, gather for report meetings as a home group activity, while meeting new witnessing contacts. A trinity consisting entirely of existing members can be referred to as a "B3," a trinity composed of three blessed members, and is in the Abel realm. The members of the trinity are either blessed members,

[Figure 1-4] A gathering of 12 members in a hoondok family group

or are preparing to be blessed. They and their children are all part of the Abel realm, and they have joined the trinity in order to support the heavenly tribal messiah in his work.

New witnessing contacts should be treated as VIP guests. For this reason, they are referred to as VIPs. In addition to including current members in a trinity, we can encourage new witnessing contacts to progress in their development by joining a trinity.

The process by which one becomes a heavenly tribal messiah through home group trinities is as follows: First, the existing three members (B3) create unity by regularly holding home group report meetings, while continuing to meet new VIPs. They organize a new trinity around the new contacts whom they have met. A very effective strategy is to form a trinity entirely of new members (V3). Studies have shown that new VIPs can attract even more new contacts than existing members can. As a trinity of current members unites to meet new VIPs, they should support them in recruiting 12 new persons.

This can be formulated as follows: B3+V3+V3+V3=12. Once the hoondok family group grows from three to 12 persons, it is necessary to actively support one of the three existing members, B1, B2 or B3, in becoming a heavenly tribal messiah. B1 who recruited 12 persons also should help both B2 and B3 to attract another 12 persons. Once B2 and B3 have repeated this process, a group of 36 blessed families will have been created naturally. Therefore, the hoondok family group becomes an association of blessed families, as it naturally grows and multiplies.

In this process we make the Principle our lifestyle. As members regularly participate in home group report meetings and HTM Leader School, they purify themselves and support and help each other from a sense of concern for each other. By establishing a successful foundation of faith and foundation of substance in this way, they are able to meet the Messiah, receive the Blessing, and move along the course towards holy perfection. Holy perfection means becoming a perfected human being while exchanging in direct dialog with Heavenly Parent. All blessed families who have experienced this process acquire the necessary skills and abilities to create 430 blessed families.

We should not forget that this becomes the process by which

[Figure 1-5] Hoondok Family Group - 12

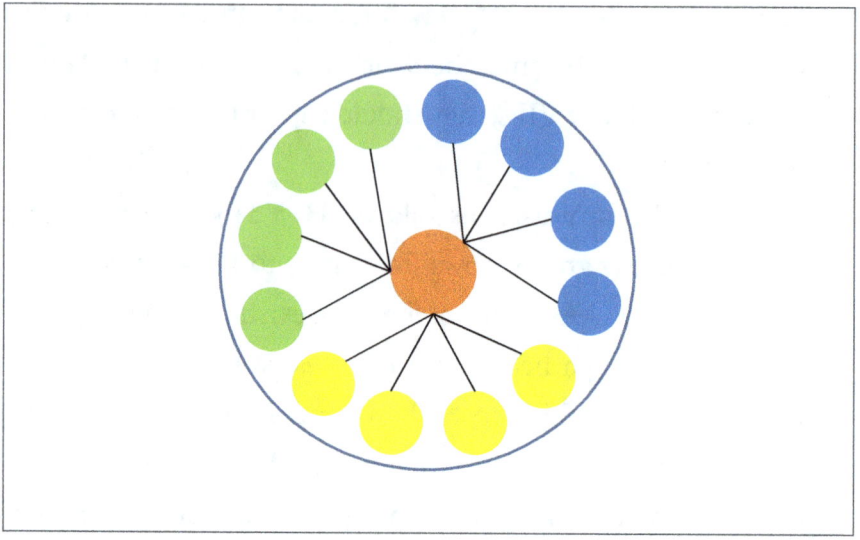

Cheon Il Guk is built, following the trinity strategy of True Parents. This process is not easily completed, since the establishment of a trinity is a training course which is accompanied by hardships and suffering. However, we cannot avoid this path. Many members give up trying to pursue this process, primarily because their ego and judgment get in the way of unity. Hence, we should invest in life by asking ourselves, "Why should we go through this process?" whenever we experience arduous courses and start thinking we want to give up.

There are various strategies for heavenly tribal messiahs to develop a trinity home group and the hoondok family group which is successful in meeting witnessing contacts and gathering 12 members.

[Figure 1-6] Selecting One Member of the Trinity and Building a 12-Member Hoondok Family Group

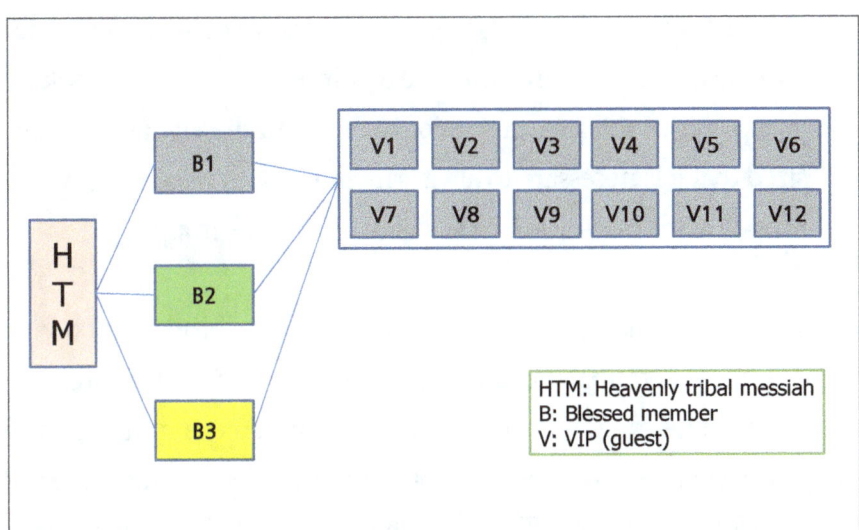

① **Selecting one member of your trinity and supporting him to recruit 12**

In some cases, the existing three persons (B3) around a heavenly tribal messiah increase their number to 12 by actively supporting one person (B1). This means that the heavenly tribal messiah who manages the trinity selects one person among the three, by mutual agreement of all of them, and strategically supports him. Even if another person has made the original connection with a witnessing contact, everyone should be ready to follow the decision made by the trinity and encourage the contact to join the group of the trinity member that has been chosen. If 12 persons become a hoondok family group centering on the trinity, they should see one another as one family. This can be achieved because they are all one family.

In the hoondok family group consisting of 12 persons, they work together to witness to others. If 12 persons are gathered already, one of the existing members (B2) works as the leader of the hoondok family group, while all of them continue to witness until the hoondok family group consists of three groups of 12 or 36 families. It has been emphasized that it is necessary to always include coaching and HTM Leader School workshops for the success of this home group.

② **The existing trinity organizes a new trinity around each VIP.**
The heavenly tribal messiah supports members of the current trinity to promote another trinity home group centering on themselves. Therefore, three new persons organize trinities of VIPs centering on each of themselves. Then, the heavenly tribal messiah helps the three trinity leaders to form their own hoondok family groups consisting of 12 persons as each member of an existing trinity generates three new members. In this period, B1, B2 and B3 are active in their heavenly tribal messiah's home group trinity while simultaneously securing 12 persons for the development of their own home group. Then, a hoondok family group consisting of 36 families is created, if each of the three trinities completes its mission. In the process, coaching is also required, and it is important to develop each member through HTM Leader School workshops, utilizing education and training beyond the home group.

③ **How to determine how to divide the families centering on the heavenly tribal messiah, when 12 persons have been gathered**
According to this method, the three persons in the heavenly tribal

[Figure 1-7] Building Hoondok Home Groups of 12 starting from each Member of the Trinity

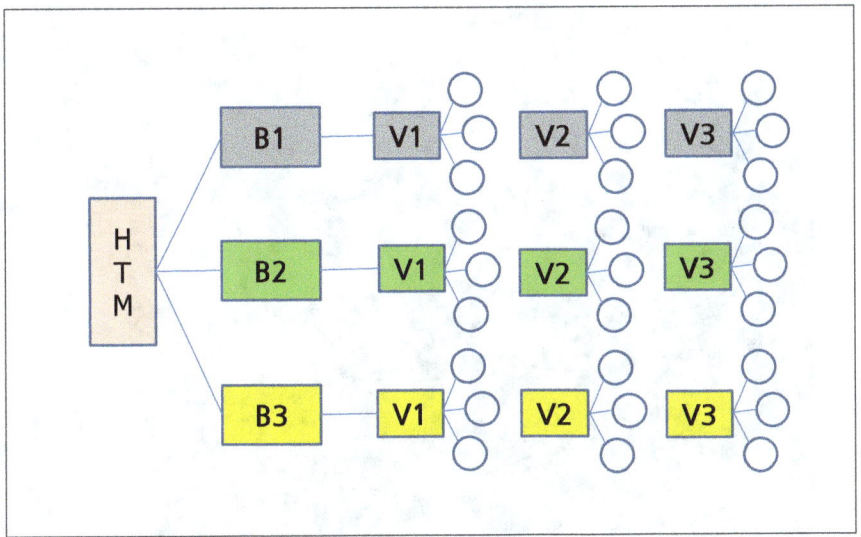

messiah's original trinity work together to build relationships with and invite VIPs and then conduct an intake process according to their own capabilities. This results in the formation of a hoondok family group consisting of 12 persons, and the heavenly tribal messiah chooses criteria for dividing his group into new trinities, taking into consideration the processes by which they were witnessed to. The heavenly tribal messiah may allow the members to form their own trinities, based either on relationships between existing members and new ones or with their relatives and tribes. In the process, members should actively support the work of the heavenly tribal messiah by recognizing all VIPs as spiritual children, even though they may not actually have joined yet. Such a method may be the most natural one, among many others. There is the possibility that

[Figure 1-8] Blessing photo of young couples from Professor Gil Young-Hwan's home group

once the groups of three are determined, some of them may have difficulty uniting, having problematic relations with each other or ill feeling toward others. Since these difficulties are not easily resolved, it is desirable to spend time to help them alleviate such conflicts, such as regular home group report meetings.

3. Building a Network of 36 Families

We have examined some methods by which a home group can grow to 12 members, starting with a trinity of members who determine to become heavenly tribal messiahs. By methods like these, the

[Figure 1-9] Building a Hoondok Family Group of 36 by Adding to Each Member of the Trinity

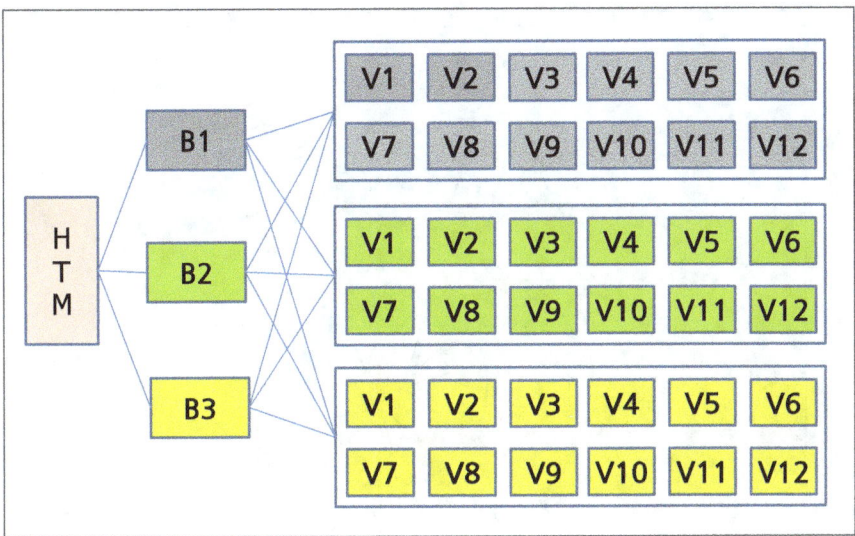

trinity will create a hoondok family group consisting of 12 persons, while continuously employing the multiplying system, including HTM Leader School.

If B1, B2 and B3 from the hoondok family group which initially contains 12 persons each build their own hoondok family groups of 12 persons, then three hoondok family groups are formed, comprising 36 members, as shown in Figure 1-9.

We have examined how to increase the number of members in the hoondok family groups from three to 12 to 36, while building trinity home groups and multiplying them. Here, we should focus on what strategies are used to assemble 12 persons. If each one looks for spiritual children only through his own abilities, he might reach his limit. However, if they work as a team, they will overcome their

[Figure 1-10] A 36-Member Hoondok Family Center

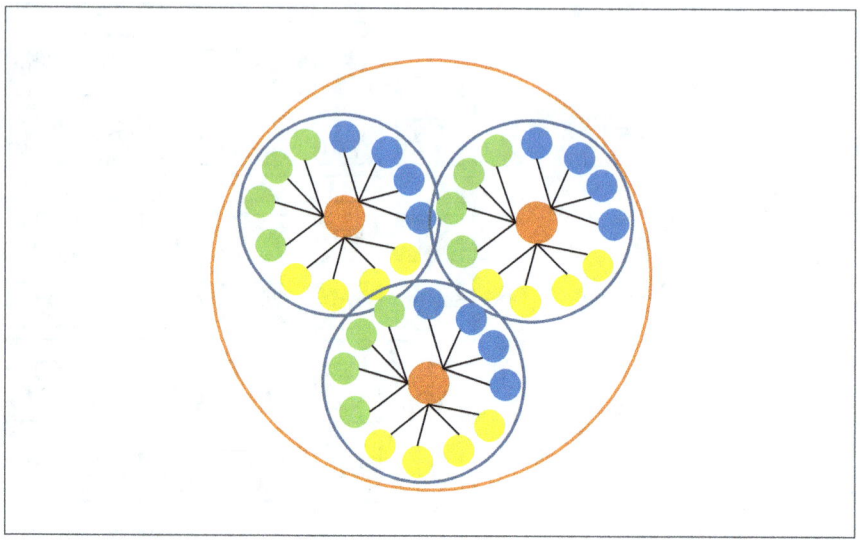

limits. Making a team and working as one group will give you several options, depending on how you recruit 12 persons.

For example, there are different ways to expand to 36 families: 1) select one person among B1, B2, and B3 and encourage him to recruit 12 persons; 2) have B1, B2 and B3 each recruit 12 persons by organizing his own trinity and multiplying it; or 3) have B3 work with VIPs to recruit 12 persons and then divide them between B1, B2, and B3 to establish them as their spiritual children.

If one person among B1, B2 and B3, perhaps B1, is selected to recruit 12 persons, this method will be continuously used: B2 then collects people with the support of B1. Now B1 has 12 persons and B2 also has 12 persons, and they all help B3 to gather and educate 12 persons. Consequently, B1, B2 and B3 each has a hoondok family group consisting of 12 persons; so a total of 36 members is the result. How is this possible? It is because members are continuously active, as the consistent witnessing system is operated. A home group system like this is necessary to increase the number of people beyond 12.

① A case in which African heavenly tribal messiahs in the field are increased to 12 persons

These are the cases of Masica, Moto Cambali, Eblin and Simpembe in Zambia.

"I have made much effort to have more spiritual children. At last, I was able to raise up 12 spiritual children who I can trust and rely on, as did Jesus. Since 2015, I have earnestly worked full time for the heavenly tribal messiah movement, together with my 12 spiritual children. Although it occurred later, it was very surprising that a series of successful results followed each other so quickly that they reminded me of the nuclear reactions I had learned about at school.

In Monges village, only one participant was blessed, and then we got a call from him and he said that he desired to hold a Blessing ceremony in Choma, the village in which he lived. In addition, in less than a week, the number of couples who were asking to participate in the Blessing increased. Parents who were impressed when they listened to lectures about the true family movement asked us to hold a workshop for their children.

After one week, we held a workshop for the children of the

couples who had received the Blessing. About 79 young people participated in the workshop. After participating in the workshop, they decided to attend a longer workshop. Among them, 22 actually attended a retreat held in the city. After coming back from the retreat, they invited their friends and encouraged their friends' parents to participate in the Blessing ceremony.

Subsequently, blessed couples again came together with their children and friends and relatives, and they also studied earnestly in two-day and seven-day workshops. Thus, the results of witnessing increased exponentially. Such really incredible events progressed according to Heavenly Parent's plan, as if they were predetermined. The blessed people served as a catalyst for founding the Youth and Students Federation. Then, blessed married women, hoping to learn more detailed knowledge of the Blessing and the Family Federation, organized meetings to learn about them. These meetings led to the inauguration of the Women's Federation for World Peace in the Choma area, on December 10, 2016. The participants, 163 married women, all signed and submitted applications to join the Women's Federation."

Unbelievable events like these have been happening in Asia and Africa. The explosive growth in heavenly tribal messiah activities is also an opportunity given by Heavenly Parent. Each team of 12 persons should become organizations of even greater potential.

4. Building a Network of 430 Families

① How 36 families each can bring 12 families

The three hoondok family groups of B1, B2 and B3 experienced the process in which 12 families are brought through the trinity home group, finally resulting in a total of 36 families. If each family brings 12 families, through one of the methods described above, a total of 432 families will be added.

As each of the blessed families has learned to bring 12 families, if they can successfully follow the patterns they have learned, 430 families can be blessed. Thus, the success of a heavenly tribal messiah fundamentally depends on creating unity among the three families in the initial support trinity and multiplying each of them to 12

[Figure 1-11] A 430-Family Hoondok Family Center

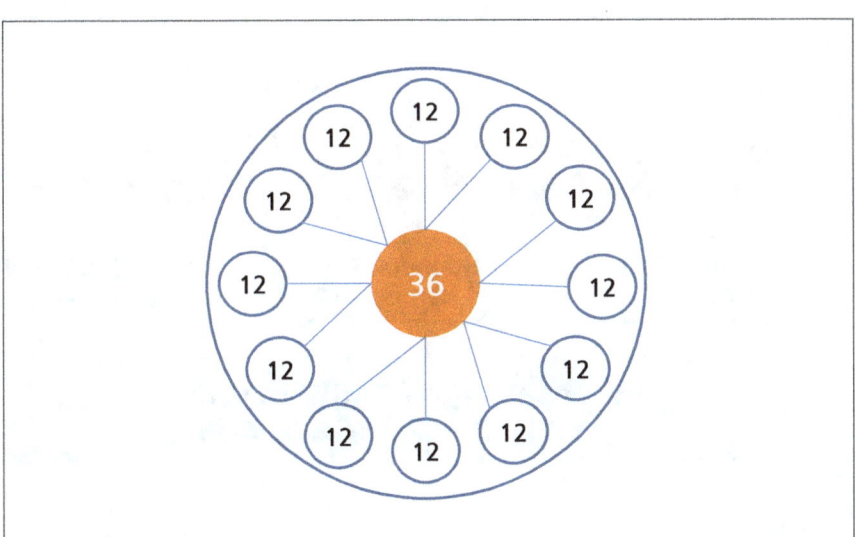

families. It is important not to forget True Parents' strategy that they can multiply without limit, if a successful hoondok family group consisting of 12 families becomes the foundation.

② How each hoondok family group can recruit 144 persons

Another method is that three hoondok family groups each multiply their own 12 hoondok family groups. If the 12 family members in B1's hoondok family group each build 12 more hoondok family groups, a total of 144 persons are gathered. Then, if the number (144) of B1 are added to those of B2 (144) and B3 (144), the result is 432.

Tribal messiahs who succeed in blessing 430 families should continuously manage and educate the blessed families in their

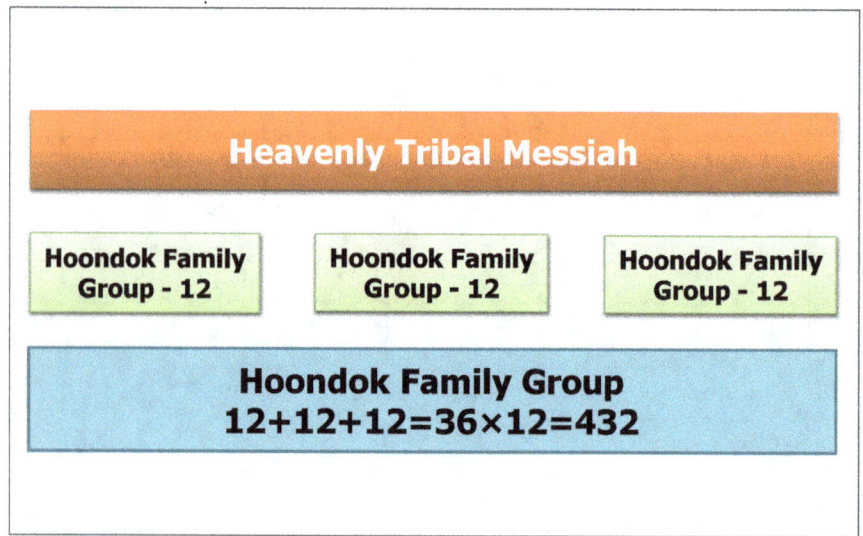

[Figure 1-12] A 430-Family Hoondok Family Center

home group through HTM Leader School. Accordingly, all blessed families should become regular members.

5. How Can 430 Blessed Families Become Regular Members?

As of December 2017, around the world, including Asia and Africa, there were 392 heavenly tribal messiah families who had given the Blessing to 430 couples. In order to do this, they had to create a strong heavenly tribal messiah home group structure.

Although these new members have received basic education and been blessed, they also need to receive true family training in the home group and HTM Leader School, in order to become regular members of the Family Federation who can put down deep roots. To this end, they should be included in the organizational system of home groups, as described above. If they have been blessed but still are not educated and organized, we must do our best to involve all 430 families in home groups, by organizing home groups around the 430 families.

Active heavenly tribal messiahs should assemble 12, then 36, then 430 families arranged in home groups. If you have expanded to 430 families by multiplying home groups, they already will be organized in home groups of about 12 families each. If not, there are various ways you can organize them. In Asia, 43 persons are selected from among the blessed families, each of whom is responsible for 10 families, with the goal of helping them to become regular members.

It is best if the heavenly tribal messiah organizes a trinity. If each of those three persons recruits 12 families, you will have 36 families, and can reach 43 by choosing just a few more.

Case in an Asian area

Let's examine the case of the heavenly tribal messiah Sangcom, in Kalasin Province, Thailand. Because heavenly tribal messiah activities in Kalisin Province have been very active, she has been thinking about a plan for the management and gradual development of heavenly tribal messiahs and tribes.

"Since we have not built a center in this province yet, the next process related to the mission is how to guide the blessed families. I must make a plan, so that I can make good use of the families who are able to take care of others. The Asian leaders have advised us to designate local leaders and build a family leadership system using home group strategies. We plan to make a system by training 43 leaders. We will begin with a small group of three persons and invite others as guests, encouraging them to join the group. We hold meetings in this group like hoondok family group meetings. In the Asian system, meetings are held not only at the center but also rotating between the homes of each leader. Tribal representatives in Thailand and other countries visit the members of their tribe in turn and interact with them using mobile apps, sharing news about True Parents and other related information.

The Thailand Family Federation headquarters recently built a center in Kalisin Province and also provided one vehicle and one full-time member. As we move toward the future, we will try to find the resources to support further improvements with our own power.

We continuously are teaching the tribe members about tithes and special donations. Therefore, a few newly blessed families have begun to tithe, in spite of their low income. Among them, people who engage in agriculture usually donate some crops such as rice. One of our local government officers has witnessed to some single members, including the head of the ward, who have applied for the Blessing. He has educated them about tithing, and they have begun to make donations. He prepares lectures on true love principles and Divine Principle education for children whose parents have been blessed and for other people in the locality. There are also some retired teachers who hope to do volunteer work for us.

I have supported my tribe and other tribes to have good results and succeed as heavenly tribal messiahs. I am working to hold Blessings in three different states, although, above all, Kalasin should be held up first as a model case. Thailand has a total of 77 provinces. If we can restore at least seven provinces, they may provide a sufficient foundation for Thailand to be restored by the year 2020. To this end, we have set up the following principles:

a. Educate 43 blessed families as home group leaders and organize the families so that each home group leader is taking care of ten

families.
b. Elect a young successor to work under the heavenly tribal messiah and empower him to raise up young people and workers.
c. Raise funds and continuously instruct all people to follow the traditions and to tithe.

In establishing a foundation for heavenly tribal messiah work, it is not easy to foster trained personnel and midlevel leaders, due to economic difficulties and other limitations. However, I believe that better outcomes can be produced, with True Parents' vision and blessing. Dr. Ronnachit Putthala, the district chief of Kalasin Province, and his wife have been making more efforts to resolve some difficult problems and misunderstandings than the members in general. The fact that we have such honorable leaders as John the Baptist figures is our great grace. They believe that their ancestors will stay close to them if they serve as tribal messiahs. They also believe that they can never achieve their ends without the support of Heavenly Parent, True Parents and absolute good spirits.

According to the thoughts of heavenly tribal messiah Sangcom, under the guidance of Regional President Yong Chung-sik, a model strategy will be developed starting in 2018, by which each country will choose 12 successful heavenly tribal messiahs who will educate all 430 blessed families to become regular members. If this project is finished, the next step will be to organize model villages and cities centered on those heavenly tribal messiahs. In order to be acknowledged as regular members, the tribe members should form trinities of selected families, and 43 or 36 families among the 430 families should receive more intense education as home group leaders.

6. Heavenly Parents, Spirituality and a Heart of Hyojeong Are Required Because a System Is Just a Tool

We have explained how to build a network of 430 families for success as a heavenly tribal messiah. However, it is not possible to achieve our objectives using only the system that we have described.

The mission of a heavenly tribal messiah is to construct the substantial Cheon Il Guk as the first line of defense against Satan. This mission cannot be accomplished without the investment of jeongseong, prayer, and the spiritual aid of Heavenly Parent to help the messiah, his family and his tribe to put down roots of hyojeong. The importance cannot be stressed enough. This is why the report meetings, when operating a home group, are held focusing on jeongseong.

2

The Work of Large-Group Family Federation Centers and Local Hoondok Family Groups

We have examined the processes for forming and organizing trinity home groups and large tribal groups of more than 430 families. Now we should understand which missions and responsibilities are those of the existing large group Family Federation, which lie with the tribe-level hoondok family home group association, and what is the mission of the small home groups. It is important to find the right horizontal and vertical relationships between them for high-noon alignment without shadows.

1. The Mission of the Large-Group Family Federation Center

What should we do if we want to bring a large group Family Federation center to settlement in Cheon Il Guk through hoondok family group activities? If we talk about the functions of Family Federation headquarters, we mean the roles, missions and activities of the

Family Federation. Foundation Day is the day when the heavens and earth were made anew. In order for such a renewal to occur, there must be an initiator of that renewal. The renewal of the heavens and earth did not occur of itself. Human beings, who are subject over heaven and earth, had to be renewed first. The initiator of this transformation is not the world, but must be the Family Federation. The Family Federation can be the initiator of the renewal of heaven and earth, only if it renews itself first. This means that the Family Federation should be significantly transformed after Foundation Day. It should be re-created as something quite different. How should it be changed?

First, a historic and revolutionary breakthrough in the function of the Family Federation is necessary. The Family Federation belonging to the age of the providence of restoration should be completely renewed to one belonging to the age of the providence of creation. Therefore, among the organizations and systems of the Family Federation, it should be transformed centering on its educational function. In order for the Family Federation to be the subject of the new heaven and earth, it needs to develop systems to provide teaching materials for hoondok family groups so that education can be conducted through hoondok family groups. In the wilderness period, it was a community bound together for the flight from Egypt and a community gathered to accomplish the conquest of Canaan. However, in the Cheon Il Guk settlement age, it must become a community gathered for settlement which can help the blessed families who have entered the garden of Eden to settle and grow according to the principle of creation. True Parents have demonstrated how the Family Federation should be reformed in the future, by showing a model in their guidance of the Family Federation in earlier times.

On September 1, 1991, True Parents instructed all the blessed families (except for the second generation) to return to their hometowns, with the goal of fulfilling the mission of tribal messiah. Then, on October 14, 1991, in the Cheongpa-dong headquarters church, they also directed the group leaders who had returned to their hometown to assemble their relatives and speak to them and to hold worship services in their own home. True Parents also taught us that the Family Federation is a place in which families can be educated so that they will be ready to gather and hold services in their home. They said that we should take down the signs that said "church" and change them to "training center." After that, the Family Federation began to use various names for its work, such as True Family Movement Headquarters, True Family Culture Center, and Local Family Center. When a hoondok family group is firmly established and ready to play its role earnestly, the primary function of the local large group Family Federation (district hoondok family group and county hoondok family group) and of the Family Federation headquarters (hoondok family group association headquarters) will be changed to providing education.

Second, the Family Federation should create teaching materials to support its educational function. Those teaching materials represent the institutionalization of the hoondok family group. It is necessary to have principles, a doctrine and ceremonies that teach and reinforce the true character, identity and tradition of True Parents.

Third, the restored Family Federation which has returned to Eden should reform its teaching methods for the hoondok family group. This is because, as the grace accompanying Foundation Day, the age of the governance of Heavenly Parent has opened. The change from the age of the providence of restoration to the age of the providence of creation means that the Family Federation, which has been following the path of the principle of restoration, must now walk on the path of the principle of creation for the completion of individual growth and the perfection of true families.

Although the Family Federation often has used the phrase "nurturing education," it is no longer the time when the growth of members can be nurtured by the Family Federation. Rather, people need to complete their growth by using their free will to accomplish their portion of responsibility, thus entering the indirect realm of God's dominion. What this means is that individual perfection and family perfection are something that cannot be done by one's teachers at school, nor by one's parents, nor even by Heavenly Parent. This means that if we use the word "nurturing," it means we do not understand the meaning of Foundation Day and the age we are living in, the age of the governance of Heavenly Parent.

Hence, the teaching methods of the Family Federation should be reformed to developmental education, rather than teaching by rote, in this age of the providence of creation. This is an age when education is needed which will help people to develop and mature their inherent potential. Coaching leadership and the Cheon Il Guk coaching style, which support this kind of learning, are part of the program taught in the HTM Leader School III.

Fourth, the education should be focused on the firm establishment of Cheon Il Guk through the hoondok family group. Education which had been focused on entering Cheon Il Guk must be transformed to focus instead on the safe settlement of Cheon Il Guk. This means focusing on education for individual growth and perfection to become the subjects of Cheon Il Guk, completing the three great blessings and realizing the value of the three great subject partners principle, and creating a basic Cheon Il Guk community by completing the four great realms of heart and the four-position foundation.

So far, we have not operated hoondok family groups according to True Parents' words. We also have not experienced a life of faith of pursuing individual and family perfection while attending Heavenly Parent and True Parents in our homes or going on to expand our families into tribes. Therefore, it is necessary to make a detailed manual for a life of faith to be practiced in our hoondok family group.

2. The Trinity Hoondok Family Gathering

True Parents connected blessed families into trinities and emphasized that the three families should live together within one home. Accordingly, each Blessing group (36 couples, 72 couples, etc.) was arranged into trinities of families. However, since it is not really practical for them to actually live in the same house, it is necessary to organize trinities for hoondok family groups that will support the establishment and settlement of Cheon Il Guk. The restoration of tribes and the establishment of Cheon Il Guk are not achieved through rapid growth or miracles but by the multiplication of the hoondok family group structure, building an association of hoondok family groups that becomes Cheon Il Guk.

True Parents determined that the trinity is the basic unit for building an organization. Therefore, the hoondok family group must be organized into trinities, as it is essential for expanding a hoondok family group into a tribal group by multiplying trinities.

As it is, blessed families rarely visit each other, even when they live in the same apartment complex. We do not relate to each other easily as blessed families, though we currently attend the same group. This is due to many reasons, including concerns about infringement of privacy, causing a nuisance or concern about visiting empty-handed. However, if we have formed a trinity and have a close relationship with the family next door or other neighbors nearby, we can visit each other freely without reservation. If the number of your family members increases from three or four to 10, doesn't that mean that there will be more people for you to love generously and more people to receive your love? If this happens, you will feel excited that your capacity for learning true love has extended and that this will become your first step toward a tribal church.

An effective way to start can be a trinity hoondok family group, consisting of nine to 12 people, that meets every Friday. A trinity hoondok family group is necessary, since a small organization of about ten people is useful for the spiritual growth and perfection of the family.

Therefore, trinities that gather for hoondok family group offer praise, do hoondok readings of True Parents' words and pray, and then confess and repent for wrong thinking, words and behaviors that they have experienced during the past week, and pray for one other. In addition, they pursue good deeds and avoid evil deeds, as a method of attaining perfection, and spend some time together training themselves in living lives of love with freedom and honesty.

As the core of the hoondok family group meeting, hoondok reading of True Parents' words is done with the goal of internalizing and embodying the contents of each message and understanding how it applies to our time and our daily life. In the same manner in which cells divide, the trinity can multiply into more trinities as new families are witnessed to and more trinity family groups are developed centering on one family.

Because a hoondok family group is a small home group and the group leader typically does not have extensive pastoral experience or expertise, it is necessary to conduct pastoral duties together as a team with neighboring hoondok family groups. With this support, trinities can multiply within the hoondok family group.

If the hoondok family groups that have multiplied from one trinity join together, it is possible to have an association of hoondok family groups that includes 36 families. With this number of people gathered, they will be able to offer education and training programs. The home group leaders can work as a team to balance each other's shortcomings in fulfilling pastoral duties. Neighboring hoondok family groups should work together to support lectures, support joint events, exchange educational materials, and host educational events. In this way, they can make up for each other's weaknesses and multiply their strengths.

However, the more important duty is to provide training to those in one's own hoondok family group to gradually expand the trinity into 36 hoondok family groups. This is the path to the completion of Cheon Il Guk through the restoration of a tribe.

3. The Local Large-Group Family Federation

The existing local large group Family Federation is a large group consisting of hoondok family groups, that is, the federation of all the hoondok family groups in the area. As such, it has the name Family Federation for World Peace and Unification (FFWPU). Therefore, each local association of hoondok family groups in a village, town, county or city may consist of dozens or hundreds of hoondok family groups.

The worship services or meetings of large group hoondok family groups characteristically should be held in the form of the reporting of joy. A local large group hoondok family group should hold open worship in which all members can gather. Such an open worship service shouldn't solely reflect the church's distinct characteristics but should be held for those newly witnessed to. It should be universal in that anybody can comfortably participate, sharing love and friendship under Heavenly Parent. Thus, it has the form of the open home group trinity. In addition, each local hoondok family group should encourage its members to create a tribe of true families by reaching out to their relatives and neighbors.

Local hoondok family groups should support the continuous education of new hoondok family group leaders, the development of education programs for children and adolescents, missionary and volunteer work and the practice of large group worship. Internet homepages may be useful for supporting these efforts.

A. Provide guidance and support for the formation and operation of 80 hoondok family groups.
B. Evaluate and support the weekly activities of the small-group hoondok family groups in the area.
C. Provide education for group leaders for small-group hoondok family groups by operating HTM Leader School programs.

In particular, what is needed from local large group Family Federation centers is a regular system of education to support the activities of the hoondok family groups. To help people develop a pure consciousness of Heavenly Parent's intellect, heart and Will, and as education for the true family movement and the expansion of tribes, they need to offer a three-month course, including 1) prayer school, 2) hoondok school and 3) leader school.

The need for and function of the deep connection between local and national Family Federation chapters and hoondok family groups operated by heavenly national messiahs will be examined further in Chapter 3.

Family and Home Group Report Programs

* The following text has integrated and modified excerpts from former FFWPU-Korea President Lee Jae-seok's book Family Church Series: Life of Faith to work with the structure of this handbook. (Author's note)

The report meeting (worship service) program described below is for report sessions separate from those included in the Home Group Three-Cycle Report Meetings that are explained later in Section 4: Hyojeong Home Group Report Process. The contents below are for meetings that trinity home groups, families or hoondok family group associations hold every day or every week to report to Heavenly Parent, or joint hoondok family group report sessions, etc. Blessed families who are living in attendance to Heavenly Parent should have a hoondok and report meeting every day in their home.

1. Fundamental Paradigm Shift

(1) Families, trinity home groups, and hoondok family group members must be united

Up until now, the home was a place where a family lived privately and the place where they privately gathered to honor Heavenly Parent. Also, it was a place where family ceremonies, hoondok and education in faith were carried out. Therefore, the family and the Family Federation had separate existences. However, now they must become one.

The home must be the place to meet True Parents, and as a place where a life of attendance is realized, it must become the home base of a life of faith to resemble Heavenly Parent.

(2) The family is the place for practicing a spiritual life.

As the home base of a life of attendance, each family must conduct the activities of their spiritual life, training for spiritual development, and work to resemble Heavenly Parent. This means that every process of preparing a holy sanctuary must be performed in each hoondok family group where families are gathered. The family is the fundamental place for spiritual training.

(3) The family is the basic unit for building Cheon Il Guk.

Each family must become a base for the growth period in the

principle of creation of individual perfection, family perfection, and the perfection of Cheon Il Guk. As our spirit develops through the stages of form spirit, life spirit and divine spirit through the exercise of free will, we move through the formation, growth and completion levels in our growth toward individual perfection, finally reaching the point where we can enter the direct dominion of Heavenly Parent. The hoondok family group is needed as the place to complete the process of individual perfection, as well as the perfection of the family and the formation of Cheon Il Guk.

2. Everyday Life of a Blessed Family

The fundamental life of a hoondok family group includes morning hoondokhae and meditation, and evening reflection on life and meditation. Let's look at some examples.

(1) Wake up at 5:00 a.m.

🏠 5:30: Morning Greeting Prayer

"Heavenly Parent and True Parents, have You slept well?"

Offer a good-morning greeting prayer naturally and respectfully, with warmth and emotion. Continue with a prayer of gratitude.

🏠 Gratitude Prayer

"Dear Heavenly Parent, now I am welcoming this new day of (today's date). I thank You for being in my life, allowing me to live and breathe. I thank You that I am alive. I will live an inspiring life with love, joy, peace, and happiness. I will live a life of joy and delight, so please become the center of my heart and the true owner of my life. Heavenly Parent, who has shown me mercy as boundless as the rivers and seas, and has allowed me to experience life with You in this body, I will live with this body, which is Your sacred temple, using it beautifully with goodness, so please guide, lead, and work with me always.

True Parents have told us to regard our experiences with You as important as our life. Since I am going to regard the experience of being the body of Heavenly Parent as important as my life, and live the life of a ghostwriter, a spokesperson, an agent, and a representative of Your true nature, please grant me Your wisdom, ability, and stamina. I report this in gratitude, in the name of (my name), a member of a blessed central family."

(2) Morning meeting at 6:00 a.m.: Hoondokhae and meditation, intellectual and emotional spiritual training

🏠 Offering a Bow

All members of the family gather at 6:00 at home and offer a bow to Heavenly Parent and True Parents, guided by one person who says, "*Charyeot* (attention)! Bow to Heavenly Parent and True Parents. ... *Baro* (at ease)!"

🏠 **Sing the Cheon Il Guk Anthem**

🏠 **Recite the Family Pledge: First verse**

🏠 **Opening Report Prayer**

"We are so grateful to You, Heavenly Parent and True Parents who have saved us and given us new lives. We are beginning our morning's report meeting. Please allow us to live in attendance to Heavenly Parent and True Parents at the center of our family, to worship and to read Your words, embody Your words and understand their true meaning, and participate in the lives of True Parents, and let us directly experience the existence of Heavenly Parent in our lives. Grant us Your mercy that we can serve Heavenly Parent and True Parents, and that we can have active and creative lives of faith.

I report this, with gratitude, in the name of (my name), a blessed central family."

🏠 **Hoondokhae: Spiritual Training for the Intellect (10 minutes)**

Hoondok reading topic: Reproduction is a principle of creation.

🏠 Hoondok reading contents:

Have you all heard about how cell division works? Starting from one cell, cells multiply until in one place you have an eye, in another place a nose, and every other part that is needed. In one place a foot appears, over and over until everything is there. All things are created in the same way. A cell that is connected with true love can have the same value as the entire universe. [Sermons, 216-288]

To maintain organic life, reproduction must be carried on continuously. Reproduction cannot be done through a vertical relationship. To reproduce, a process of separation also is needed. And there must be a horizontal relationship. Through that horizontal relationship, reproduction, multiplication, is carried out naturally. Multiplication cannot occur in a vertical relationship, such as the relationship between a community leader and a local ward head. However, when the two unite, if you are the community leader and the ward leader works in one accord with you, then multiplication can be carried out. This is the principle of creation. [Sermons, 17-278]

Reproduction can be possible, if a subject partner and an object partner perform give-and-receive action focused on the same goal. No matter how perfect a subject partner might be, it is not possible for multiplication to occur with one party only. A condition of relationship must exist in order for multiplication to occur. This is the principle of creation. [*Sermons*, 43-74]

🏠 Explanation of the hoondok reading

True Parents spoke about the process of cell division and connected it to the true love of the universe. This means that as the cells of our body endlessly reproduce, we must become a reproducing body of true love. Isn't it true that our body's cells are constantly reproducing, even while we are unaware of it? In that case, today our families need to look for where the cells of love are present, and how they are reproducing in places we are both aware and unaware of.

🏠 Contemplation on the hoondok reading

Now we will focus more deeply on one term from the hoondok reading: "cell reproduction." In order to understand this more deeply, let us ask Heavenly Parent to speak to each of us. We will wait to hear the message that Heavenly Parent has for us. We are ready to gain enlightenment. We do not want to just read the passage and let it go by. We want to be enlightened by Heavenly Parent on the meaning of the reading and, in this way, make the reading part of our being and essence, which will give us physical purification. Let us contemplate the meaning of "cell reproduction or multiplication."

The person leading the meeting concludes the hoondokhae section after 10 minutes.

🏠 Meditation

Now we will continue with silent meditation. We will have a 20-minute meditation session. Prayer is our connection to Heavenly Parent. Therefore, the most effective spiritual training is prayer. Prayer includes individual prayer, silent prayer, unison prayer, contemplation, meditation, and so on. There are various kinds of meditation too: *Hwaduseon*, *Mookjoseon*, transcendental meditation, *Vipassana* meditation (mind-watching meditation). And among the types of mind-watching meditation, there are breathing meditation, wisdom meditation, merciful meditation (in the Buddhist definition, this actually means "to give joy and remove grief"), and so on.

Transcendental Meditation

Meditation is an essential way of training, in order to become the external form of Heavenly Parent as His temple through spiritual training. It is best if you sit in a natural position. Stretch your spine, do some abdominal breathing naturally, and close your eyes slowly.

It is natural to have distracting thoughts. If such distracting thoughts are formed, go back to a mantra to help get rid of them. Repeating a mantra (e.g., *Ommani*, *Shimmani*, etc.) is the way to connect to the existence (Heavenly Parent). It is a wagon that carries your heart.

As you breathe and repeat your mantra, let your mind relax,

without being concerned about your breathing and mantra occurring together. Just let them go as they will. Transcendental meditation is not about being focused or trying too much. It is just letting go of your consciousness and thoughts. If your face feels itchy during the meditation, just scratch it. You don't have to bear or suppress it. Your head might be lowered or bent backward during the meditation. You may fall asleep. This may happen according to your body or health condition. If you notice something like this happening, just sit up straight again and return to your mantra.

A quiet place is good for meditation, but it is also possible in a subway or on a bus.

If something happens (doorbell or telephone rings, etc.), pause for a moment. But you should come back and finish your meditation time of 20 minutes.

It is most effective to meditate in the morning, and before dinner on an empty stomach. You should meditate for 20 minutes, twice a day.

The phenomenon gained from the meditation is subjective. It may work well or may not. Such things can be affected by the surrounding environment, your health, or your interests. You do not need to try to match the experience of others.

The desired result of the meditation is a peaceful body and mind as you forget about the breathing and even the mantra while retaining consciousness. You may also experience transcendence over your consciousness. However, this state of being is not achieved every time. You may spend the entire time struggling with distracting thoughts, and 20 minutes may seem a very long time. Yet it is very important to do it every day, and if you feel that your mind becomes peaceful and light, the meditation is successful. If you continue practicing transcendental meditation, you will be able to transcend the material world and enter God's territory. If you achieve this, God's characteristics and spirituality will saturate your heart. Transcendental meditation is a passive method to forming spirituality.

If you only commit to a 20-minute meditation twice a day, you will feel swells of joy and impulses of love and devotion from the very center of your heart. Once your meditation is over, finish with a prayer of gratitude.

(3) Evening prayer at 8:00 p.m.: Reflection on life and meditation

Reflecting on our life is an intentional form of spiritual discipline. It is a way to rid our mind of selfishness and self-centered thoughts and to fill it with spirituality. It is practical training in true love. The family gathers in the prayer room at 8:00 in the evening, and the head of the household leads the meeting.

🏠 *Gyeongbae* (bow)

🏠 Opening Prayer

8:00 in the evening is a time for everyone in the family to reflect on their day. It is a time to think about whether we are living according to True Parents' words and the growth period, as described in the principle of creation, and to pray with a heart of repentance and determination to make a new beginning.

🏠 Reflection on our life

Reflection on our daily life is a kind of prayer in which we take an internal look at what we have done, to distinguish what is right or wrong, good or evil.

Reflecting on our day involves general reflection and special reflection. General reflection is a self-examination of our every action during the day. Next, special reflection is directed at a particular problem, thinking about what needs to be fixed or about a virtue that needs to be developed. These two kinds of reflection can be carried out simultaneously. In this way, every action of the day is reviewed carefully, and when an important error is discovered, a special reflection is done to seek a solution. The next step is to record our observations in a journal every day.

General reflection

General reflection, which is necessary to improve and understand oneself well as an eager and dedicated believer, includes the following five key points:

First, we must thank our Heavenly Parent for the grace we have received. The practice of expressing our appreciation becomes a great comfort and sanctifies us at the same time. It reveals clearly any ingratitude that we have, which allows us to repent and maintain our trust in Heavenly Parent.

Second, we recognize our sins and ask for help in defeating this sin in our heart. Therefore, it allows us to assess ourselves accurately so that we can improve ourselves. Without the grace of Heavenly Parent, we cannot understand or improve ourselves.

Third, we must ask Heavenly Parent for forgiveness for our sins. The most important element of reflecting on our life is repentance, and we must not forget that this repentance becomes the cause of Heavenly Parent granting us special grace.

Fourth, we resolve to correct our sins with the help of God's grace.

Finally, we complete the process with a prayer.

Special reflection

Special reflection is perhaps more important than general introspection or prayer. This is because it lets us find each of our flaws and allows us to overcome them easily. Not only that, if we do a thorough self-examination of an important good deed we have done, we will find our conscience is aware of that deed, and that makes it easier for us to continue with other future good actions related to that deed. Therefore, to advance in the virtue of being obedient is to follow the way of humility, self-denial and devoted faith.

Likewise, if we practice the virtue of humility, it helps us practice obedience and loving from God's viewpoint, which cleanses and purifies us. At this time, arrogance may be the strongest interference in practicing the love mentioned above.

Choosing a focus for reflection on daily life

Generally, reflection helps us to overcome our flaws by guiding us to carry out a good action that opposes a big flaw which is controlling us, helping us take a step toward eliminating that flaw. Such flaws are significant spiritual obstacles, and if we learn how to overcome them, we will be able to defeat any kind of enemy.

If we have chosen a subject for reflection, we must challenge any wrong action that is revealed during the course of our reflection. We should work at getting rid of everything that hurts others, everything that is evil.

If "love" was chosen as the subject for reflection, start by suppressing and decreasing any words or actions that oppose love.

Next, do not delay too long, but quickly search for the internal cause of the flaw. For example, emotional jealousy or the desire to show off during a conversation may be revealed as the cause of the flaw. And it is important to sincerely carry out a good action challenging our flaw and to not limit our efforts to only a passive struggle. A flaw cannot be eliminated if we do not take a righteous action that challenges it.

Lastly, to ensure that our advance toward true love progresses, we must distinguish carefully between the subjects to be examined, according to the various levels of good actions. Not every type of good action should be included: only the actions that are necessary for us.

For the virtue of humility, we first must practice self-surrender. So when we have a conversation with others, we should speak less and help the others speak by asking thoughtful questions. Also, we must be careful not to reveal the private things we have heard, because love includes helping people keep their private things unrevealed.

Such methods of reflection may seem a little difficult, but after doing it a few times, we will find it is not difficult. If there is no time for a long reflection, the period can be shortened. For example, spending only two or three minutes each evening will still allow us to make a simple examination of our day.

Preparing for reflection on our life

First, seek a heart of gratitude toward Heavenly Parent, who protects us from sin and temptation and embraces us. Without His grace, we will commit many sins.

If we are sincere in our reflection, we surely will need to repent, as we realize how we have ignored and abused the grace of Heavenly Parent. An attitude of repentance will confirm the understanding of our weakness, helplessness and unworthiness that we have gained from reflecting on our life, allowing us to have true humility. And it is the way to end the shame we feel at repeated wrongdoing.

Reflecting on our life in this way allows us to form a strong determination to improve and mature ourselves. It also dulls the passions of pleasure which are a cause of sin, thus helping us to avoid committing sin and atone for our wrongs through repentance. Going further, it helps us to understand how we can reduce our sinful acts to improve ourselves.

The determination we gain by this kind of reflection helps us to be careful, not relying too much on our own intentions and strength. It also helps us rid ourselves of arrogance, which blocks us from receiving grace and causes us to fall into new mistakes and brash actions. This determination helps us to have faith in the infinite goodness and omnipotence of Heavenly Parent, who is always prepared to help us when we feel inadequate. Through self-reflection on our attitude and our wrongdoings, our soul gradually will change under the influence of Heavenly Parent's grace. (Finish within 10 minutes.)

🏠 Meditation

Next, practice breathing meditation, a type of Vipassana meditation, for 20 minutes (mind-watching meditation).

Training to control self-centered thoughts

Vipassana meditation is an active training method in mindfulness. The practitioner observes the phenomena that occur in the body and mind in order to move away from egocentricity and selfishness. Therefore, Vipassana training is also called mindfulness training. It is a discipline that allows one to notice negative feelings and then change it to divine nature by controlling it.

Breathing meditation method

- Take a seat on the floor or in a chair.
- Straighten your backbone to allow free breathing.

- Relax your body and mind.
- Focus on inhaling and exhaling, and the feeling on the end of your nose, chest and abdomen.
- If a distracting thought comes, recognize it and continue to focus on your breathing and mind.
- The consciousness and the breathing become one.

Becoming one means that the mind is not separated from the breathing, being fully immersed in breathing. Then the mind is stable and in a state of peace.

Once it is stabilized, focus your attention on inhaling and exhaling only, not letting your focus move between the nose and chest any longer, but remaining on the end of the nose, where only exhalation and inhalation can be felt.

When you reach a deep silent and static state, the mind stops moving. Thus, the only target that remains is the breath.

This becomes the beginning and foundation of the training and continues to the next stage. Therefore, in any place or at any time, you can practice this breathing training. It is important to remain aware of your state of mind.

- Finish after 20 minutes.

Walking meditation is a very good form of meditation to master this breathing meditation.

(4) Evening greeting at 10:00 p.m.

🏠 **Evening Greeting**

"Dear Heavenly Parent, True Parents, have a good night."

🏠 **Prayer of Appreciation**

"Dear Heavenly Parent, I offer You my appreciation for allowing me a joyful and happy life within Your grace. I offer endless gratitude and honor to You, who have allowed me to have the morning service and evening prayer and led me to great enlightenment and understanding to live a meaningful life. Thank You.
I report thankfully in the name of (my name), a blessed central family."

3. Weekly Program for Hoondok Family Group

(1) Family service and life introspection prayer session

For five days of the week—Monday, Tuesday, Wednesday, Thursday, and Saturday—the family gathers for family service and life introspection prayer sessions. On Friday, the members of the trinity hoondok family group have a joint meeting. This means that every Friday, there is a time to reflect on the hoondok family group for the week, and to develop each hoondok family group through discussion and testimony. This report session is different from three-cycle report sessions.

(2) Friday trinity home group joint meeting

The purpose of True Parents' assigning blessed families into trinities is so that they could go the way of the Will unwaveringly by uniting with one another centering on True Parents' will. The trinity is the basis and the foundation on which the family, society, and nation can stand firmly. Foundation Day has allowed us to live in a new era, the era of achieving Cheon Il Guk. For Cheon Il Guk to be established, we must build home groups and hoondok family groups based on the trinity. We must form trinities in order to expand the hoondok family groups into tribal churches. God's Will is fulfilled on the foundation of the trinity. For the settlement of Cheon Il Guk we recommend organizing your trinity home groups by district.

① Significance of trinity family group meetings

Trinity hoondok family group meetings are, first, the actualization of the four great realms of love that are practiced in one's hoondok family group, in the tribe and in society. The hoondok family group is where one's family expands its range, to build a tribe through practicing the four great realms of love between three object partners: husband and wife, parent and child, brothers and sisters. If we love only our family, it becomes self-centered. Therefore, expanding the four types of love to our tribe is training to give the true love practiced in our family to other families.

The second purpose of trinity hoondok family groups is mutual cooperative spirituality training, while sharing what the members have experienced in their hoondok family groups or home groups. For the purpose of mutual support, everybody has conversations to encourage, to advise, and to consult with each other.

The third purpose is to work hard to expand and create new hoondok family groups. There are two dimensions of spirituality training. The passive way is to become free from sins, and the active way is to put true love into practice. Spiritual training requires following God, fulfilling God's righteousness, holiness and love, and becoming the embodiment of God.

Overall the purpose of trinity meetings is a chance to reflect and speak openly with each other about our wrong words, thoughts, and actions, and to pray for one another. It is a time for free and honest spiritual training to pursue good actions and avoid bad.

In the hoondok family group meeting, the first important element of spiritual training is striving for internal and individual spiritual purification; the second is making an effort for mutual cooperative spiritual training; and the third is eliminating evil actions and performing good actions that express true love.

② Advantages of trinity hoondok family groups

Of course, it may be difficult to find a time and day on which the trinity home group can meet every week. Nevertheless, finding a way to hold regular meetings as a trinity hoondok family group can have many advantages. First, it provides a stable path of faith. Many elements in modern society make our religious life difficult. We may encounter difficult issues that an individual cannot handle alone. If a trinity of families is united, they will have the resources to overcome any difficulty. A trinity hoondok family group is a place where we can find comfort when we are facing hardships. Each of us will become a windbreaker for the others. The trinity hoondok family group is not simply a social group that gathers and separates once a week. It is a group of people united by a common purpose, who can embrace and support each other's destiny.

Second, it is a place where we can overcome difficult trials. Just as True Parents encountered many tests in their course, there are always tests in a religious life of faith. Whether an interpersonal challenge or a test from Heavenly Parent, after every blessing there is always a new test. These tests are a challenge, but they are also the vehicle for our growth and development. It is all too easy to give up when a challenge comes and just seek to escape the situation. However, in our trinity we can find the wisdom to overcome the tests and challenges we face. If we speak honestly and ask for counsel from the others, their wisdom will become mine. With this wisdom we can overcome the test and continue on the path to becoming a holy person.

Third, we can feel the heart of Heavenly Parent through the harmony in the trinity. The members of a trinity hoondok family group share their lives, actions and values, and they all move in the same direction. When the members of the trinity cooperate and harmonize with one another while living a life centering on Heavenly Parent, they can connect to Heavenly Parent's heart. One can experience His heart in the trinity hoondok family group. Since every member of the trinity hoondok family group has Heavenly Parent's heart within them, they will be able to experience more aspects of His heart if they harmonize and unite.

The trinity hoondok family group is the destiny and duty for all Family Federation members, in alignment with the settlement of Cheon Il Guk and the perfection of the family. It is the best way to maximize the success of our family in realizing the Will of Heavenly Parent.

③ The trinity hoondok family group joint meeting manual

With the guidance of the leader of a trinity hoondok family group, three families gather regularly in one of their homes or a designated place.

◆ **Trinity family group meeting part 1:**

Begin in the same way as the morning service of the hoondok family group.

The hoondok family group leader should lead the service.

- 🏠 *Gyeongbae* (bow)
- 🏠 Hymn or Holy Song
- 🏠 Opening Prayer

🏠 **Hoondok reading:**

"Prayer is a command. No matter how hard it is, we deal with it and make a promise, fulfill it and come back, make a new promise and pray. In the process we grow and develop. 'Dear Heavenly Parent, I did not fulfill what I have promised today.' We repent, and pray, 'Tomorrow I will go forward without fail.' When we have a meal after such a prayer, you should look at your meal and we say, 'Hey, rice! You must become my energy to realize my love and push me in the right direction!' And when you look at your clothes, you should say, 'Hey, clothes! I need to wear you so I can do this job. I am wearing you to defend myself, push myself forward and protect myself!' That's what we should be like."
[*Sermons*, 112-58, 1981.03.29]

🏠 **Silent meditation**

Meditate silently on the words you have just read. Think deeply on a part of the text (or single words) or implications that you resonate with. Talk about your experience or realizations with others.

◆ **Trinity hoondok family group meeting part 2:**
During the evening prayer session, self-reflect and meditate.

🏠 **Reflection on our life**

For life introspection, look back on what has happened in the past week, reflect and repent, ask for forgiveness and make a new resolution (5 minutes).

🏠 Meditation
Do a 20-minute session of mindfulness meditation, using breathing meditation. Then talk about mistakes you have made in your life, and encourage and give advice to one another (20 minutes).

🏠 The trinity family group's time for conversation
Take time to confess the sins of your life to each other, and to encourage and advise each other. (20 minutes)

🏠 The path to becoming god's external form

🏠 The grace of God seeking us before we seek Him

🏠 Questions for spiritual sharing
Even before you realized it, have you experienced the grace of Heavenly Parent, who visits and leads you with passionate love? What do you think the mission is that Heavenly Parent has entrusted to us, according to His Will, for us accomplish during our lifetime?

🏠 Questions for repentance and completion
Is there any experience you have had in your life which causes uncertainty, not knowing if it was a sin or not, in your relation-

ships with other people or in any of your words, actions or attitudes? How are you working for repentance and trying to change the direction of your life?

Each person offers a prayer of promise that he or she will make a new start. Sing hymns, offer a prayer of gratitude, and finish the session.

🏠 Example of joint prayer

"Dear Heavenly Parent who has graciously allowed us to be transformed from the path of death to that of eternal life! Please come and dwell inside each of us; please exist fully in us to become the master of our hearts, and reside in every part of our lives to become the true owner of our hearts, that we may live with vibrant life and faith.
Let us be filled with the wisdom to learn Your words as reborn children; let us be filled with passionate emotion to love our neighbors; and let us live in the way You want us to live, not the way we want to. Please change us with Your holy, beautiful, and good nature, and let us be grateful for all matters, and let love, joy, and peace become the fruits of our spiritual training."

(3) Sunday: Hoondok family group joint service

The hoondok family group worships Heavenly Parent during service every morning as a family, but on Sunday the family does not hold its own service due to the local hoondok family group joint service. Therefore, we recommend having a family worship service at 6:00 in the morning. This is also a very important tradition in True Parents' family.

◆ **The hoondok family group's Sunday pledge service**

Guidelines on clothing and appearance
We should have a clean body and a reverent mind for pledge service. Also, our clothing should be clean and tidy.

Pledge service order
- Bow.
- Recite the Family Pledge.
- Recite the hoondok family group's mission statement.
- Report prayer
- Simple word of request
- Individual prayer

Guideline for pledge service as a blessed family
There are a few considerations when carrying out a pledge service as a blessed family. The blessed family MUST include the Family Pledge as part of the 6 a.m. pledge service. All the members of the family bow once to the altar. Then they recite the Family Pledge together. Then a representative, either the husband or wife, says a

prayer.

The husband and wife stand face to face and offer a full bow to each other once, and sit down facing the children (on the floor or on a seating cushion).

One of the children leads the other children in offering a full bow to the parents. If time permits, the parents tell any story that would work as internal guidance for the children, or a personal testimony, or something they would like to tell, or some news about True Parents.

Through the external action of bowing, all the members of the family can gain a heart of respect for one another. This is an opportunity for the family to make a new resolution to attain reverent love and ideal family relationships.

True Parents have emphasized in *The Way of God's Will* the importance of educating children during pledge service about a life of attending Heavenly Parent.

> "From now on, every Sunday the family should offer a bow to Heaven. Blessed families must set an example of serving Heavenly Parent. When the weekend approaches, you should clean your body and mind and wait eagerly for Sunday morning or the first day of the month to arrive. Sunday must become the day that the children look forward to. The parents should create an environment in which they can joyfully welcome this day with their children."

Children at pledge service

Young children should attend pledge services as early as possible. For example, a baby over six months can attend a pledge service in a parent's arms. It is important to plant such traditions from the time the children are very young. Through these traditions, the children can learn the life of serving God. Although the first child may have a harder time understanding and maintaining this tradition, eventually after having a moving experience, the oldest child will help the younger children to learn the tradition.

Hyojeong Home Group
Report Process

4

In addition, the most important duty of the trinity home group is to get together regularly for report sessions on witnessing activities. This allows the group to organize and receive education in becoming citizens of Cheon Il Guk.

The trinity home group should hold report meetings regularly, focusing on the building of relationships with witnessing contacts—inviting them, nurturing them, and multiplying in numbers through jeongseong (devotion)—as its foundation. After setting a goal, this home group expands from a small group to a large group by performing the whole three-step process over a period of 12 to 16 weeks. Since this home group aims at the expansion of Cheon Il Guk and multiplying, the report meeting also should be held on these topics. This three-step process is called a three-cycle report session, which means that this process should be repeated continuously, just as the wheels of a bicycle turn continuously.

The above process can be explained by the following diagram,

[Figure 1-13] The Elements in the Three-Cycle Report Meeting

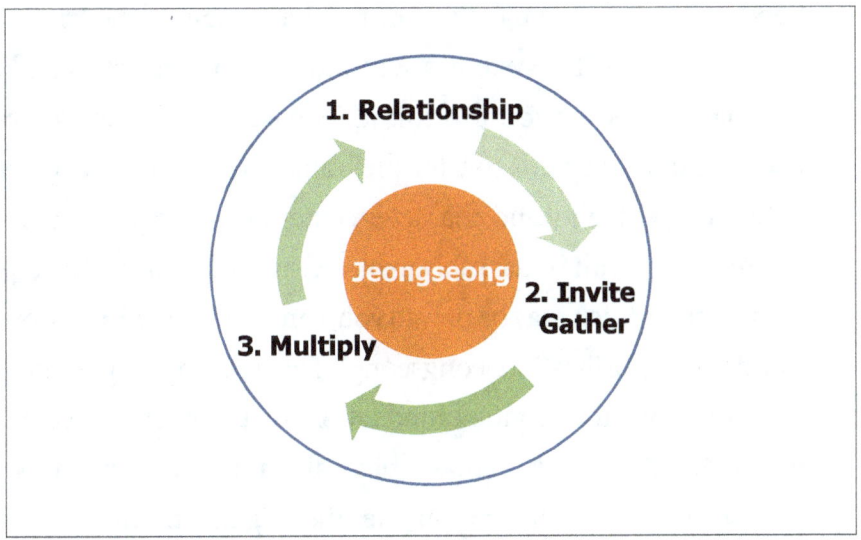

which shows the things that should be focused on in a report meeting session. This process will be described in detail later. For now, brief explanations will be given on building relationships based on jeongseong, inviting, gathering and multiplying. Basically, the home group checks the activity of the trinity through the three-cycle report meetings and works to promote the activities.

1. Purification Jeongseong

Not only before or after organizing a trinity home group, but also in everyday life, jeongseong (supreme loving devotion in both thought and action) has special meaning to heavenly tribal messiahs. It can be said that jeongseong is the water of life in a deep mountain, because it is an essential element for the success of the trinity. No matter how good the system is, it cannot last for long without a basic driving force or lubricant to run it. Jeongseong offerings of prayer and devotions play this role for the home group. They are a combination of spirituality and character centering on hyojeong, which is a core energy with remarkably explosive growth ability. One type of jeongseong, which may be new to you, can be described as "hoondok mind–body purification jeongseong." The types of jeongseong, such as meditation and hoondok meditation, that were explained earlier in this book were also about spiritual training that cleanses and purifies one's evil mind and pursues the original mind.

What we cannot overemphasize is that even when there is a methodology to establish a system and an organizational structure, it is necessary to have the spiritual strength that can move this structure and move the original mind.

(1) Hoondok mind-body purification jeongseong: Course for perfection of character

The common element of all the processes for becoming a heavenly tribal messiah is cultivating ourselves spiritually toward accomplishing individual perfection. This is much like fastening the first button the right way when getting dressed. If there is no such process, it is like building a castle on the sand. If you received the marriage Blessing without this process, it is difficult to expect family

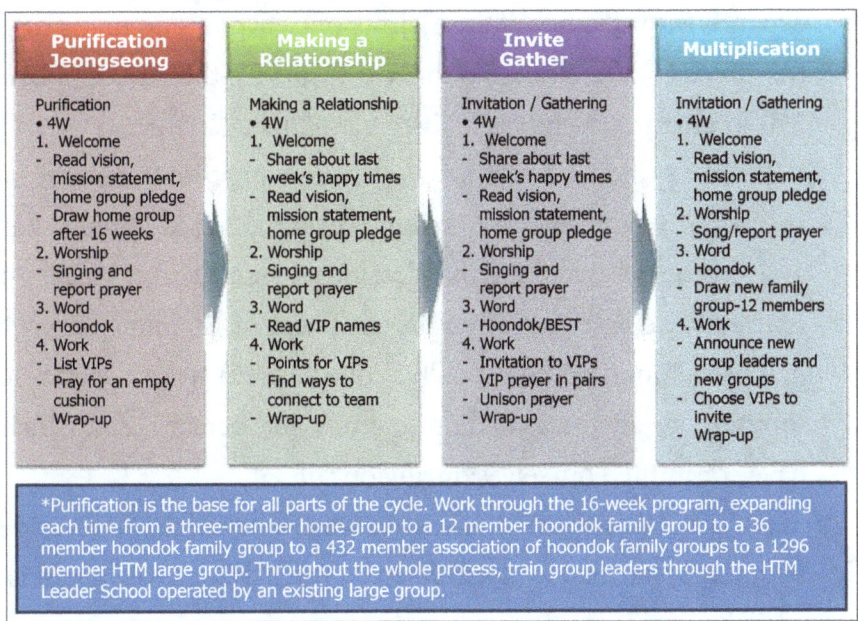

[Figure 1-14] A Three-Cycle Report Meeting Beginning with Purification Jeongseong

perfection or perfection of dominion. In other words, the root of the three great blessings is that we cultivate ourselves spiritually. In order to accomplish this purpose, we read the Word, purify our body and mind, and offer our jeongseong to drive forward the process of our individual perfection. The key to multiplying the home group is jeongseong that combines the power of the Holy Spirit of hyojeong and one's character.

Hoondok mind-body purification jeongseong requires that we "read the Word and offer jeongseong with mind-body unity to achieve the first blessing (perfection of character). To unite the mind (the original mind) and the body we should carry out acts of faith that constantly purifies the evil mind, sanctifies the body and expands the influence of the divinity of Heavenly Parent inside us in the process." We cleanse ourselves to purify the mind. (Matthew 5:8) To purify ourselves is to live a life of *aju* (我主).

From a principled perspective, this is "a practice to remove fallen nature." If we receive the Blessing, original sin is cleanly washed away by the holy wine and the Blessing we receive from True Parents. However, we have to wash away the stains of hereditary sin, which has been inherited continually; collective sin, which came down through our ancestors and our culture, and personal sin, which we have committed ourselves during our life.

As True Mother said, we have to wash away all the faults and sins with clean, purified, water created by the light of hyojeong. It is not until, having washed away our sins in this way, we enter the path of sanctification on our own and talk directly with True Parents and Heavenly Parent that we reach the perfection of character.

Learning this process is at the root of the home group endeavor, and the core of this process is jeongseong, which is the way for all members to experience Heavenly Parent. In order to undergo spiritual experiences of Heavenly Parent, we have to widen the space for Heavenly Parent inside ourselves. Our body and mind have to become *aju* (我住), the house where Heavenly Parent lives.

When the "I" inside us is cleansed, that is, our inner ego is purified, then Heavenly Parent is liberated and we can become one with Heavenly Parent. We can become people who live with the original mind. The original mind is the mind of Heavenly Parent, who is the subject of conscience. The original mind is the owner of unchanging principles.

When we become one with the original mind, we become fragrant "true selves" full of freedom, happiness and joy. To become such a person, we need the practice of hoondok mind-body purification jeongseong. The goal of the trinity's activities is to unite as a team, create a home group and continue its activities, rather than performing activities alone. Expansion and reproduction of this process become the way to save all the suffering people in the world.

The gathering of the trinity—in other words, the gathering of a home group—exists in many forms. However, among them, there is a core report meeting like the worship service report meeting of a large group. This report meeting is one method of expanding Cheon Il Guk by continuously repeating the three processes of building hyojeong relationships with Heavenly Parent and people based on jeongseong, inviting, gathering people, and multiplying the trinity. We call it a three-cycle process, because it reminds us that it must keep moving continuously, like bicycle wheels. We have to turn the bicycle wheels by moving our feet. We are riding the bicycle, and we are on the move every hour of every day. This is the three-cycle process of a home group. In other words, it is building relationships, inviting, gathering and multiplying centering on jeongseong. In this regard, hoondok mind-body purification jeongseong is the root, the center, and the base of the home group report meeting, fulfilling the jeongseong that is the core and anchor of the entire process.

① Hoondok mind-body purification jeongseong that develops hyojeong

The term hoondok mind-body purification jeongseong is a combination of the words "hoondok," "mind and body," "purification" and "jeongseong." It looks like a new term, but actually it is not. There are many ways to offer our jeongseong. The term "jeongseong" includes a wide range of activities and is not easy to understand. This activity may become a vague if we are not carful. Therefore, it is named with the combination of the words "hoondok," "mind-body unity," and "purification jeongseong," which are key elements to a hyojeong culture.

In particular, purification jeongseong was asked repeatedly of all blessed families on the 48th Heavenly Parent's Day on the first day of the first month of the third year of Cheon Il Guk (February 19, 2015, by the solar calendar). True Mother said, "I sincerely hope that all blessed families will become clear water that purifies their surroundings." The blessed families first must become clear water, and then they can purify their surroundings and the world. This clear water is the "clear water of hyojeong," which can purify the filth of the world. Therefore, hoondok mind-body purification jeongseong is a driving force of jeongseong that develops hyojeong (a heart of filial piety) and brightens the world with its light.

At the second anniversary of the Seonghwa of True Father, the True Parent of Heaven, Earth and Humankind (7.17 by the heavenly calendar, August 12 by the solar calendar) True Mother gave us True Father's words, "Forgive, Love and Unite." All blessed families have to live according to these Words with a heart of hyojeong. We should think of what happened to others or what happened to ourselves as our own responsibility, seeking forgiveness from Heavenly Parent, loving and uniting. In addition, we have to live a life of reporting to Heavenly Parent, the owner of our body and mind.

Hoondok mind-body purification jeongseong is a process of reading the Word, using key words to summarize the most important part of the message—the part you want to remember—and living a life of purification through contemplating on it every second of every minute of every day. You also may purify your life through physical actions and practices such as offering bows.

> Hoondokhae is a time when True Parents guide us toward perfection. Hoondokhae should become a hobby, and we should eat spiritual food through it. Through Hoondokhae, our family and our spiritual life can grow. After the return of the realm of spirit world to earth, the spirit world that has helped True Parents can help us. [*Sermons*, 292-17, 293-108, 293-106, 295-274]

Hoondok mind-body purification jeongseong is a time to interact with Heavenly Parent within our lives. During this time, we can listen to the voice of the conscience, the voice of the original mind within us. It is a time to communicate with Heavenly Parent, who is not only inside us but also inside everyone. It means to read the Word, meditate on the Word and practice the Word. Heavenly Parent is not elsewhere. Heavenly Parent is with us. Heavenly

Parent is not somewhere else, Heavenly Parent is in our heart Therefore, when we pray, we should talk with our heart. Heavenly Parent is at the root of our heart. If we continuously reach into our heart, we will see that Heavenly Parent is right there at the root of our conscience. [CSG, p. 33]

How can we meet Heavenly Parent and live within God? Meditating for 20 minutes twice a day is one part of the process. At first we can meet God with our heart, and then we can experience God through the five senses. [*Hyeokmyeong-jeok Dae Jeonhwangi (Revolutionary Great Turning Point)*, Sung Hwa Publshing, 2012, p. 112]

How can we find Heavenly Parent's answers in our mind? Sometimes we cannot hear any answer, and other times we hear so many answers that we cannot tell which is from Heavenly Parent. We need to choose the voice of the conscience from the root of the mind, the voice of the original mind, which is the more fundamental. If we write down the story of our day's work while living such a life, the record is called a hoondok mind-body purification jeongseong journal, that is, a shimjeong (heart) journal (reflection journal).

A person with a pure mind can see Heavenly Parent. Purification means making the mind clear. Making efforts for this to happen is one kind of jeongseong. There are two types of purification: 1) We take responsibility and purify our mind; and 2) Heavenly Parent intervenes and purifies our mind. It is said that Heavenly Parent does things that humankind cannot do through the expansion of

His divine infinite power. Surprisingly, this purification not only makes our mind clear but also cures illnesses of the body that have been caused by the mind and brings us an experience of joy.

Among True Parents' words, there are places where spiritual experiences with Heavenly Parent are described. We should live every day as described below.

"When you are hungry you say, 'I'm hungry! I want something to eat!' But for whom do you want to eat? Do you want to eat for God, or for yourself? You must eat for God. By doing this, you make your body a perfect holy temple of God. You should think, 'God inside me is hungry and is telling me to eat.' When you eat with this mindset, your meal becomes sacred. It is the same when you breathe, when you use the toilet, or when you do anything else. When you listen, you are not listening alone. Likewise, when you see or touch something, do not think that you are doing it alone. When you relate to people, even when you relate to Satan's world, you need to think that it is God who is relating to them through you. When you speak, you should think that God is speaking through you. When you are totally one with God, you can live. Even though your living, thinking and loving are centered on yourself, it still will be lawful. Even though you live, think and love centered on yourself, your living, thinking and loving will be centered on God. That is the principle." [CSG, 11.1.2:6]

① What are the methods for hoondok mind-body purification jeongseong?

Methods of jeongseong may vary depending on the person. We can choose a time and then pray, bow, and sing Holy Songs at the specified time. Living a life of jeongseong means remembering the contents of the hoondok we read in the morning, and purifying ourselves by thinking of key ideas from the Word every second of every minute of every hour of every day. In particular, purification jeongseong is a way to accomplish the first blessing of uniting the mind and body. Hoondok mind-body purification jeongseong means reading True Parents' words, standing at the center of Heavenly Parent, and purifying and sanctifying our mind and body. Therefore, we need jeongseong of the body and the mind. We can do jeongseong of the mind in the ways described below. However, everyone is different, and we can develop various methods that suit us best and use them. Here are some typical examples.

a. How to purify the mind in daily life

When something happens or you think of something, ask your Heavenly Parent inside you. For example, if you become angry, ask, "Heavenly Parent, I'm angry now. What do you want me to do?" and "What do you want me to be like now?" Then, face your current situation.

When you think in this way, it will purify you and you will see yourself talking with Heavenly Parent. Moreover, your anger will abate, and you will see yourself giving messages of gratitude and love to yourself. Speak repeatedly to Heavenly Parent within you when you are angry, "Forgive me. Thank You. I love You. I will unite." At the moment, you will notice that you are already purified. Then, recall the key words from the Hoondok, and feel gratitude and love so that feelings of "Thank you" and "I love you" can reach the depths of your mind. You will be surprised when you look at yourself as your anger changes into gratitude and love. This is hoondok mind-body purification jeongseong which trains your mind in the course of your daily life.

Purification jeongseong is the root within a home group for making relationships, inviting, recruiting, and multiplication based on jeongseong, which is the core of a home group report meeting. When you have accomplished your individual perfection through hoondok mind-body purification jeongseong, many people around you will follow. It is the same way that flowers attract bees and butterflies. Flowers with fragrance and honey do not go to the bees and butterflies. This is because bees and butterflies are bound to come to the flowers.

The process is illustrated in Figure 1-15.

Once a consistent hoondok mind-body purification jeongseong is achieved, "building beautiful relationships" is next. When meeting a wholesome person, each relationship will form a trinity relationship and multiply. Then, after each trinity focuses on Heavenly Parent and forms a four-position foundation, those in the four-position

[Figure 1-15] The Process of Purifying the Mind through Hoondok Mind-Body Purification Jeongseong

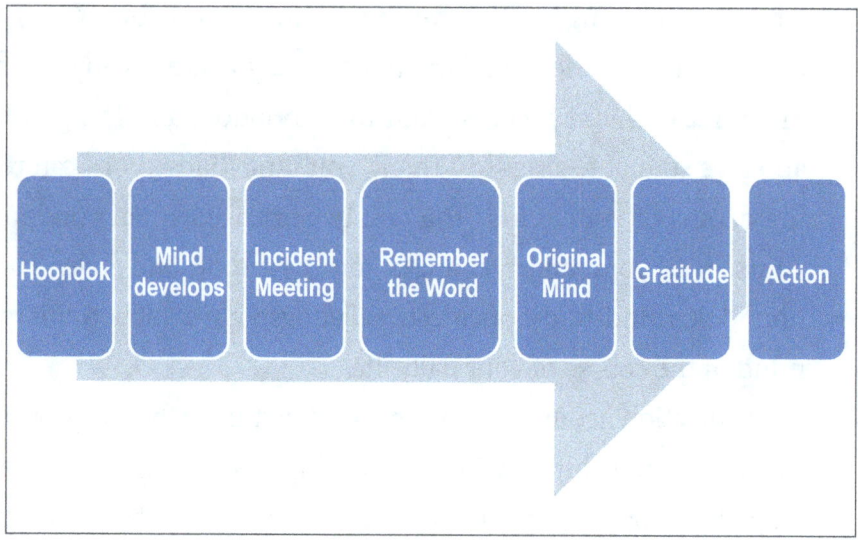

foundation will be able to personally manifest the first blessing and True Parents' ideologies.

"You need to know the greatness and power of prayer. (In) the Bible (it says) ... if three people join together in prayer, they have great power." [CSG, 9:3:4:31]

Building beautiful relationships leads to inviting. If you gather those who are invited and they become members of a home group, there will be automatic multiplication.

b. Maintaining prayer teams in a large group

Purification jeongseong by individuals and trinities is powerful teamwork in a small group, that is, a home group. However, a "purification jeongseong prayer team" is absolutely necessary, even in a large center. It is generally recommended to Family Federation churches or district headquarters, that is, to large groups, that longer-term elderly members or spiritually sensitive members form an "intercession prayer team." The prayer team makes a schedule to pray in the prayer room through teamwork so that the candles of jeongseong never go out in the center.

The prayer team serves publicly to offer jeongseong for the achievement of the purpose, goal, vision, and mission of the group. Moreover, if a midsize group or home group requests prayers, the prayer team leader adds them to the prayer request list and provides prayer ministry to the team members. In addition, it also provides personal intercessory prayers. He or she can pray for a personal wish, for health and for successful achievements in their business. The prayer team makes a "prayer box" to collect prayer requests and places it at the entrance of the center to allow members to put their prayer requests in the box when entering or leaving the center. When they come to the center to offer jeongseong, the prayer team collects the prayer requests from the box, the prayer team leader will hold a meeting and distribute the prayer contents to the members of the team. In this way, large, middle and home groups, prayer and jeongseong should become a root of support for our work. These habits eventually will inspire us to participate in the CheongPyeong great works to provide additional spiritual support for our work.

c. Going the way to discover our true self—feeling the presence of Heavenly Parent

A heavenly tribal messiah starts the day with hoondok mind-body purification jeongseong, forms trinity relationships with people within and outside the large and home groups, and invites tribe members and neighbors to a place of happiness to receive the Blessing. This is not a one-day task or program but a continuing way of life, like eating three meals a day. In this way of life, hoondok mind-body purification jeongseong is a core element of daily life. If we offer jeongseong, we will feel Heavenly Parent. We should talk with Heavenly Parent at all times. Belief in spiritual experiences is a necessity. The closer we reach the deepest state, the closer we get to Him.

Heavenly Parent, who is within me, is the True Parents of Heaven, Earth and Humankind. There are both divine character and human character within us. We need to discover the divinity within us. We know in our head how Heavenly Parent exists and what kind of divine entity Heavenly Parent is, because we have listened to the Divine Principle. However, if we know this only in our head, we cannot feel Heavenly Parent. We should feel Heavenly Parent in our heart. Do we feel as much as we know? No, we do not. There is a huge difference between knowing and feeling. There is a very big difference between knowing and spiritually experiencing what we know.

At the very beginning of *Cheon Seong Gyeong*, we can find these statements:

"Through my life of constant prayer and meditation from an early age, I finally encountered God." [CSG, 1.1.1:1]

"God existed before we came into existence. He existed before we could think, and He leads our senses and our whole being. This awareness is more important than anything else. The basic point is that awareness precedes knowledge, not the other way around. If we are cold, we feel cold before we know we are cold. Likewise, since God exists, we should be able to feel His existence in our very cells. Achieving that awareness is what matters. The issue is how we achieve that awareness, the ability to experience these things." [CSG, 1.1.1:2]

In this way, we should be able to feel, spiritually experience and physically experience the divinity inside us with our own ability. We should discover Heavenly Parent in us. Thus, as hoondok mind-body purification jeongseong reaches a deeper stage, we can have a more profound experience. This is our own responsibility. If hoondok mind-body purification jeongseong reaches a much deeper stage, we can discover not only Heavenly Parent inside us but also Heavenly Parent inside others. Continuing this practice means pursuing the path of individual perfection, which is the attainment of the first blessing given to us by Heavenly Parent, "Be fruitful." However, what does our life look like in reality? Are we living a joyful life in which we feel free and happy while feeling Heavenly Parent with a heart of hyojeong?

Ask yourself these questions: What kind of person am I? I do not feel comfortable. I have anxiety and fear. I have hate, jealousy and envy in me. Sometimes I get sick. At times I exist only for myself. I have preconceived ideas that I believe are right. I make judgments and act based on stereotypes. I need to know who I am. What are all the things I am anxious about or afraid of? It is me obsessed with the past or things I have to accomplish in the future. I am the one who is holding myself back. I try to draw who I am, but in fact, what I draw is not the image of Heavenly Parent. It is my own current image that I cannot take off. That image is my reality and your reality. If that is the case, who am I in this condition and who are you in this condition? It is "you and me," wrapped in ego, not my true self or your true self. My true self is covered, restricted and restrained by my condition. What I need is to feel that my true self is Heavenly Parent and my divine original mind. Because of my false self, my original mind is hidden and sad. My false self is suffocating and imprisoning my true self.

Who is my false self? Is it the part of me filled with trauma, hate and fear? A jealous and envious me! Who on earth am I with such qualities? Such a person is my evil mind, which is self-centered and follows evil nature that judges others according to my will. Who is this person? He is "me with Satan." It is called an evil mind. The evil mind lives by feeding on anxiety, fear, jealousy, envy, misunderstanding and wrong desires. Without purifying these things, joy and peace will not come inside me.

We have to change quickly. When we notice these things, we only need to acknowledge the wrong "me." We have to acknowledge and support the divinity of people who are around us. The people who really accomplish the perfection of their character know that Heavenly Parent is next to them, so their behavior changes. This is the way to the completion of the first blessing. It is not that others let me go the way but that the divinity in me becomes more influential if I do the jeongseong to purify myself and reduce the influence of my false self, the evil mind inside me. If I reach this stage, the divine in me dominates my body. In me, Heavenly Parent becomes the owner (*Aju* dwelling in me), and Heavenly Parent resides in me. *Aju* means to become one with Heavenly Parent.

When my body becomes one with the divine, illness and pain disappear and my body becomes the body of Heavenly Parent. Sometimes, even if I feel a sickness in my body, I will think of the body as a sacred body, and even the pain will be thought to be brilliant pain and holy pain. If I reach this stage, I can say, "Thank you," even though I feel sick. Since I think of my pain as the pain of divinity, I can say this time, "I'm sorry, my body became sick because I mistreated it. Please forgive me. Heavenly Parent, I still thank You so much that I am alive and breathing. Thank You. I thank even this pain for giving me illumination. Thank You. Thank You. Thank You." If this gratitude goes beyond the boundaries, love naturally enters my mind so I can say, "I love You. I love You. I love You," and I will experience that the divinity exerts such influence over me that I actually feel my body heat up with it, making me feel refreshed so I can become an incarnation of joy, and then I can say, "I became one with Heavenly Parent."

Many members in Korea and Japan have been tasting joy and happiness through hoondok mind-body purification jeongseong. There are more and more members who actually have experienced the presence of Heavenly Parent. There was a member who was suffering from cancer and was afraid, and she said that she felt calm in the deepest part of her mind while offering purification jeongseong. She said that her fear was worse than the pain in her body, but after being liberated from fear, her prayers became very free.

Many others have given testimonies about their experiences. They are delighted because the hate and fear they felt toward people disappeared, the moment they offered hoondok and purification jeongseong. The divinity within them worked and exerted influence. We really need to thank our True Parents for letting us know this. At home, many conflicts between parents and their children are healed. At this time, we have to restore the heart of hyojeong, like True Parents say, "Forgive, Love and Unite."

d. Purifying the body

What do we mean when we talk about purifying the body? Until now, we have focused primarily on purifying our mind. However, our body also should be purified. For example, purifying the body is learning how to do a pledge service of offering jeongseong and doing True Parents' physical training exercises in order to purify the body properly so that the energy of divinity circulates well. Our mind becomes the subject and focuses on purifying our body. We can feel by ourselves that the energy of the divine flows in our body and heals and purifies not only ourselves but also others.

By doing this we should be able to sympathize with Heavenly Parent and feel the empathy of true love. However, with whom do we feel empathy every single day? We need to look at ourselves frequently. When we call God, "Heavenly Parent," do we really receive the answer "Yes, child"? We cannot get a response because we are not one with Him and all that comes to us are our own thoughts. Therefore, we easily give up on jeongseong and prayer or offer only habitual prayer and jeongseong.

e. Practicing purification

Here is how to purify yourself based on what you have learned so far. First, it is important to have time to think of who you are. It is recommended that you purify yourself in a quiet place through meditation and meditation prayer. There are many ways to do this, but here is a method of purification through writing and meditation. It also would be good to purify through a hyojeong workshop in the large, middle and home groups.

In general, when people ask, "Who are you?" everyone says their name. In addition, if they are asked to write a self-introduction letter, everyone writes as follows.

The following things roughly represent who you are.

☰ Writing 360 answers to the question "Who am I?"

Who are you? Write down who you are.

Name	
Age	
Home Country	
City of Birth	
Schools you went to	
Family	
Occupation	
Position	
Other	

For example, you may have written something like this:

Hong Gil-dong, forty years of age, CEO, father of ∘∘∘, husband of ∘∘∘, son of ∘∘∘.

Are these things really you? Take time to think quietly and continue to write down who you are. To complete this process, you should write 360 answers to the question "Who am I?" Generally, when most people have written about 100 answers, they stop writing or give up. If you continue until you have written down 360 answers, you will be enlightened.

Who am I really?
Where does the answer "me" come from?
This answer comes from my thoughts or my evaluations.

Where did my thoughts and evaluations about my wife, husband, children, relatives and witnessing contacts come from?

These are evaluated by things that are consciously and unconsciously stored in our brain. By the way, scholars say that everything we assess and define is saved in the brain. However, they say that rather than exact facts, it is personal thoughts, judgments, the environment and other circumstances that are saved. In conclusion, the truth is sometimes omitted, and distorted contents are delivered consciously or unconsciously. Sometimes memories of things that didn't happen are saved as well. We cannot deny that we judge and condemn others with the "me" that we know, with our subjective judgments, our thoughts or our beliefs. Unforgettable experiences like trauma become embedded in our unconscious mind and trouble us. All these things are gathered together and form the so-called "me." What can Heavenly Parent, the owner of the original mind who should be able to live within us, do when we are in this condition?

Heavenly Parent is imprisoned within us. The Divine Principle says that the owner of the evil mind is Satan. Isn't Heavenly Parent, the owner of the original mind, trapped by our own self which is tied down with the memories of ourbad past, distorted judgments and our ego? Can Heavenly Parent breathe well? What will happen to Heavenly Parent inside us if we do not purify ourselves?

In the end, hoondok mind-body purification jeongseong liberates Heavenly Parent in us, and when He is liberated, we can become sacred, cultivate our own temple within us, and cleanse everything.

The divinity within us can awake when we are purified. That's "the way I live."

Heavenly Parent exists in a state of confinement within you. [CSG, p. 96].

If this is true, it means that ultimately I am the very person who confined and restrained the divine Heavenly Parent of the divinity in me. Therefore, I am a sinner.

According to the Word, we should have the mind to think, "Everything is my fault." How have I been so far? My wife? My husband? My children? Tribes? Witnessing guests? We need to think of whether there were wrong judgments or thoughts about them. What thoughts did I have?

It is said that Christianity is a "redemptive religion." Jesus died on the cross for humankind. He took up the cross instead of them. Jesus did not blame them and even asked God to forgive their sins. What did True Parents do? True Father said, "While in prison I was whipped, beaten, tortured and bloodied, yet I never resented those who beat me." [CSG, 3:3:3:25] Buddhism teaches that we should abandon all greed within ourselves. Emptying the mind means that we should purify our evil mind.

Are we really capable of doing that? How are we doing? In the end, becoming a heavenly tribal messiah means becoming a person who resembles True Parents. Can we take responsibility even for the faults of other people or illnesses as our own faults? We should be able to think, "Everything is my fault."

The True Parents gave the Words, "Before seeking dominion over the universe, perfect dominion over yourself." No matter how great something we try to do is, if we cannot have dominion over ourselves, in the end it will come to nothing. Purification jeongseong is a process of enhancing the strength to have dominion over ourselves, centering on True Parents' Words.

≡ Listening to the Voice of the Original Mind 1

Before listening to the voice of your original mind, question yourself. If there are serious mistakes you have made that you can think of, write them down. Think of people involved in your home, center, and workplace, as well as yourself. Think of people you have hated, disliked, feared and do not want to talk with, or recall the preconceived ideas that you have considered right and acted upon.

There are your stereotypes that limit you, such as: "_____ is never allowed!" or "_____ must be like that!" What are those things? How many times have you asked Heavenly Parent in you about whether these things are right or not?

Now, with the understanding that the cause of our apologetic feelings and wrongdoings is our own self, let's write down our various mistakes as they come to mind. Then we will read each subject three times in a quiet voice.

_____ is my fault. Please forgive me.
_____ is my fault. Please forgive me.
_____ is my fault. Please forgive me.
_____ is my fault. Please forgive me.

.... is my fault. Please forgive me.
.... is my fault. Please forgive me.
.... is my fault. Please forgive me.

All these mistakes come from our false self that is embedded in our mind and body, not our true self. This version of ourselves was passed down from our ancestors before we existed, and unconsciously acquired from our family and the environment. It is the false self which has unconscious beliefs based on desires of the body rather than the true heart. It is "me centered on myself." It is our stereotypes, not our original mind, which is Heavenly Parent who originally exists within us. Everything that is wrong came from my false self.

Listening to the Voice of the Original Mind 2

Quietly close your eyes, sit upright and take time to examine your false self. How does Heavenly Parent feel looking at you? Why can you not sympathize with and feel empathy with the heart of Heavenly Parent in you? Try to focus on yourself in the now.

Purification jeongseong begins with observing yourself in the here and now and seeing yourself accurately. We need to recognize our mistakes and wash away the layers to find the original self. If tears come out, just shed tears. Feel the voice of the original mind and experience what is going on spiritually. If we do not remember what we have done wrong, it is because of the persistent dirt in , which is dull and solid and sticks without moving. We should realize this and repent. This should be purified. Wash it away with tears and prayer. Then, feel the eyes of True Parents that are watching you do this.

We should increase the divine influence of Heavenly Parent in us. Having spiritual experiences is to feel and react. Look into "pitiful me" with your own unfilial mind. Then, think of what is "hyojeong me" and confess to yourself with the right attitude, "Heavenly Parent, I'm sorry. Everything is my fault. Please forgive me. Heavenly Parent, please forgive me." Then forgive yourself.

Accept this feeling deeply, and continue to feel it while waiting until this feeling is delivered to your body. If not, wait until you can feel it and then try again. Try again and again each day until you can make it.

Wait until your heart is filled with emotion and until you feel warm in your heart. Your cells and body will react and change. When tears come out, do not keep back your tears but shed them freely.

Listening to the Voice of the Original Mind 3

Now you need to proclaim loudly:

"The wrong things were not done by my true self."

"From now on, I will never be led by my false self."

"Never!" "Never!" "Never!"

Heavenly Parent does not leave you or the people you love, but remains within you and in them. Feel it again.

As tears fill your heart, you will feel gratitude for Heavenly Parent who would not abandon you even when you were your false self. Now you will never be led by your false self.

Listening to the Voice of the Original Mind 4

Now give your love and thanks with a heart of hyojeong and a report of love. Thank You. Thank You. Thank You. Please express your gratitude deeply with a word of gratitude in order for the word of gratitude to permeate your mind and heart and then spread throughout your whole body through the blood bursting forth from your heart; this will give your whole body the spiritual experience of the word of gratitude. Thank You. Thank You, Heavenly Parent in me.

Now, think of gratitude and love that spill over into feeling and happiness in your life. Feel a lot of gratitude and love for you, your family, relatives and VIPs. Think of what made you feel gratitude and love, and express thanks and love in writing as you feel it. Then, read each one three times with your heart.

Expressing Gratitude and Love in Writing

	Thank You. I love You.
	Thank You. I love You.
	Thank You. I love You.
	Thank You. I love You.
	Thank You. I love You.

> Thank You. I love You.
> Thank You. I love You.

Speak words of thanks every single day, and express "gratitude and love in writing." A life of thankfulness, keeping a gratitude journal, a shimjeong journal and giving a gratitude report every day will turn you into your "true self." Words of thanks and a life of gratitude produce surprising and mysterious results.

This heart of gratitude soon leads to eager love. In other words, it becomes *gamsarang*, the combination of *gamsa* (gratitude) and *sarang* (love). Now experience and enjoy that Heavenly Parent and you have become one. In addition, at the closing stage, proclaim that you have become one with Heavenly Parent or others. And feel that your mind, which is the original mind, and your body have become one.

Proclaiming Oneness

> I become one with
> I become one with
> I become one with

So far, we have learned how to liberate Heavenly Parent in us and how to listen to the voice of our original mind, based on True Mother's words "Forgive, Love and Unite." This training should be experienced by all blessed families. It is recommended to do this frequently during jeongseong report sessions in home groups.

[Figure 1-16] The Process of Achieving Oneness

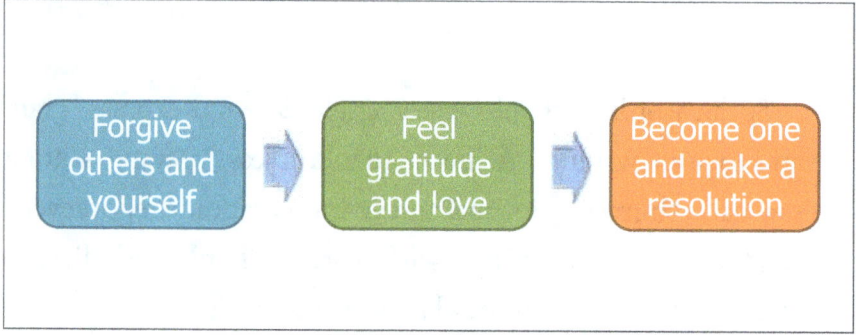

Moreover, if members periodically participate in the shimjeong training sessions or the hyojeong training session which is part of the HTM Leader School program or large group center education program, it can have a profound effect.

f. Holding a hyojeong training session

It is recommended that large, midsize and home groups organize the training components described above and hold a hyojeong training session, working in small groups or teams within home groups, large groups or leader school workshops. In the past, shimjeong training sessions were held without established standards. However, existing members as well as new members should look into themselves through a hyojeong training session to feel and spiritually experience Heavenly Parent and True Parents, and they should participate in many training sessions to come closer to their original mind.

In particular, it is necessary to learn the technique of "original mind coaching" in the hyojeong coaching leadership session that is part of HTM Leader School III. This becomes a tool for solving many problems in a home group or when meeting new people.

g. Case stories of purification jeongseong

Many cases of purification jeongseong have been reported in Korea and Japan. There are a lot of cases of purification occurring among members who did not have the will to witness as well as purification between husband and wife so that they could restore the atmosphere of a true family.

Here is the case of a member in Okayama, Japan.

> There was a woman living in fear because her husband beat her. After participating in the workshop, she chose to offer jeongseong. She had been beaten all her life, so in her terror, she had even considered suicide. However, she chose to offer purification jeongseong. Thinking of Heavenly Parent in her and of Heavenly Parent living in her husband, she offered jeongseong. She thought, "The one who fears my husband is myself. What are the thoughts of the original mind in me?" She was full of fear and dread of her husband, but when she felt her original mind, something amazing happened. She was saddened as she felt pity for her husband, who had lost love, so she shed endless tears. Then she confessed to Heavenly Parent within her, "I'm sorry. Please forgive me. Thank You. I love You."
>
> At that moment, she was touched with pity for her husband and

her heart was filled with love. On the following day, her husband also beat her as always. In the past, she ran away and screamed for help because of fear and dread. However, on that day, when she was hit, she held her husband and eagerly confessed to Heavenly Parent in her husband.

"Heavenly Parent, all these things are my fault. I am sorry. Forgive me." At that moment, hot tears flowed from her eyes, and even while she was being beaten, love entered her heart. "Thank You! I love You!" The tears were not tears of fear and dread but tears of love. At the moment she was being beaten, she chose to have a heart of gratitude and love. This gift can come only from Heavenly Parent.

She felt pity for her husband, who did not know that there was a divinity in him and who was acting at the bidding of his evil mind. She used to be scared when she saw her husband's eyes, but she was very surprised because her heart was so peaceful. She cried because she felt pity for her husband, not because she was afraid of his eyes and angry punches. She asked God to forgive her husband. As she looked at her husband, she felt that he had softened and the forbidding look on his face was gone. What surprised her the most was how much she had changed. Moreover, the members around her were so surprised when they saw that her purification jeongseong changed her environment as well as herself, even though the external situation had not changed at all. Changes like these are very common around us.

2. Home Group Three-Cycle Report Meeting

We have learned about hoondok mind-body purification jeongseong, a way of perfection of character, which is the most important core factor in the process of becoming a heavenly tribal messiah. After becoming a perfect person, what should we do then? What is the perfection of the individual for? It is for a hyojeong relationship with others. In other words, we should succeed in making a relationship of a foundation of substance with other people, with individual truth incarnation, on the spiritual foundation of faith built between Heavenly Parent and ourselves.

Heavenly Parent yearned for the heart of hyojeong and did not want to exist alone, so He created all things and humankind as His substantial object partners of filial piety. Individual perfection eventually should be followed by a stage of building hyojeong relationships. No one can live alone in this world. Blessed families can be on a route to the perfection of the family only if beautiful give-and-receive relationships between subject partners and object partners are established.

(1) Home group three-cycle report meeting—meaning and effect

Members of the trinity get together and have a home group report session. A jeongseong report meeting, which is rooted in hoondok mind-body purification jeongseong, is a report meeting with three-cycle reports on building relationships, inviting and gathering and multiplication, in rotation. Specific details and manuals for this report session will be presented in the following chapter. A home group report meeting is a meeting with a clear purpose of the reporting on and supporting these activities.

The home group report session, held on a weekly or daily basis, enables new members to transform their character and heal relationships. Therefore, this enables them to be born as new people of character who are able to solve problems on their own, both individually and in their families. In this process, they undergo a process of becoming a core member of the Family Federation. The existing regular members of the Family Federation also gain spiritual children through a process of new self-transformation, which allows them to live their life as a heavenly tribal messiah, forming a heavenly tribe together with the new members.

(2) Characteristics of non-growing home groups

① Home group gatherings that do not include three-cycle reports

Nevertheless, many experiences have shown that it is not easy to run a home group. According to the reports of visits to members who run home groups, many home groups hold gatherings without including the three elements in the cycle of making relationships based on jeongseong, inviting and gathering, and multiplication. These were not home group report sessions but general district gatherings, small groups or social gatherings.

These gatherings strengthened relationships among small groups, so it was possible to maintain the gatherings, but these did not have healthy growth with multiplication for the formation of new home groups.

Gatherings of a small group have many purposes. Home groups differ from general small groups in that they have distinctly defined purposes and directions. In particular, these are witnessing-oriented and Cheon Il Guk multiplication-oriented. These aim to offer jeongseong for witnessing guests, establish healthy hyojeong relationships with, invite them and gather them as members. The home groups have a report session with these specific purposes for Heavenly Parent. If a home group does not have these, it can be a home group gathering but cannot be a "home group report meeting."

② Dictatorial leadership by home group leaders

The role of leaders in operating a home group is very important. Leaders have to be competent to run small groups. The leadership qualities required to run a home group are different from those required for large groups. In a home group, a small number of people who are adjacent to one another have gatherings in a small space; therefore, careful and detailed care and consideration are required.

In particular, the manual of the three-cycle report meeting includes coaching-type questions, support materials and operational methods for seeking directions, not instructions or commands. However, if leaders preach at great length like leaders in large groups, or if they dictatorially control the report sessions for a long time, the home groups will lose their creativity and originality. Therefore, leaders should run the group's meetings as report meetings that can help members of the home group discover methods by themselves through jeongseong, by raising questions, and that can lead them to understand what they need to do.

The role of the participants is also important. If seniors participate and want to teach the members as if they are disciplining them, the home group gatherings will become passive and non-active. Sometimes the participants need to develop their ability to adjust well, if there are a lot of statements which they do not understand or which differ from what they have been taught so far.

③ Report meetings with a different purpose

Home groups are small group gatherings. Every small group has its purpose. For example, there are gatherings for the purpose of studying the materials in HTM Leader Schools I, II, III, and there are also gatherings for advanced study of the Divine Principle. This means that a home group report meeting should keep to the purpose and content of the report only. There should be no learning or study of the Word in this gathering.

In the process of operating a home group, there is time to read the Word. This is intended to support the action of the three parts of the cycle by centering on the Word. Therefore, the Word has to lead to practice and action. This means the home group should pay attention not to become a home group to study the Word by spending too much time on the Word.

Home group report sessions have their specific direction for multiplication, so if a home group has difficulty in performing the above process, it should seek the help of a coach.

④ Lack of hyojeong love in the trinity

An abundance of hyojeong love in the trinity is the most important requirement for multiplication. According to True Parents, the trinity's three members should be more strongly attached to one another than to their own family members. If one member or one family is in a difficult situation, the problem should be solved and then all the members of the trinity should be united. Experience has shown that Heavenly Parent works steadily through well-run home groups after the formation of a trinity. In united home groups, Heavenly Parent's presence can be felt, and powerful work occurs due to His divinity. When members come together and offer jeongseong, they can experience exciting work by Heavenly Parent, such as the sick being healed and goals being accomplished. On the contrary, if members of the trinity complain, are not congenial and feel difficulty, the home group eventually will disappear.

⑤ Home groups that meet intermittently

In studying the reasons for home groups failing, it has been shown that one of the reasons for failure was that the home groups were holding their meetings sporadically, stopping and starting. They would get together for a while and then stop, then gather again if the group leader called them. The members did not develop close relationships and did not experience Heavenly Parent working through the group, so eventually they gave up and stopped gathering. On the other hand, actively developing groups that were having lively experiences with Heavenly Parent often met twice or even three times a week. Persistence is a very important factor.

Home groups that frequently changed the time and place of the report sessions also fluctuated. These home groups frequently changed the meeting time or place based on circumstances and needs. When this happened, the groups also tended to weaken. The reason is that the home-group report meetings need to have the same order of priority as weekly worship services with Heavenly Parent. The time and place of report sessions of worship services of a large group do not change. The home group report sessions need to have the same importance as large group report sessions. They are just different in size. Members of the home-group report meeting should be able to prioritize those meetings and think of them from the same perspective as those of the large group report sessions. Therefore, the home-group report sessions should set a clear time and place in order to establish the sessions with consistency.

In particular, large continents such as Asia, Africa and South America do not have as many large groups as Korea and Japan, and even places where the home-group report meetings are held may be very far away. Therefore, home-group report meetings should be considered to have the same characteristics as large group report sessions. In Thailand's Kalasin Province, a central member provided his house as a home group meeting place. Therefore, his home is a location for a home group but serves as a large group.

[Figure 1-17] Growing Home Groups and Non-Growing Home Groups

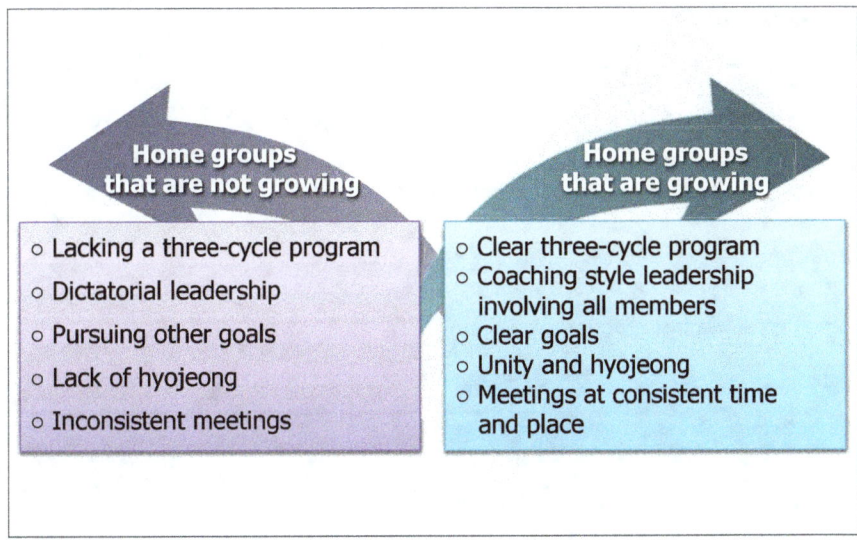

Here is a comprehensive summary of the above details.

First, growing home groups should hold regular report meetings with the systematic cycle of jeongseong, relationships, invitation, gathering and multiplication, supported by spiritual activities.

Second, when operating a home group, it is necessary to use a coaching-style operating method appropriate for small groups so that all the members of the home group can participate without dictatorial control by an individual.

Third, report meetings should be conducted with a clear purpose and direction.

Fourth, members of the trinity should be united and there should be the heart of hyojeong in the home group.

Fifth, the home group report sessions should have a set time and place, like the worship service of a large group, and should be held consistently.

Chapter 2

How to Conduct Home Group Report Meetings

Understanding Home Group Report Meetings

(Three-Cycle 16-Week Course)

The home group report meeting is a small-group worship service for the growth of Cheon Il Guk and the establishment of heavenly tribal messiah work. In other words, it is the time to report to Heavenly Parent about our life and activities during the past week on a small scale at an appointed time and place. It is different from other types of small group or home group meetings. Through home group report meetings, we communicate with Heavenly Parent and True Parents, experience spirituality and strategize to achieve the vision of Cheon Il Guk. It is like breathing together in small groups. As large groups grow through enthusiastic large group report meetings, home groups also grow through home group report meetings.

The core of home group report meetings is reading and studying, along with spiritual purification and jeongseong. This report meeting is an organic Cheon Il Guk growth system that nurtures families and fosters the development of home group leaders. It offers purification and jeongseong to new family members (VIPs), builds relationships among trinity members through internal and external exchanges of love and goodwill, and organizes invitations to happy-day or other training events. During Weeks 4 to 16 in the cycle, there will be activity reports giving guidance for basic activities, including relationship-building, invitations and outreach, along with a foundation of continuous jeongseong.

1. Two Features of Home Group Report Meetings

A home group report meeting may be a gathering of individuals or a gathering of families. A gathering of individuals refers to small groups that have gathered primarily to support witnessing and outreach activities, and invitations to the Blessing, while a gathering of families is more like a home group, primarily focused on nourishing the families already in the group.

A gathering of individuals is a group of members of similar age and experience. For example, it may include a small group of CARP students and youth, children and Seonghwa students, single young men, single young women, blessed husbands or blessed wives, or any other type of group of the same gender and similar social status. Groups gathered in this manner are usually effective in working together to reach a goal. If the members of a meeting are of different genders or different social classes, it is not always easy for them to discuss their personal thoughts openly in the meetings. Organizing members of the tribe in this way is an effective way of supporting the growth of the tribe, with each group reaching out to new participants in the same social status.

In home group report meetings, the blessed families may hold meetings in the form of home group meetings, or meetings centered on outreach activities, centering on the three-cycle process. In any case, the structure of each meeting should include reading and studying, spiritual purification and jeongseong. For a heavenly tribal messiah hoondok family group, which has achieved the goal of gathering 12 members or 12 families, it is advisable to use a balanced schedule that includes both home group and outreach meetings.

2. Hoondok Family Group Report Meetings

Hoondok family group report meetings are usually a gathering of families. Their focus is on completing and expanding the process of creating beautiful blessed families. Let's examine the program for these meetings.

① Gather together for a simple meal like a big family, or discuss with each other informally.
② Sing some holy songs together, followed by an opening prayer by the appointed person.
③ Read the Family Pledge and your hoondok family group mission

statement, slowly and thoughtfully, and offer a bow of reverence to True Parents.

④ Hoondok: read a selection from True Parents' words.

⑤ Offer your thoughts regarding the hoondok reading. Report on your experiences and thoughts of the past week. Include time to report on your witnessing activities during the past week. During this time, you also can have a full witnessing report meeting.

⑥ Sing a holy song to dedicate the donations. (Donations can be gathered before or during the meeting.)

⑦ The home group leader offers the closing report prayer, or you can have a closing unison report prayer.

⑧ Make any necessary announcements and declare the meeting finished.

The hoondok family group report meetings are held mainly in family units of couples plus children. They sometimes are called home group services. If a family group is located far away from the nearest Family Federation center where large group meetings are held, the hoondok family group report meetings may end up replacing large group report meetings. If this is the case, you should work to expand the hoondok family group to a medium-size or large group. For families located closer to a large group, the family should do both large group meetings and small home group meetings. Sometimes, for new members, it is good to have smaller, home group hoondok family meetings for a while first, before attending large group report meetings. In Japan and South Korea, where there are many large family group communities, all hoondok family group members also should attend large group meetings. This will provide a well-grounded system of vertical alignment, a two-wing system of connection.

In Asia, Africa, South America and other places where there are few active large local groups nearby, the heavenly tribal messiahs should work toward expanding into larger groups by the multiplication of heavenly tribal messiahs.

3. Three-Cycle Report Meetings

Three-cycle report meetings, also called "outreach home group report meetings," focus on the success of heavenly tribal messiah outreach. The goals of these report meetings include building relationships, inviting people who have a connection to the people in the home group, and helping them develop into leaders of families. In other words, it is a meeting that shares the solid Will of Heavenly Parent and True Parents, that is, the expansion of citizens of Cheon Il Guk, which is one of the purposes of the home group gatherings. The creation of a witnessing environment and the cultivation of capable future leaders should be focused on creating the people of Cheon Il Guk. Continuing this process will lead naturally to the process of outreach home groups.

Where large groups are active, you should experience the home group process with your pastor's guidance. It is necessary to gather the members of large groups to form trinity home groups and to activate three-cycle home groups. Pastors must be involved in the process as top leaders of large groups. Here, the family members who have experienced home groups should choose mobilization areas for heavenly tribal messiah activities and help organize trinity home group report meetings.

For Seonghwa students, college students and other young people, these report meetings are the most effective. They can be organized quickly and are an easy way to expand hyojeong leadership. If you can master the process of running home group report meetings, using them to set your vision and practice your mission, you can grow into a stronger leader in your society, the nation and the world.

4. Program for Three-Cycle Report Meetings

Home group report meetings should be conducted in four steps: Welcome, Worship, Word, and Work. Home group report meetings require good preparation in order to be successful. The home group leader and the other two members of the trinity should offer jeongseong to support the work of the home group. If the trinity is not yet formed, you should work quickly to organize the trinity in order to have the group work well. Prepare materials for working with the home group, including membership and management forms, supplementary texts and testimonies. Transportation needs

[Figure 2-1] Program for Home Group Report Meetings

must be taken into consideration. Make sure there is no inconvenience regarding transportation for the people who are coming. Prepare a simple meal or refreshments, song sheets, sufficient chairs or cushions including extra seating, and other things for the meeting ahead of time. Extra seating should be prepared so that not only guests but also family members of those in the group can feel welcome. Place a VIP card or something on a vacant seat or cushion to welcome future family members. The home group leader should think through the content of the report meeting in advance. If possible, it is good for the trinity to have a meeting in advance. In one Japanese missionary's home group in South Korea, a large teddy bear was set on a vacant seating cushion during meetings. This was because her VIP guest always liked to hold that teddy bear. In this way, they had a strong expectation that the VIP would come again to attend the next report meeting.

(1) Welcome—greeting and conversation (about 10 minutes)

This creates an atmosphere so the attendees can concentrate on a successful report meeting. It is the time to greet each other comfortably.

One method is to share a funny story or joke as an icebreaker. The group members can tell each other funny things. Such things can be found easily in a book or in a small group kit. This creates a friendly atmosphere. It is effective when used in accordance with the atmosphere in order to strengthen the connections between the group members, allow them to get to know each other, start a conversation, help a newly invited VIP feel welcome, and so on.

(2) Worship—singing and report prayer (about 10 minutes)

Worship should be the content that makes the atmosphere of the home group meeting spiritual and emotional. If a VIP is there, making the atmosphere less familiar, the home group leader should lead the worship so that the members may hear the voice of Heavenly Parent. You may choose pop songs to sing alternatively, but it is best to invoke a feeling of shimjeong (heart) as much as possible. It is good to have a separate worship leader who can give a short inspirational message during the worship segment and lead the singing with a gracious voice. Sometimes choral harmony can be formed in two or three parts, which is more beautiful and better than singing in unison. For this, the trinity may need to choose different voices and take time to practice singing outside the meeting time. It is best to choose familiar songs for offering praise more deeply. It can be helpful to prepare MP3 tracks of the songs to sing along with.

(3) Word—Reading and Discussing True Parents' Words (about 30 minutes)

This time for reading True Parents' words at a home group report meeting is different from the time for studying their teachings. It is the time to prepare passages related to the theme of the report meeting and inspire the group members. It is not a time to teach, but a time to generate inspiration and compassion. Also, the time for discussion should be balanced so that everyone has a chance to speak. The time should not be dominated by one person. To accomplish this, the group leader needs to learn the coaching style of conversation. The group leader should be in a position to build up the group members by asking well-directed questions, so that the discussion does not stray toward judging or correcting the participation of others in the group. Other members of the group also will learn these techniques through participation.

For the discussion, it is good to catch some keywords from the message, announce the topics chosen for the report meeting, and invite feedback from all the members regarding their own life. Home group leaders and home group members should find ways to engage the members who are not talkative in comfortable feedback by asking them questions, asking them to offer their thoughts. It is important to keep private matters that are discussed here from leaving the room. It is recommended that you conclude the discussion time with a report prayer.

(4) Work—Activity Reports and Plans (about 20 to 30 minutes)

This is the core of the home group report meeting. It is the time to discuss what to do in the coming week in response to the reading on the home group topic. The goal of the home group ministry is to carry out heavenly tribal messiah work and support the vision of expanding and creating home groups. Relating weekly experiences and testimonies can be an effective way of supporting these goals. Also introduce VIPs, and do jeongseong together to focus body and mind. Some of the time should be spent planning your ministry as a team, working together to develop strategies for jeongseong, relationships, and invitations.

The content of hoondok should be chosen to relate to the ministry goals of the group. This will make it easy to move from the reading to discussion and on to ministry plans, and also to find ways to support and inspire group members in their ministry.

Closing (5 minutes)

After you have ministered to the guests and made your ministry plans for the week, the final part of the meeting is the closing. The closing should be a time for heart-to-heart interactions with each other, such as offering prayers in pairs, hugging each other, or types of support through physical contact with each other. In addition, you may give prayers for VIPs, prayers for fulfilling your mission, and purification and jeongseong to keep a spiritually elevated atmosphere.

The program described above is also called the "4W" home group program. The four Ws are WELCOME, WORSHIP, WORD, and WORK. As you develop your group, it is helpful to give testimonies about the home group experiences you have had. This program can be used and adapted whenever and wherever a home group has a meeting.

5. Using the 16-Week Meeting Cycle

The home group report meeting will continue to touch on developing relationships, invitation and expanding the tribe, centering on jeongseong. We have organized the course into a 16-week cycle. At college, it is recommended to match the semester schedule, revising it to a 12-week course if necessary. At the end of the 12th or 16th week, we begin a new cycle, reporting about the course we have just completed.

In large groups, we need to announce the schedule for our home group report meetings, and at the end of each 16-week cycle, we should have a special welcome event for new members who have come during the cycle. Similarly, if we have established a CARP chapter or other providential organization, we should have a welcome event at the end of each 12-week or 16-week cycle, in order to help keep the group vibrant and active.

Jeongseong Report Meetings—Understanding and Practice

1. LESSON 1—A Practical Guide to "A Day of Jeongseong"

> **Purpose :** Practice the completion of the first blessing by cultivating the habit of offering jeongseong.
> **Focus :** a time of self-purification, purification prayer for VIPs, and meeting the Heavenly Parent living within us
> **Preparation :** Prepare VIP card, vision, mission statement, home group pledge, vacant seating cushion, report on living up to one's principles, and a sound system.

A day of jeongseong starts when members begin their day with jeongseong and love with the light of hyojeong and end the day with jeongseong and love. That's why the first meeting in a home group has the theme of jeongseong. A life with deep jeongseong helps us achieve the first blessing. This jeongseong means while doing hoondok to spiritually cleanse the mind and body, having a heart of hyojeong until our Seonghwa (ascension). Jeongseong is the root of a home group and is a stepping-stone to becoming a successful heavenly tribal messiah. While offering daily prayers, we should read out the names of our VIP contacts.

(1) Welcome—Introduction (10 minutes)

✔ **What was your happiness score for last week, on a scale of 0 to 10? Let's discuss this together.**

This is the time for home group families to meet and greet each other for the first time. It is also known as an icebreaker. It should be a time for families to get to know and help each other get settled in, so that they do not have any inconvenience at their first meeting. This process may take longer if the number of home group members is close to 12. A home group leader may divide the larger group into small groups of three to four persons each and choose a leader from each group so that the discussion will take less time. If you have only three to four persons gathered, you may have discussion in just one group.

The home leader will ask the leaders for their average weekly happiness score and gather all the group members to support the team or family with the lowest score, to make the whole group's atmosphere more vibrant.

✔ **Read together the home group's vision and mission statement and home group pledge.**

The vision and mission statement should be prepared in advance. A new home leader will hold a meeting with the group members, before the home group starts its activities, to create the home group's vision and mission statement and then create a home group pledge. The vision and mission statements should be memorized through vision workshops for about three months before the home group starts its activities. All these tasks should be prepared not by the home group leader alone but together with the members. The vision and mission statement should be simple and clear, so that family members can memorize it. It is recommended that, each time the home group gathers, the group members should stand and read the statements together before sitting down.

✔ **Close your eyes to envision together the future of the home group after 16 weeks.**

This is the time to envision the future of the home group. It is also a good idea for a home group leader to play meditation music, if available. The members will have time to draw a picture of a group of 12 people gathered together, along with VIPs, thinking about the increase in members after 16 weeks. Things may happen as you draw. In the case of a home group composed of only one trinity, the home group leader should mentor them so that they can draw the image of a hoondok family group. In a center, you will see after 16 weeks that each trinity will have increased to 12 persons, and at this time each home group will see a vision of forming a hoondok family group. The home leader may speak quietly of the process as they are in a meditative state.

- ✔ **Let's close our eyes quietly. Now, let's try to see what our home group will look like after 16 weeks. When and where are you having the group meeting? What people are gathering? What is the atmosphere like? They are beautiful and happy. Please enjoy your meeting!**

The important thing to remember here is that each time you start your first meeting, you should let the members draw a picture of being with a new member after completing a 16-week home group session. This is to let them visualize in advance the results that will come after 16 weeks. However, you can choose to do this or not, depending on how much time you have and how many people are at the meeting. If you have a home group with about three or four persons, you will be able to do it. However, if you have more than 10 members, you should conduct this part in the next jeongseong session so that they can see the future clearly.

(2) Worship—Singing and Reporting (10 minutes)

- ✔ **Let's sing the holy song "○○" while longing for the True Parents with a heart of hyojeong.**

Sing a holy song, hymn or gospel hymn. After singing, the home group leader will offer a short report prayer.

(3) Word—Reading and Discussing True Parents' Words (20 minutes): "The Power of Prayer"

✔ **We read a passage from True Parents' words. Today's reading is "The Power of Prayer."**

"We must know how great the power of prayer is. I, one person, have prayed here, and still the prayer is powerful enough to be able to mobilize the spiritual side of this substantial world, the infinite spiritual world. Therefore, prayer acts like a magnet. Since prayer is as powerful as a magnet, if you become a leader in the future and truly pray for the members for 24 hours a day, believing that something will be done soon, you will see it done. Prayer actually has this kind of power. This is why the Bible says, 'Wherever two or three are gathered, I will be there.' When three people pray together in unity, you can have great power." [*Sermons*, 76-298]

After completing the reading, the home group leader shall have the other home members offer their opinions briefly. Also, people should relate any spiritual inspirations or important thoughts that have come to mind during the reading.

✔ **Let's speak about the feelings and words that touched your heart during the reading.**

After reading, offer comments as described above. When there are just a few members in the group (three to six persons), let each of them offer their inspirations one by one. When there are more than 10 people, it is better to have each one say a single word that represents what they felt and experienced, and have everyone repeat the word aloud in unison.

✔ What does offering jeongseong mean to us all? Could you tell us about any experiences you have had in achieving your goal after offering purification jeongseong?

(4) Work—Activity (20 to 30 minutes)

Prepare lists for individual and VIP purification jeongseong that will support the success of the home group. Ask people to relate anecdotes and testimonies about their witnessing work.

✔ Let's create a VIP list for purification jeongseong.

✔ Imagine that one of our VIPs is actually sitting in that vacant seat. Let us pray deeply to meet the Heavenly Parent within them.

The jeongseong report meeting is the core of the three-cycle report meetings. Therefore, during these meetings, every effort should be made so that all the trinity or group members can be deeply involved in jeongseong related to their witnessing contacts and the group's goals. Rather than doing many things, it is important for the group leader to help the group members focus on the jeongseong and on meeting the Heavenly Parent within. In order that the meeting be more successful, the home group leader should offer additional jeongseong in advance.

In this time, the home group leader should coach the members in the home group to help them report about themselves, their families B3 and VIPs. Group coaching is similar to individual coaching, with extra help so that those in the group understand and support each other.

Since the purpose of the meeting is for new contacts and for expanding the home group, it is important for each member of the home group to bring a VIP card to place on the vacant seating cushions and offer jeongseong together with them. Put the VIP cards on the vacant cushions and lay hands on the cards while saying unison prayer or meditation prayer. It is recommended that everyone carry VIP cards in their wallet, along with True Parents' picture, and take them out to remind them of their faces, whenever possible, and to offer purification jeongseong for them. It is also recommended to offer purification jeongseong frequently, not just during the meetings.

Closing (5 minutes)

This is the time for problem-solving. Make the most of the reports on activities. These should include reports on members, home, trinity, and home group activities, and center and community service during the past week. The best time to check on these things is during the home group meetings.

It is recommended that the members who are having various difficulties—such as forming home groups, their own participation, and bringing VIPs—develop the habit of writing these points down in advance and bringing them to the meeting for prayer. The purpose of the purification jeongseong stage is to give home group members training in offering intense prayers and jeongseong.

✓ Let's ask each other to pray for our VIPs. And let's meet Heavenly Parent by offering prayers by pairs.

Then close the meeting with prayers by pairs with earnest and warm hearts. After concluding the home group meeting, the home group leader will talk about what things need to be prepared for the next meeting. It is recommended to stick to the schedule for the home group meeting and take care of other matters after the close of the home group meeting.

Preparing for the Next Home Group Meeting

Give VIP cards, a purification and jeongseong list, and reports on activities and practice to your members. Then take about 20 minutes to have your home group members who are starting the cycle for the first time watch the PowerPoint presentation about the 16-week cycle and the vision for the home group. It is best to take a short break after the closing of the home group meeting before making the presentation. It is also very important to find time outside of regular group meeting time for HTM Leader School II to help the members recognize the home group vision and mission. In conclusion, it is difficult to expect that the group will expand quickly with just weekly meetings. Those home groups that have expanded quickly usually meet at least three times a week.

LESSON 1—A Day of Jeongseong

(1) Welcome—Introduction (10 minutes)
◇ What was your happiness score for last week, on a scale of 0 to 10? Let's talk about this together.
◇ Let's read the hoondok family group pledge together.
◇ Close your eyes to envision together the future of the home group after 16 weeks.

(2) Worship—Singing and Reporting (10 minutes)
Sing holy songs, hymns, gospel hymns, or pop songs to match the mood, speak from the heart, and offer report prayer.

(3) Word—Reading and Discussing True Parents' Words (20 minutes)

"We must know how great the power of prayer is. I, one person, have prayed here, and still the prayer is powerful enough to be able to mobilize the spiritual side of this substantial world, the infinite spiritual world. Therefore, prayer acts like a magnet. Since prayer is as powerful as a magnet, if you become a leader in the future and truly pray for the members for 24 hours a day, believing that something will be done soon, you will see it done. Prayer actually has this kind of power. This is why the Bible says, 'Wherever two or three are gathered, I will be there.' When three people pray together in unity, you can have great power." [*Sermons*, 76-298]

◇ Find key words to discuss with others.

(4) Work—Activity (20 to 30 minutes)
◇ How would you grade your day's life of jeongseong and what grade would you like to have? (coaching)
◇ Prepare a VIP list for offering purification jeongseong.

Closing (5 minutes)
◇ Conclude with passionate and earnest prayers.
◇ Confirm the hoondok family group's (home group's) mission statement and pledge, getting signatures from each other, and prepare VIP cards.
◇ Show an explanatory PowerPoint about comprehending and managing hoondokhae and witnessing in hoondok family groups (home groups).

The Relationship-Building Report Meeting—Understanding and Practice

1. LESSON 2—
A Practical Guide to BUILDING RELATIONSHIPS

> **Purpose :** Get acquainted with serving and building hyojeong relationship with VIPs.
> **Focus :** How to help VIPs by recognizing their needs in terms of when, where, how, and what
> **Preparation :** VIP cards, report and a progress log, behavior analysis table (DISC—a behavior assessment tool used by psychologists), vision and mission statement, and home group pledge.

Building relationships should be one of the goals and actions in the daily life of home group family members. Building Cheon Il Guk is based on the people of Cheon Il Guk. Therefore, we should become people of Cheon Il Guk by strengthening our true love relationships with our neighbors. Practice to make building relationships a daily habit.

A healthy home group is characterized by a deep interest in the following four things:

First, we understand witnessing as a PROCESS, not as an event or goal. Witnessing is not an event to achieve a goal, but something to be done as a matter of course like a farmer working in the fields. Farming is like life itself for a farmer. Some research has shown that witnessing done in the context of an existing relationship is much more likely to succeed than witnessing through large-scale evangelistic events or programs.

Second, in witnessing we focus on raising heavenly tribal messiahs, that is, leaders, rather than bringing people to the Blessing. This kind of thinking helps us to be successful leaders, first of our own lives, and also of our family and society. Since everyone has divinity, we only need to help them to become true selves by purification and jeongseong—that is, helping others to realize their true heart. When they are faithful to this, people will change, and witnessing and blessings will occur naturally. (Ask, "What is the fruit of an apple tree?")

Third, witnessing focuses on building relationships rather than delivering and teaching knowledge. Through the relationships with the people in our lives we let them know that Heavenly Parent is within both us and them. This is like creating a relationship bridge of true love. In fact, building relationships does not just involve building relationships with external VIPs. The first step is to establish a strong giving-and-receiving relationship with the Heavenly Parent within us. This is our inner relationship. To accomplish this, we need purification and jeongseong. Next, we work to make the connections with our VIPs healthy and beautiful relationships. In relationships, a strong network of relationships is formed as they move from the inside to the outside. This is called INSIDE–OUT.

Fourth, all the works related to the CIG home groups will be in coaching style. The home group leader must be a CIG coach when dealing with VIPs as well as with the existing members of the home group. Coaches are those who play the role of bringing out the divine power that sleeps inside the object partner. Therefore, we should help people to recognize the divine power in themselves with respect, jeongseong, and love rather than holding onto a consciousness of giving answers or teaching. This help should be mostly in the form of listening and questioning. Even when running home groups, the leader should not become a teacher to the home members but rather a coach in order to help them to grow stronger. For this, all CIG HTM leaders should be coaching leaders. Looking at the content of the 16-week home group program, the home group leader should almost always just ask questions, listen, praise and support.

It is important to note that the 16-week manual was created based on this basic understanding of coaching. The operation of a 16-week home group becomes difficult if it is not in coaching style but in teaching style, which reduces effectiveness and causes difficulties right away. Therefore, all families should endeavor to find out what they can learn from each other with effort and perseverance instead of trying to teach each other.

For example, to build a respectful relationship, the way the home group family members greet each other should be changed. For example, "Good afternoon, VIP!" is recommended. And building relationships is more effective when a team is involved behind each individual. To build a relationship is, in fact, to establish a sturdy relationship between the inside (B3) and the outside (V3). It is important to know your partner, to help him to get what he needs, and to establish a win-win relationship.

So what is necessary for success in making a relationship? There are many important elements, but first of all, it is important to take the time that is needed to establish the relationship. Where home groups work well, a lot of time is committed to building relations with home members. Before the day's work begins, decide on a person whose relationship will be focused on during your morning purification jeongseong. Choose someone (a witnessing candidate) to build your relationship with, write down how you will go about it, than share this with B3 (the other blessed members). It is very important to set a time and a place to meet, offer jeongseong to understand and support the contents of the meeting, and make time for the meeting. We should confirm how important we consider the time we spend meeting VIPs. It should be a part of the time we consider important during the day. The story of many family members complaining of difficulties was that they had no time to meet people. It is related to the value of their lives. These people also need to take time management programs, which is one of the leadership programs. If they cannot make time, they cannot accomplish anything.

Second, it is important to make time, but what is more important is to determine our attitude toward the people we meet in our daily life. Even if they are not the people we meet for witnessing, our attitude and way of behaving and looking at the people we meet must be different from the past. In building relationships with people, we need to think about the feelings of our Heavenly Parent. This means when we meet people, we must think of them as our object partners for purification jeongseong with the hope that we can widen the scope of Heavenly Parent's presence inside all the people associated with us.

Third, it is important to build relationships based on need. This refers to a person-centered approach in relationships. Evangelists often use an approach centered on the contents they want to teach, rather than what people need, and that is why their object partners don't become interested. However, the principle of successful relationships is to find out what our VIP needs. In other words, it is critical to build a "needs-centered relationship" to meet the needs of VIPs. According to True Parents, witnessing is good when it benefits the other person. This means responding to what he needs after finding it out.

In order to perform the above well, we decided BUILDING RELATIONSHIPS should be the second stage of the home group.

(1) Welcome—Introduction (10 minutes)

✔ **I'm curious how the week went for each of you. Let's talk about this with one another.**

There is a reason to ask each other if we had any good experiences. Families are dominated by the outside environment in their daily lives. In other words, we are often under the control of our environment. Because of this, our mood and life may be easily controlled. Even if the outside environment (weather) is rough, it is very important for the people of Cheon Il Guk to be able to live with "inner good weather" and successfully pay attention to each other. In particular, the life of hyojeong breaks down if we are not interested in each other. Families that are not interested in one another soon collapse. This means that the focus of our daily life should be hyojeong.

✔ **Let's read the home group's vision and mission statement and home group pledge together.**

While reading them, remain standing to create a different atmosphere. When the home leader announces numbers one, two, or three, the atmosphere becomes enthusiastic when the family recites the numbers. This is an expression of the strong commitment to live a life centered on each numbered purpose.

✔ **Let's make a nice acrostic poem in the name of the neighboring person.**

This sometimes can be difficult. The home leader should present his poem first, even if he has only had time to complete the first few lines. In particular, Japanese family members and other family members may have long names. Therefore, you may want to make the acrostic poem with a shortened version of their name. The purpose of this is to make you realize that you should be interested in one another. Sometimes it may be hard to carry out this process. At this time, it is recommended that the home leader have the members gather together, think about each other deeply, write acrostic poems to each other and send text messages via smartphone message services.

(2) Worship—Singing and Report Prayer (10 minutes)

Sing holy songs, hymns, or gospel hymns. After singing hymns, the home leader will begin with a report prayer. In South Korea, prepare to learn the body movements for songs such as "Three Bears" and "I Love You." In other countries, sing joyfully with amusing movements. However, it is recommended that the home leader also select holy and moving songs. In the opening report prayer, the home leader will give a short message on the importance of relationships.

(3) Word—Hoondok Reading and Discussion (about 20 minutes)

People have a natural desire to go toward something that will serve or benefit them. When we focus on giving something to the people around us, they become closer to us. At the least ,we should serve our neighbors for their benefit. The key words here are "serve," "benefit" and "for the sake of."

When you read the selected paragraphs, it is good to have the people in the group find the main words in the reading, reflect on them, and call them out. After you have finished reading, find ideas in the message that relate to the lives of your VIPs. Next, tell the group about your VIPs, and have the other members of the group repeat their names. The reason for telling the group about your VIPs during the meeting is so that all the group members will be comfortable with the VIPs when they attend meetings in the future.

(4) Work—Activity (about 20 to 30 minutes)

This is a time for the home leader and the home group members to discuss how they can help their VIPs. This is the most important time in this stage. The members of the group tell the others in the group about their VIPs and their plans to help their VIPs. This becomes the goal and focus for the upcoming week. Members should try to explain how they are developing relationships with their VIPs—for example, having meals together, helping with housework, going to a sauna together, going grocery shopping, watching a movie or a play together, and so on. If you help the others in the group to become familiar with your VIPs, the VIPs naturally will become united with the rest when they enter the home group. If VIPs are invited and no one knows anything about them, it will not be an effective invitation. The foundation of building relationships is service. It is important to know that the basis of building relationships is finding out what you and the group can do for them and then treating them and helping them as if they were your own brothers and sisters, with a spirit of service and hyojeong.

✔ **How high is my HOW TO BUILD A RELATIONSHIP score on a 0-10 point scale?**

We will check how many points each person has in relationship-building skills, make a goal as to how many points they would like to have and then a plan about how to attain those points through group coaching or individual coaching.

This will be the time for the home group members who have not been able to do many activities yet to look back at themselves. It should be a time to advise and help each other so that successfully making relationships with VIPs can be a part of our daily life. It is necessary to give newcomers spiritual help and support. Group members promise to invest themselves to achieve the desired scores with the help of the home leader.

Relevance coaching is recommended. (See Part 6 of the appendix, on balanced coaching.)

Now it is time to make plans to invite your VIPs. Around four to seven weeks after you have met a new VIP and had a happy-day event with them, you should be ready to invite them to join a 16-week love home group. Refer to the "BEST" process in the "HOW TO INVITE" section to invite them to the home group, which is Stage 3. Or discuss ways to invite people for other memorable experiences.

Let's learn what "BEST" is. BEST is a fun way of welcoming a new VIP to a home group by leading him to reveal his reasons for coming to the home group. "B" stands for "before"—a VIP talks about his life before; "E" stands for "event"—a VIP tells what things or events occurred; "S" stands for "salvation"—the motivation for the VIP to be saved; and "T" stands for "today"—what he has become today.

Existing home group members should make their own two- or three-minute long "BEST" response and practice it. It can be used as a storytelling technique during the home group meetings to guide a VIP, a new family member, to naturally talk about the way his journey has gone, while others also tell their stories, using the same formula. At this time, the new member will tell his story by following the lead of the existing family members. It is a good idea for the existing family members to talk about the things that have moved and changed them.

Finally, we look for the ways to make team relationships. Since this is the core in BUILDING RELATIONSHIPS, it should be a time to look closely at the personal details of the new family members, as well as look for ways to help them in detail. It is also recommended that you discuss and arrange this stage in accordance with the report and a progress log.

A member appointed by the home leader gives the closing prayer. He should offer a sincere prayer, placing VIP cards on vacant seating cushions.

Closing (5 minutes)

Inform the home members of concrete plans, including the time to help each other in building relationships. And inform the members of the next week's meeting, preparations and home group members' major family events.

LESSON 2—Building Relationships

(1) Welcome—Introduction (10 minutes)
◇ Let's tell each other what happened last week.
◇ Read the home group's vision and mission statement and home group pledge together.

(2) Worship—Singing and Reporting (10 minutes)
◇ We will sing holy songs, hymns, or gospel hymns. After singing hymns, the home leader will offer a report prayer.

(3) Word—Hoondok Reading and Discussion (20 minutes)

"You have to explore the philosophy of the 'living human.' Always think about how you can lead people to me or to our church. There is only one way to do this, and I know how to do it. It is a spirit of serving others. For humans, there is a natural tendency to go wherever there is something that is profitable for them. If the person you are contacting gets some benefit and you give it to him, you will be able to naturally lead another person. If, on the other hand, you want to profit from them, you will have difficulty. If you serve someone, he will come closer to you. Even if you cannot put all your energy into one person, you have to determine, 'I will do my best at least up to this much.' That's the mindset that you need to have." [*Pastor's Way*, p. 408]

◇ Read key Words, introduce VIPs with whom you have relationships, and say their names out loud together.

(4) Work—Activity (about 20 to 30 minutes)
◇ Talk about how many points you have in BUILDING RELATIONSHIPS in your life, how many points you want, and how you can reach your desired score (coaching).
◇ Plan strategies for inviting VIPs.
◇ Find out how to make a relationship as a team (coaching).

Closing (5 minutes)
◇ Ask your group members to pray for your VIPs.
◇ Inform the members of the next week's meeting, home group members' family events, and so on. Close the meeting with a representative prayer and prayers by pairs with fervent hearts.
◇ Remind the members about upcoming invitations by placing a seating cushion to help them visualize invited VIPs.

The Invitation Report Meeting—Understanding and Practice

1. LESSON 3—
A Practical Guide on "HOW TO INVITE OTHERS"

> **Purpose :** make an invitation that VIPs will love the most
> **Focus :** Find a way to make a memorable meeting in which the VIPs will not feel awkward.
> **Preparation :** VIP nameplates, bouquets with welcome message, VIP seating cushions, VIP cards, and BEST document.

The home members already have been working hard to make relationships with VIPs, individually or as a team. After enough work, they have a VIP invitation event. This is the step before the harvest. People like to be safe and comfortable, so the invitation gathering should provide this kind of environment.

The invited VIPs should be welcomed with the hospitality of a family so that they can join us with a joyful heart. Because they already have met home members a few times through happy days and building relationships, the VIPs may not feel awkward. This is the stage in which we provide some space for the VIPs to realize on their own the investment in them from members of the home group. If they do, the VIPs will come to trust the members all the more deeply.

However, if no VIP is invited at the invitation meeting, the home members may practice BEST in the Ministry section, or continue on with building relationships. However, even if you do not have an invited guest now, you should perform the content that can be performed in the HOW TO INVITE in expectation of the invitation in the next week.

(1) Welcome—Introduction (10 minutes)

✔ Let's each talk about something that made us happy last week.

✔ Read the home group's vision and mission statement and home group pledge together.

Reading a home group pledge or mission statement can put pressure on the VIPs when a VIP is invited. Nonetheless, it may allow the VIPs to grasp the nature of the home group. One thing that will help them feel comfortable is if your mission statement includes "service and caring for our neighbors." In fact, we are proud of our home group activities because they are a part of the effort to make true families, and love and service for my neighbors are the goals of the home group.

✔ **Where do you want to be invited the most in your life?**
This content will make you realize that the place or environment to which VIPs want to be invited is the same as the place where you want to be invited. It is important to recall your own experience of being invited to the home group so that your plan to invite and meet VIPs will be prepared well.

(2) Worship—Singing and Reporting (10 minutes)

We will sing holy songs, hymns, or gospel songs. After singing hymns, the home leader will offer a short report prayer.

If VIPs have been invited, you may impress them if you find out their favorite songs in advance and sing them. We also recommend singing pop songs and designating a song your home group likes to sing as your own, much like a country's national anthem or a school anthem.

(3) Word—Hoondok Reading and Discussion (about 30 minutes)

Find key words within the hoondok reading. For example, the message says, "The home group should treat its guests well if it wants to receive good fortune." We can think that the home group will be ruined by bad luck if it does not take care of the guests who have come. A home group should be a group that people want to visit repeatedly.

Among invitation events, there are some occasions when VIPs are invited to the home group meetings and other times when they are not. It is necessary to distinguish clearly between these two kinds of situations. Even if you do not have an invited VIP, place vacant seating cushions and proceed as if VIPs were there. It is important to know that inviting VIPs is like a struggle against Satan to bring them to our side.

- ✔ **What kind of atmosphere and places do our VIPs want to be invited to?**

It is important to plan ahead and prepare carefully when inviting VIPs. You will find that even those who have not met VIPs yet become enthusiastic to have their own VIPs. Or, it is good to tell your own thoughts on VIP invitations to others. You may directly proceed to BEST, depending on the time.

- ✔ **Let's talk about BEST in the position of the invitee.**

BEST stands for Before, Event, Salvation, and Today. The reason for doing BEST in the third-week phase is to naturally draw a story of self-testimony about their own past (Before), what experience (Event) led to their connection to the group (Salvation), and how they are doing nowadays (Today). Usually the home leader should prepare a one- or two-minute speech about BEST. It is also aimed at making it easier to find out how the VIPs were invited. That's why it is good to prepare BEST documents in advance at the invitation stage to make things easier.

(4) Work—Activity (about 20 to 30 minutes)

Together with your family members, plan a beautiful and bold invitation for VIPs. You need active help from your home group family members for VIP invitations. You will even need them to make a small contribution. If a small amount of money is collected from family members of the home group for the VIP invitation, you will be pleased with each other to find out that all the family members contributed to the invitation.

✔ **Let's find out how to reap the harvest as a team (invitation coaching).**

When you meet a VIP for the first time, you can meet him one on one for about four weeks. However, for meetings before their first home group invitation, it is recommended that you plan to meet the VIPs at a good place outside the center. At this time, it is important that you meet the VIPs' needs in advance, preparing a conversation or topic that may benefit them, so that it can be a very effective invitation. Or make strategies as a team to invite them to a happy day (a guest-friendly worship service for outreach purposes that can be held on any day, except during the Sunday Service time, and includes fun activities). Even if they have not been invited to a home group meeting yet, it may be time to discuss the happy day invitation.

Japanese and Thai families living in Bangkok have had good experiences hosting home-cooked dinner feasts as happy day events for their home group. These gatherings include new and existing family members. The members made interesting plans for a happy day—such as making Japanese food, wearing kimonos, making photo lines to take pictures together. The members attracted the interest of VIPs, while also giving a brief lecture on the struggle between the original heart and evil mind.

In Malaysia, the "Aza Aza" program has become very well known, so that it is now very easy to invite students and parents. Events like this provide a natural first experience for VIPs with the members of the home group before they attend a regular home group meeting.

Closing and Preparation

✔ **Let's pray for VIPs, praying in pairs.**
Praying by pairs may bring a very blessed atmosphere. You may talk to each other about your weaknesses and pray to overcome them. You can create an atmosphere of greater grace if you pray for one another while holding hands. It is a good idea to prepare quiet music to create a gracious atmosphere at this time.

✔ **Let's close the meeting with a unison prayer with a hearty spirit.**
Even if no VIP has taken part this time, you must complete this

stage with the conviction that you can have your VIPs next time. To this end, place a seating cushion prepared for this in between home group members. Then put everyone's VIP card on the seating cushion with their hand on top. And pray fervently, looking in its direction.

✔ **When you have a new family member, you can prepare your own home group PowerPoint presentation and describe your vision and mission with others.**

LESSON 3—How to Invite Others

(1) Welcome—Introduction (10 minutes)
◇ Read the home group's vision and mission statement and home group pledge together.
◇ Talk about where you want to be invited the most in your life.

(2) Worship—Singing and Reporting (10 minutes)
◇ After singing gospel songs or other easy songs together, the home leader will offer a report prayer.

(3) Word—Hoondok Reading and Discussion (30 minutes)

"If your household is to receive good fortune, you must treat your guests well. Right? And, when serving guests, if you give them the leftovers from your own meal, you will be punished. If there is such a house that treats its guests well, even the neighboring dogs come to the door of the house, and the flying birds come to the house and try to nest there. If you do so, your home will be blessed. However, if you do not take care of the guests who come to your house, the house will be punished. The home's fortune with decline.

Our house should be the kind of house that people in the neighborhood want to visit without any obvious reason, want to depend on, want to come to often, and want to gather in." [*Sermons*, 44-163)

◇ Let's talk about BEST from the position of the guest.
◇ BEST: Before, Event, Salvation, Today
   The reason for doing BEST in the third-week phase is to naturally draw out a story of self-testimony about their own past (Before), what experience (Event) let to their connection to the group (Salvation), and how they are doing nowadays (Today). Usually the home leader should prepare a one- or two-minute speech about BEST to educate the regular members. This content should be conducted at the invitation stage in the third week (stage).

(4) Work—Activity (20 minutes)
◇ With the group members, plan beautiful and bold invitations for the VIPs.
◇ Think about out how to reap the harvest as a team.

Closing (10 minutes)
◇ Ask for prayers for VIPs and pray in pairs.
◇ Close the meeting by offering unison prayer with a hearty spirit.

Multiplication Report Meeting—Understanding and Practice

1. LESSON 4—A Practical Guide to Multiplication

Purpose : prepare for the birth of a new home group
Focus : eliminate any awkwardness caused by the multiplication of the home group and make it hopeful
Preparation : home group report and a progress log that was kept, and deliver it to the new home group

This is the fourth stage in home group operations. At this stage, it may branch off to a new family or may not. It is recommended that the home groups starting first proceed with this step with the mindset that they are being trained and learn as they go. Nonetheless, at this stage it is necessary to envision the appearance of home group multiplication that will take place after 16 weeks. After 16 weeks, the new family members will become active regular members through happy day and leader school.

The pastor may intentionally try multiplication by putting a large group as the center of the home group instead of new members coming in. In other words, he may try to include other existing families that were not included in the previous home groups. This kind of home group can be understood as a result of self-multiplication but not as leading VIPs to home groups on site. There are also cases in which the three cycles that were started by a pastor spread within a large group itself. In 2004, a home group called "Love Society" was formed with the pastors who were taking courses at the Unification Theological Seminary in the United States. The pastors were led into the home group, thus achieving multiplication. The home group meetings were unforgettable, and the process at that time became the root of today's program. There have been many failures of home groups when large groups suddenly switched to being home groups without gaining genuine support from their members. Therefore, when it comes to the stage of multiplication after the first group formation, it is desirable for pastors to form hoondok family groups by gathering the existing family members while completing the 16th week.

If a home group is born by pioneering, we have to create an atmosphere like that of a festival. It is a good idea to give our congratulations and encouragement to new leaders and family members who are branching off to a new home group.

Characteristics of Hyojeong Home Groups and Spiritual Children

Initially, we started with the existing trinity B3 (B1, B2, B3) through their efforts going through happy day, leader school, and so on. There is a way for B1 to form a hoondok family group with 12 persons first with the help ofB2 and B3. It consists of 12 members, namely, B2, B3, and V1-V9. How does hoondok family group multiply? We must cooperate and sacrifice together until we have three, 12, 36 persons, and so on. In B3, there are family members who are good at evangelism and others who are not. But overcoming this is what the hyojeong home group ought to do. A hyojeong home group is where true family love is practiced. In other words, if there are brothers and sisters who cannot have children, we should be able to give them our own children. This is the basis for B1, B2 and B3 to each become a heavenly tribal messiah. This is the hyojeong team spirit. Of course, the originally established B1 hoondok family group needs to help build toward independence of the B2 and B3 hoondok family groups. There are many ways to do this.

For example, a 12-person hoondok family group may consist of B1 + V1 + V2 + V3 = 4, B2 + V1 + V1 + V1 = 4, and B3 + V1 + V1 + V1 = 4. In this case, a hoondok family group has been formed, but each B1, B2, and B3 has only three VIPs. In this case, it is necessary to decide who among B1, B2, and B3 will be successful in achieving the first 12-person hoondok family group and support it. Then they support each other to accomplish that goal. In this situation, we must have a heart of hyojeong to share our spiritual children with each other, or to give our child to a family that has no children.

Through this process, you can become a hyojeong home group to experience and practice exchanging hyojeong. In the process of sharing and supporting their children from the standpoint of a family until a 12-person home group is reached, hyojeong can be experienced physically. It is as if a baby grows in support and encouragement from the family of hyojeong after an easy birth. It is the hyojeong home group where the pain that they feel when giving their own children to a family who cannot have children turns into love. True Parents gave us the Blessing and then formed trinities for us. They told us that if a family in our trinity could not have their own biological children, we should give one of our children for them to adopt. This is the family of hyojeong. Likewise, in order for all blessed families to become heavenly tribal messiahs, they must master this kind of branching off to a new family with love. We will carry on with this operation until the trinity first started becomes the heavenly tribal messiah with 12, 36 households and so on. When this happens, the home group will have more than 430 homes creating midsize groups and large groups. It is important for all 12 members to have the experience of making 12 members, since they have gone through the home group three-cycle report, happy day, and leader school courses. Over time, this group will have the power to grow. All of these are done on the basis of jeongseong and became possible because of the divine power generated in the home group and the presence of Heavenly Parent.

If the time for branching off to a new family has not come yet, the cycle must go on, so it should be time to firmly establish the basis for branching off to a new family.

(1) Welcome—Introduction (10 minutes)

Read the home group's vision and mission statement and home group pledge together. You may read only the home group pledge without the vision and mission statement. If there is any change or need to change the home group pledge, vision, or mission statement, we will summarize it at this stage.

✔ **Let's give three words of praise to two persons.**

This is to cultivate among family members the habit of praising each other in daily life. At this time, praise should not be vague but concrete. If you want to praise the other person for what he or she has done, it is a good idea to praise him or her specifically for the process rather than results, or how to reach the results. For example, "Looking at your child's success, I can see that the unseen support of his mother has been a great source of strength for him," and so on.

(2) Worship—Singing and Reporting (10 minutes)

✔ **Sing "The Three Bears" as follows with gestures.**

Three bears are in a house
Papa Bear, Mama Bear, Baby Bear
Papa Bear is chubby

Mama Bear is thin
Baby Bear is soooo cute
(shrug, shrug) you are doing well

Sing a song standing up with joy, and then simply start with the home leader's report prayer. If you are in a country other than South Korea, you can sing a fun children's song from your country, or a pop song, or folk song. Also in South Korea, you do not have to stick to the children's songs mentioned above. Be creative!

(3) Word—Hoondok Reading and Discussion (20 minutes)

Find key words within the hoondok reading. And try to pick out the main themes. Let us focus on "witnessing is for multiplication," and try to understand the cells. It is also good if one person out of the trinity prepares and makes a presentation. Then talk about "cell multiplication" together. It is also a good idea to have someone in your group who knows about cells talk about the characteristics of cells. It is good if they mention the idea that the biological basis for cell membranes, DNA, and cell nuclei—that is, the basis of the principle of creation—is also a foundation for growth, or home groups. The reader now asks what the cells of our home group look like. This is to show that the cells that resemble the current home group are multiplying. Also, think deeply about the message, "Evangelism is done on a horizontal line, not on a vertical line." Envision what your home group that is branching off to a new group will look like.

(4) Work—Activity (30 minutes)

If it is possible to branch off to a home group, we will determine and announce the home group leader and new members. In addition, B3 groups that are already proceeding well should behave as if they have branched off and share information with other groups. And discuss their expectations of their own hoondok family group, imagining what it will look like in the future.

If it is possible to branch off to a new group, you should talk with your home group leader and pastor or coach a week in advance, branch off to a family, and pray. Announce the list and have them encourage each other. Even if branching off to a new home group did not occur, coordinate the groups that include preliminary new home group leaders and members, so that branching off to a new group will be possible after four weeks.

✔ Let's take a look at the future, becoming heavenly tribal messiahs with all 12 children.

Make time to ensure that all members of the family who participated in the multiplication can understand and cooperate with the process of a hoondok family group. We need to proceed with the report meeting in a heartfelt way so that the family members who attend it can clearly visualize the contents outlined above in their minds.

In both branch style and B3 style, the first step is to achieve a trinity. The method of branching off to a new family is more directly involved with the parenting and care of the master leader than the B3 style. Until it is time to branch off to a new family, we can advance to very stable faith-keeping and multiplication by having meetings regularly.

However, the B3 home group style may be able to operate another emerging home group very quickly, depending on the ability, along with the formation of trinities. This is because B3 may operate their own V3 or cooperate with each other to give help. The feature of the B3 style is to operate the home group by consistently forming B3 among the members centering on the master home leader, and then each B1 will create another home group. This is a place for B3 and collaborative ministry, rather than the help of a master leader. It is fast because it has to grow on its own, but there is a tendency to be task oriented rather than to grow through spiritual activities. After this process, have a hearty closing with report prayers.

Closing (10 minutes)

Write your own difficulties on a paper, exchange the papers, and pray for each other for a week. Then admit your own difficulties during the past week and ask your family members to pray. If you pray in pairs, you will be greatly blessed. The family members with prayer requests will promise to pray together at an appointed time in the week.

LESSON 4—Start of a New Life

(1) Welcome—Introduction (10 minutes)
◇ Read the home group's vision and mission statement and home group pledge together.
◇ Give three words of praise to two persons.

(2) Worship—Singing and Reporting (10 minutes)
◇ Sing "Three Bears" with gestures.
◇ The home leader will offer a report prayer.

(3) Word—Hoondok Reading and Discussion (20 minutes)

"You know about cell multiplication, don't you? Out of this single cell, your eyes, nose, hair, feet and all the others will come out. Everything will come out the same. The cells connected to true love are of equal value to the universe." [*Sermons*, 216-288]

"Organic life must be endlessly reproduced in order to be sustained. There is no multiplication in a vertical relationship. In order to breed, it is necessary for each to be separated and independent. And each should be on the horizontal line. If they are connected on a horizontal line, multiplication will start automatically. Multiplication does not happen in a vertical relationship, such as the relationship between the local head and the district head. However, when they are joined together, if the local head becomes the center and the district head cooperates with the local head, multiplication starts. This is a principle of creation." [*Sermons*, 17-278]

"Multiplication occurs when subject and object partner correspond with each other centered on one purpose. No matter how perfect the subject is, it is not sufficient with the subject alone. A relationship must be present for multiplication. This is the principle of creation." [*Sermons*, 43-74]

◇ Envision how the home group will look like if it branches off to a family with 12 new members.
◇ Group members should offer suggestions about what will have to happen in order to achieve a new branch home group.

(4) Work—Activity (30 minutes)
◇ Organize and announce a preliminary home group leader and members. This is a virtual group.
◇ Select a VIP who you can build a relationship with and invite that is not already a member.

Closing (10 minutes)
◇ This is a time for problem-solving, so write down your own difficulties on a paper, exchange the papers with each other and pray for each other for one week.
◇ Pray fervently for a new home group.
◇ Identify where new home groups are gathered.

[Figure 2-2] A Home Group Holding a Report Meeting

We have looked at the contents of the report meeting of the trinity home group that multiplies through invitation, building relationships, and multiplying with jeongseong as the root. The home group will hold this report meeting on a weekly basis or as scheduled. Next, we will deal with a 16-week program.

Home Group 16-Week Program Week

Program:

Week 1 is A Day of Jeongseong,
Week 2 is Building Relationships,
Week 3 is How to Invite Others,
Week 4 is Start of a New Life,
Week 5 is Members Who Dream,
Week 6 is Home Group Eog Mansei!,
Week 7 is Fountain of Jeongseong,
Week 8 is Making Family Relationships,
Week 9 is Harvesting Together,
Week 10 is Adding a Home Group and Congratulations,
Week 11 is Accompanying God,
Week 12 is Making Good Habits,
Week 13 is Overcoming Challenges,
Week 14 is Jeongseong and Relationships,
Week 15 is Gathering and Multiplication, and
Week 16 is True Home Church.

LESSON 1—A Day of Jeongseong

(1) Welcome—Introduction (10 minutes)
◇ What was your happiness score for last week, on a scale of 0-10? Let's talk about this together.
◇ Let's read the hoondok family group pledge together.
◇ Let's close our eyes to envision together the future of the home group after 16 weeks

(2) Worship—Singing and Reporting (10 minutes)
Sing hymns, gospel chants, or pop songs to match the mood, speak from the heart and offer report prayer.

(3) Word—Reading and Discussing True Parents' Words (20 minutes)

"We must know how great the power of prayer is. I, one person, have prayed here, and still the prayer is powerful enough to be able to mobilize the spiritual side of this substantial world, the infinite spiritual world. Therefore, prayer acts like a magnet. Since prayer is as powerful as a magnet, if you become a leader in the future and truly pray for the members for 24 hours a day, believing that something will be done soon, you will see it done. Prayer actually has this kind of power. This is why the Bible says, 'Wherever two or three are gathered, I will be there.' When three people pray together in unity, you can have great power." [*Sermons*, 76-298]

◇ Find key words to discuss with others.

(4) Work—Activity (20 to 30 minutes)
◇ How would you grade your day's life of jeongseong and what grade would you like to have? (coaching)
◇ Prepare a VIP list for offering purification jeongseong.

Closing (5 minutes)
◇ Conclude with passionate and earnest prayers.
◇ Confirm the hoondok family group's (home group's) mission statement and pledge, getting signatures from each other, and prepare VIP cards.
◇ Show an explanatory PowerPoint about comprehending and managing hoondokhae and witnessing in hoondok family groups (home groups).

LESSON 2—Building Relationships

(1) Welcome—Introduction (10 minutes)
◇ Let's talk about what happened last week.
◇ Read the home group's vision and mission statement and home group pledge together.

(2) Worship—Singing and Reporting (10 minutes)
◇ We will sing hymns or gospel chants. After singing hymns, the home leader will offer a report prayer.

(3) Word—Hoondok Reading and Discussing (20 minutes)

"You have to explore the philosophy of the 'living human.' Always think about how you can lead people to me or to our group. There is only one way to do this, and I know how to do it. It is a spirit of serving others. For humans, there is a nature that wants to go wherever there is a thing which is profitable for them. If the person you are contacting gets some benefit and you give it to him, you will be able to naturally lead another person. If, on the other hand, you want to profit from them, you will have difficulty. If you serve someone, he will come closer to you. Even if you cannot put all your energy into one person, you have to determine, 'I will do my best at least up to this much.' That's the mindset that you need to have." [*Pastor's Way*, p. 408]

◇ Discuss key Words, introduce VIPs with whom you have relationships, and say their names out loud together.

(4) Work—Activity (about 20 to 30 minutes)
◇ Talk about how many points you have in BUILDING RELATIONSHIPS in your life, how many points you want, and how you can reach your desired score (coaching)
◇ Plan strategies for inviting VIPs
◇ Find out how to make a relationship as a team. (coaching)

Closing (5 minutes)
◇ Ask your family members to pray for your VIPs.
◇ Inform the members of the next week's meeting, home group members' family events and so on. Close the meeting with a representative prayer and prayers in pairs with a fervent heart.
◇ Remind the members of upcoming invitations by placing a blank seating cushion for each VIP.

LESSON 3—How to Invite Others

(1) Welcome—Introduction (10 minutes)
◇ Read the home group's vision and mission statement and home group pledge together.
◇ Talk about where you want to be invited the most in your life.

(2) Worship—Singing and Reporting (10 minutes)
◇ After singing gospel chants or other easy songs together, the home leader will offer a report prayer.

(3) Word—Hoondok Reading and Discussion (30 minutes)

"If your family is to be blessed, you must treat your guests well. Right? And, when serving guests, if you give the guests the leftovers from your own meal, you will be punished. If there is such a house that treats its guests well, even the neighboring dogs come to the door of the house and the flying birds come to the house and try to nest there. That is when the house is blessed. However, if you do not take care of the guests who come to your house, the house will get punished. The house will be crumbling. Our house should be the kind of house that people in the neighborhood want to visit without any obvious reason, want to depend on, want to come to often, and want to gather in. [*Sermons*, 44-163]

- ◇ Let's talk about BEST from the position of the guest.
- ◇ BEST: Before, Event, Salvation, Today

  The reason for doing BEST in the third-week phase is to naturally draw out a story of self-testimony about their own past (Before), what experience (Event) led to their connection to the group (Salvation), and how they are doing nowadays (Today). Usually the home leader should prepare a one- or two-minute speech about BEST to educate the regular members. This content should be conducted at the invitation stage in the third week (stage).

(4) Work—Activity (about 20 minutes)
- ◇ With family members, plan beautiful and bold invitations for the VIPs.
- ◇ Think about out how to reap the harvest as a team.

Closing (10 minutes)
- ◇ Ask for prayers for VIPs and pray in pairs
- ◇ Close the meeting by praying in unison with a hearty spirit.

LESSON 4—Start of a New Life

(1) Welcome—Introduction (10 minutes)
◇ Read the home group's vision and mission statement and home group pledge together.
◇ Give three words of praise to two persons.

(2) Worship—Singing and Reporting (10 minutes)
◇ Sing "Three Bears" with gestures.
◇ The home leader will offer a report prayer.

(3) Word—Hoondok Reading and Discussion (20 minutes)

"You know about cell multiplication, don't you? Out of this single cell, your eyes, nose, hair, feet and all the others will come out. Everything will come out the same. The cells connected to true love are of equal value to the universe." [*Sermons*, 216-288]

"Organic life must be endlessly reproduced in order to be sustained. There is no multiplication in a vertical relationship. In order to breed, it is necessary for each to be separated and independent. And each should be on the horizontal line. If they are connected on a horizontal line, multiplication will start automatically. Multiplication does not happen in a vertical relationship such as the relationship between the local head and the district head. However, when they are joined together, if the local head becomes the center and the district head cooperates with the local head, multiplication starts. This is a principle of creation." [*Sermons*, 17-278]

"Multiplication occurs when subject and object partner correspond with each other centered on one purpose. No matter how perfect the subject is, it is not sufficient with the subject alone. A relationship must be present for multiplication. This is the principle of creation." [*Sermons*, 43-74]

◇ Envision how the home group will look like if it is branching off to a family with 12 new members.
◇ Group members should offer suggestions about what will have to happen in order to achieve a new branch home group.

(4) Work—Activity (30 minutes)
◇ Organize and announce a preliminary home group leader and members. This is a virtual group.
◇ Select a VIP who you can build a relationship with and invite that is not already a member.

Closing (10 minutes)
◇ This is a time for problem-solving, so write down your own difficulties on a paper, exchange the papers with each other, and pray for each other for one week.
◇ Pray fervently for a new home group.
◇ Identify where new home groups are gathered.

LESSON 5—Members Who Dream

(1) Welcome—Introduction (10 minutes)
◇ Read the home group's vision and mission statement and home group pledge together.
◇ We will close our eyes to envision together the future of our home group after 16 weeks. (meditation music, hymn)

(2) Worship—Singing and Reporting (10 minutes)
◇ Turn on the CD player and sing hymns together.
◇ Prepare hymns as well as meditation music.
◇ The home leader will offer a report prayer.

(3) Word—Hoondok Reading and Discussion (20 minutes)

"All existing substantial entities started by making dreams in the mind into reality. If a person wants to make something, first he makes a clear plan in his mind. If he wants to build a house, he will set up a certain goal and make a plan and a detailed blueprint. A plan or a blueprint is just what appears on the paper for recording purpose, but is actually from the mind." [Unification Thought, 127–128]

"Likewise, dreams and visions are the beginning of everything." [Speech, 5.18. 2002]

"A person without vision cannot overcome any difficulties in daily life. On the other hand, a person with a strong vision will be able to overcome troubles in life well, no matter how hard they are. If someone who has a new vision is facing difficulties or even working in a solitary position, such a person may inherit the future and overcome the path of suffering in the future. But those who are just in a position of sympathizing and following may not be able to do it." [Sermons, 42-180]

◇ When waking up tomorrow, you see three miracles happening. What could they be?
◇ Which one are you going to choose out of the three miracles?
◇ Explain why you chose the miracle.
◇ What does it have to do with our home group?

(4) Work—Activity (20 minutes)
◇ Envision together our home group after 16 weeks

Closing (10 minutes)
◇ This is a time for problem-solving, so write down your own difficulties on a paper, exchange the papers with each other, and pray for each other for one week.
◇ Close the meeting by praying in unison with a hearty spirit.

LESSON 6—Home Group Eog Mansei!

(1) Welcome—Introduction (10 minutes)
◇ Read the home group's vision and mission statement and home group pledge together.
◇ Take turns in talking about something that is growing near you, and present your story with physical movement.

(2) Worship—Singing and Reporting (10 minutes)
◇ Sing "Tadpole" (song).
◇ Turn on the CD player and sing hymns together.
◇ The home leader will offer a report prayer.

(3) Word—Hoondok Reading and Discussion (30 minutes)

"When spring comes, the sun rising from the east will make the air warm, and all things will be prepared from the depths of the earth to show the value of their own existence, and to show themselves proudly on the new heaven and earth. When they are finished growing, it reveals how much effort they have made for their accomplishment. After a year, they show how much they grew in the meanwhile. One clump of grasses, acacia trees, bush clover, and pine trees grow up after a certain period of time and fulfill the Creator's desires." [*Sermons*, 12-65]

◇ How would you explain the meaning and nature of growth?
◇ How high is the growth index of our home group when measured on a scale of 1 to 10?
◇ How high is the growth index you hope for, and what do you need to do to get it?

(4) Work—Activity (20 minutes)
◇ What kind of troubles will happen if living things do not grow?
◇ What will happen if the home group does not grow?
◇ What are the characteristics of a growing home group?

Closing (5 minutes)
◇ This is a time for problem-solving, so write down your own difficulties on a paper, exchange the papers with each other, and pray for each other for one week.
◇ Each member speaks about the home group's wishes one by one, shouting, "Home Group, Eog Mansei!"
◇ Preparation: Set up special conditions for the jeongseong meeting of LESSON 7.

LESSON 7—Fountain of Jeongseong

(1) Welcome—Introduction (10 minutes)
◇ Read the home group's vision and mission statement and home group pledge together.
◇ Read the following and have them answer in Twenty Questions style.

"I am a servant for great people and servant for all failed people. Actually, I am the one that made great people great. I am not a machine. I am as accurate as a machine and move with human intelligence, but you can make use of me to make profit or you may go completely bankrupt. I do not care what you do. Please choose me. Please tame me. Please be stern toward me. Then I will win the world. But if you treat me too lightly, I will destroy you. Who am I?"

(2) Worship—Singing and Reporting (10 minutes)
Singing hymns or pop songs in accordance with the mood, expressing our heart.

(3) Word—Hoondok Reading and Discussion (30 minutes)

"Prayer is like a tall water jar. The atmosphere of prayer is like breathing in our physical life. When you are praying, you should do it with a sincere and earnest heart, as if an infant misses milk when hungry." [*The Way of God's Will*, Chapter on Prayer]

"Prayer is believed to be the most powerful. It is what can make the impossible possible. The Unification Church emphasizes prayer but does not pray in any other special ways, even though its content is different. 'Do not pray for yourself.' This is my teaching. I teach that people should pray for their missions and for others, and their prayers should be devoted to God in words of comfort." [*Sermons*, 91-117]

◇ From the time of the maturation of my love until now, what is the depth of my mature love on a 1-10 scale?
◇ Please tell me your testimony of purification and jeongseong.
◇ What has changed in your life through your prayer life, and what do you hope to achieve in the future?

(4) Work—Activity (10 minutes)
◇ Speak of your wishes and pray fervently for each other's wishes in pairs.
◇ Group members should fill out VIP cards describing their potential guests and organize prayer partners for them.

Closing (5 minutes)
◇ This is a time for problem-solving, so write down your own difficulties on a paper, exchange the papers with each other, and pray for each other for one week.
◇ Ask the members to pray for VIPs.

LESSON 8—Making Family Relationships

(1) Welcome—Introduction (10 minutes)
◇ Read the home group's vision and mission statement and home group pledge together.
◇ Participants draw names by lot, and compose and recite an acrostic poem using the name of the person that they have picked.

(2) Worship—Singing and Reporting (five minutes)
◇ Singing hymns or pop songs in accordance with the mood, expressing our heart.
◇ The home leader will offer a report prayer.

(3) Word—Hoondok Reading and Discussion (30 minutes)

"Today we are called a family. At our own homes, we also call members of our homes family members. Then on what ground can we call ourselves a family? We are saying that we are the members of the family centering on God's love and God's original ideal of creation. Since a relationship of brothers is formed through a family, the family indeed can be the foundation for the creation of the kingdom of heaven. Family, what a holy noun! The heaven and earth will disappear, but this noun shall not disappear. This noun and these entities shall remain." [*True Parents' Life Course 3: The Way of Unification Church Family*]

- ◇ Family members should have a relationship of heavenly love.
- ◇ How high is the family relation index regarding the VIPs with whom you have relationships on a 1-10 scale?
- ◇ With what activities are you and your VIPs connected? Let's explain through VIP contact cards (include cards).

(4) Work—Activity (20 minutes)
- ◇ Fill out the progress logs that were distributed earlier and share them with each other (people you met, number of meetings, relationship contents, and situation).
- ◇ If you do not have time to create such a relationship, encourage and pray for each other so that you have more opportunities.
- ◇ Make a plan together to form family relations.

Closing (5 minutes)
- ◇ Each person gives the names of the witnessing contacts and then asks the group to offer jeongseong for the witnessing contacts.
- ◇ Close the meeting with unison prayer and prayers in pairs with enthusiastic hearts.
- ◇ Remind the members of the invitation by placing a seating cushion representing a VIP.

LESSON 9—Harvesting Together

(1) Welcome—Introduction (10 minutes)
◇ Read the home group's vision and mission statement and home group pledge together.
◇ Place a VIP seating cushion next to you and write down the VIP's name on a card.
◇ Speak out the name of the VIP, and introduce the name by making an acrostic poem with it.

(2) Worship—Singing and Reporting (5 minutes)
◇ Select and sing hymns or songs about harvest.
◇ The home leader will offer a report prayer.

(3) Word—Hoondok Reading and Discussion (20 minutes)

"You should not go out alone for witnessing. You have to work together with people who have not gone out for witnessing. Thus, the front and the rear people must cooperate with each other. The person in front must fight, and the person in the rear should cooperate mentally and materially with all due diligence. That is what we should do. The family members who can't join going out for witnessing must participate in other ways. We must drive out Satan in the four-position foundation. We have to be loyal with the conviction that the world of Satan surely will collapse. Just as you are loyal to God, you have to be loyal to your will." [*Sermons*, 11-210]

"Will it work if you say, 'I will suffer alone. I can go out alone to do witnessing, can't I?' No, you can't. When you are doing it alone, it means you are doing it wearing Satan's tail. The witnessing must be done by God's command." [*Sermons*, 25-208]

◇ Think about the methods of harvest that you have used so far. Describe it in one word and get feedback.

(4) Work—Activity (20 minutes)
◇ Let's find out how to reap the harvest as a team (how and where to throw a net).
◇ If a VIP is invited, carry out BEST. Or practice BEST.

Closing (5 minutes)
◇ Tell each other the difficulties of the harvest and pray in pairs.
◇ Remind the members of invitation by placing a vacant seating cushion as well as a VIP card on it to invite VIPs.

LESSON 10—Adding a New Home Group and Congratulations

(1) Welcome—Introduction (10 minutes)
◇ Read the home group's vision and mission statement and home group pledge together.
◇ If you have achieved the vision of your home group, what do you think you will do now?

(2) Worship—Singing and Reporting (10 minutes)
◇ A team that will branch off into a family can sing hymns or songs.
◇ The home leader will offer a report prayer.

(3) Word—Hoondok Reading and Discussion (20 minutes)

"Do you remember how difficult it was when you came out of your mother's womb? No. Why did she give birth, risking her own life? Why did you do that, why? It was to materialize amazing love. A mother is happy about the fact that she is having a baby. Instead of being unhappy, she is happy. A father does not understand it at all. He does not know how much she has suffered. He cannot know better than the mother. That is why a mother is the best person to really know the taste of love." [Sermons, 107-43]

"The way of regeneration starts from the state where it is sad and lonely. You should busy yourself with witnessing in such a way that rumors will spread saying, 'He is crazy. He is like a goblin haunting in broad daylight.' You should bustle from one house to the next. When we fall short of grace, a better way than prayer to raise our grace is witnessing. If we fall short of grace by going back and forth between two houses, try to go back and forth between four houses. What I mean is you should witness to four houses. This way, your fallen grace will go up again. Actually this way is better than prayer." [Sermons, 36-122]

◇ Use one word to describe common characteristics of parents when giving birth to their children.

(4) Work—Activity (20 minutes)
◇ Let's talk about the necessity of trinities and the strength of our home group's trinity.

Closing (10 minutes)
◇ Organize and announce a group of interns and new members. This is a virtual group.
◇ Give a message of congratulations and encouragement to the home group that is getting ready for new life.
◇ Give fervent prayers for new home groups.
◇ Confirm the place where new home groups will gather.
◇ Have a celebration party.

LESSON 11—Accompanying God

(1) Welcome—Introduction (10 minutes)
◇ Read the home group's vision and mission statement and home group pledge together.
◇ Congratulations! You've got a VIP. What would you like to do first for them? Speak of just two things.

(2) Worship—Singing and Reporting (10 minutes)
◇ Singing hymns in accordance with the mood, expressing your heart. It is recommended to choose gutsy songs.
◇ The home leader will offer a report prayer.

(3) Word—Hoondok Reading and Discussion (20 minutes)

"I ask you to do home church activities now, but I do not force you to do what you dislike. I give you an order to do it to lead you to a world of love. I want you to practice true love centering on home church. You need to know that it is best for you to build your own fence and nest quietly with love centering on home church. That is to devote you to the love of the true master centering on home church. How many times will God visit your home church because of your jeongseong? Have you ever thought about that? Think about it. God is able to defend your future and follow you. You must always think about whether God can reside in your home church. Then the home church will definitely welcome you." [Sermons, 115-326]

"Wherever God wants to realize His love, God will accompany the people there. God is not a delusional or idealistic God. God is not an abstract God. God is with us as the master of our life with His own authority. He is not there always to be served. God is a living God with us, centered on collective love." [Sermons, 168-111]

◇ True Parents began their home church residing with God in Beomnaetgol. Where does the amazing ability of home church come from?

(4) Work—Activity (20 minutes)
◇ How can we know that our home group is walking with God? What do you think should be done in order to accompany God?
◇ Group members should fill out VIP cards describing their potential guests, and organize prayer partners for them.

Closing (5 minutes)
◇ Speak of your wishes in pairs and pray fervently for each other's wishes in pairs.

LESSON 12—Making Good Habits

(1) Welcome—Introduction (10 minutes)
◇ Read the home group's vision and mission statement and home group pledge together.
◇ Let's praise each other for two minutes without stopping, and let's share each other's feelings.

(2) Worship—Singing and Reporting (10 minutes)
◇ Select and sing joyful hymns or songs.

(3) Word—Hoondok Reading and Discussion (20 minutes)
◇ Getting acquainted with the habit of praising

"Praise a baby in front of his mother and father. Tell them what their baby is like and how he looks but also that he looks better than his mom and dad. First you have to say the baby is cute. Shower them with praise by complimenting his looks, saying he looks adorable and that his personality is fine spirited. Is there anyone who dislikes compliments? Don't you also? Even if it is obvious to you that you aren't that good, it's pleasing to receive praise. Right? Isn't it? If you praise their son, they'll be in a good mood. Then analyze the son's personality for them, and tell them how you believe they should educate the child. Tell them these things explain that the mother and father should do that in the future. You also ask them whether they have been doing something like that. … In this way, they may feel friendlier toward you. They may like it. … Then say, 'If you teach him that way, this baby will not only lead this town in the future, but also become a good man of virtue for this country.' Then the mother will be glad to hear that. … That's how to do witnessing." [Sermons, 73-130]

◇ It is necessary to learn good habits for the growth of the home group. Discuss what good habits are.
◇ If your family has good habits for witnessing, express them in one word.

(4) Work—Activity (10 minutes)
◇ Open up to each other about personal obstacles and obstacles to the development of the home group in detail in pairs, and pray fervently to overcome these obstacles.
◇ Home group members send a "message of praise" to each of their VIPs. (If you do not have any VIPs, send it to your spouse or family.)

Closing (5 minutes)
◇ Remind the members of the numerical value of qualities by entering the jeongseong—relationship—invitation—multiplication process from the 13th week.
◇ Close with a fervent prayer.
◇ Go out with the members of the group to a restaurant known for its good food.

LESSON 13—Overcoming Challenges

(1) Welcome—Introduction (10 minutes)
◇ Read the home group's vision and mission statement and home group pledge together.
◇ Divide the members of the home group into pairs.

(2) Worship—Singing and Reporting (10 minutes)
◇ Sing gospels or hymns that are about overcoming difficulties.
◇ The home leader will offer a report prayer.

(3) Word—Hoondok Reading and Discussion (20 minutes)

"We should be able to say, 'Of course, thank you,' no matter what difficulties, indignation, and injustices we encounter. God will raise His arms to bless such people." [Sermons, 8-34]

"You have to go through a process to be challenged and to overcome difficulties always. We must realize that we cannot advance to a higher developed world otherwise, and it is a divine principle of development in our view of history and social life." [Sermons, 113-214]

"A pioneer is not a person who promises things that are limited to reality, but a person who has faith and a view of life and the cosmos that can transcend reality and promise the value of the future. In other words, he is neither a person searching for something sweet in the real-life zone nor a person avoiding the path of fighting to plant the value of tomorrow based on present reality. But he should be a person who keeps on challenging. You cannot be a pioneer unless you are such a person." [Sermons, 45-302]

◇ Let's talk sincerely about the problems that our home group needs to overcome one by one. Overcoming means that we can grow more if we solve this problem well. What should we overcome?

(4) Work—Activity (20 minutes)
◇ There are five levels in the growth of a home group. They are birth, conflict, community, ministry, and multiplication periods. The community period is a time when the home groups become one, and the ministry period is a time to go out to bear witness. The multiplication period is a time for new people.
◇ Which of the above stages do you think our home group is in? What is the basis for confirming that stage? Talk about what we need to do to get better.

Closing (5 minutes)
◇ Give earnest unison prayers to solve the problems of home groups.
◇ In order to commemorate the overcoming of the home group's problems, send your VIPs a message of encouragement and hope directly through your mobile phones.

LESSON 14—Jeongseong and Relationships

(1) Welcome—Introduction (10 minutes)
◇ Read the home group's vision and mission statement and home group pledge together.
◇ Show images of our home group with our home group family together, using images of animals, plants, minerals and so on. Example: honeybees, lions and so on.

(2) Worship—Singing and Reporting (10 minutes)
◇ Singing hymns or pop songs in accordance with the mood, expressing your heart.
◇ A new home group member will offer a report prayer.

(3) Word—Hoondok Reading and Discussion (20 minutes)

"If we need more people, we will keep praying all night long without sleeping. They will walk to us. We may see them coming. Our spiritual power is alive. It's not dead. If we say they will come tomorrow morning, they will come. We need to know how strong the power of prayer is." [Sermons, 185-322]

"When I started a church, tears never stopped falling from my eyes. It was so strenuous. While I was praying for 400 family members, calling each name, I already knew someone was healed.

I called and asked him whether such and such things happened, then the answer was "Yes." I prayed, calling all the names of my family members. Before I call their names, I see them in my head already. It takes 40 minutes just to call out all the names. They may appear with a smiling face, an anxious face and so on. So I knew what happened to everyone." [*True Parents' Walk of Life 3.-3. Raising Families with Blood, Sweat, and Tears*]

◇ What kind of spiritual power within you do you want to see revived?
◇ What do you want to do with your revived spiritual power?

(4) Work—Activity (20 minutes)
◇ How did your relationship with VIPs change your daily life?
◇ Talk about what you want to do for deeper passion of jeongseong and relationship.

Closing (5 minutes)
◇ Sing hymns and close with praying in pairs.

LESSON 15—Gathering and Multiplication

(1) Welcome—Introduction (10 minutes)
◇ Read the home group's vision and mission statement and home group pledge together.
◇ Mention the name of the family member in the home group who has affected you the most, and how that person has affected you. And if the person is there, he or she may express gratitude.

(2) Worship—Singing and Reporting (10 minutes)
◇ Sing a closing rejoicing hymn.
◇ The home leader will offer a report prayer.

(3) Word—Hoondok Reading and Discussion (20 minutes)
"We have to invest all our tears and bloody sweat. So you have to create an object partner like yourself. You have to create the existence of an object partner like yourself. You may do it by saying, 'Let him be like me! Let him be like me!'" [*Sermons*, 168-324]

"In the beginning, no one is like you. You had better raise them as you gave birth and raised your own children. Do your sons and daughters grow up all of a sudden? No, you have to toil for them for decades. You have to raise them like that. So if you have raised one, then you send him off with trust and have him repeat with others what you did for him. Next, you have him bring other people, and then you raise them as well. One-third of the people will be raised by him, and two-thirds will be raised with the help of yourself. If he does this, he will become like you. Suddenly there are four. You raise one of the four persons. In other words, three of the four will be raised by him and one of the four—your direct spiritual child—will be raised by you. The other three only need to connect to him, to connect to you. After that, this process can double, and when it comes to the third or fourth time, you do not even need to teach any of them but just talk. If the current teachers focus only on the standards that are being taught, all of them can be put in place of you. So, you do it. That way, multiplication will go on." [Sermons, 254-149]

◇ What comes to your mind when you think of your beloved spiritual parents (supporters, evangelists)?

(4) Work—Activity (20 minutes)
◇ If VIPs need to grow up to become family members like you, at what point do you want them to be like you? Discuss what you can actually do for that.
◇ Talk about important elements of intake and multiplication from your experience with family members.

Closing (5 minutes)
◇ Confess your weaknesses in VIP intake and multiplication to your partners, and pray in pairs fervently to overcome those weaknesses.
◇ Ensure that the group secretary has recorded and organized the progress from week 1 through week 15.

LESSON 16—True Home Church

(1) Welcome—Introduction (10 minutes)
◇ Read the home group's vision and mission statement and home group pledge together.
◇ Express your words of blessing with family members who have been working for 16 weeks.
◇ Clap and shout for joy while announcing the names of VIPs who have connected to the group over the past 16 weeks.

(2) Worship—Singing and Reporting (10 minutes)
◇ Sing the most popular songs among the songs sung during the past 16 weeks.
◇ It is recommended to sing a series of fun and memorable songs.
◇ The home leader will offer a report prayer.

(3) Word—Hoondok Reading and Discussion (20 minutes)

"Families should have parents, husbands and wives, and siblings. These are requirements for anyone. If you lack any of these, you're missing out on requirements in terms of the environment and family. It means you are unhappy. It cannot be perfect without a brother. You have that parent–child relationship from birth no matter what. You do not want to have parents other than your own. A person must be a son or a daughter, a brother or a sister, a spouse, and the parent of someone. This is the formula of heavenly law. If one of them is missing, it is impossible to form a spherical ideal system in the direction of the north, south, east and west. Then, it is a problem what kind of settlement can be accomplished by the heart of children, brothers and sisters, a couple, and parents. That is a home." [Sermons, 262-122]

◇ A home group is a family community, a heaven on earth to encounter in advance, that restores the ideal of a family under the one and only God.
◇ If we have DNA in our home group, what would it be like?

(4) Work—Activity (20 minutes)
◇ Describe five key features of the home group and rate each one between 1 and 10 points.
◇ Talk about what these scores tell us and what you think is most important when you start your next home group.

Closing (5 minutes)
◇ Time for discussion will become longer. This is the basis for a healthier home group, so have a session to carefully evaluate 16 weeks.
◇ Stand up and shout "_____ Home Group Eog Mansei!" and have an earnest unison prayer.

Chapter 3

HTM Organization Management through Multiplication of Home Groups

What is a Hyojeong Home Group?

The term "home group" is a way to describe a dynamic small group, yet its makeup is too diverse and extensive to explain in a few words. Let's think about what this small group, the home group, is and, focusing on the history of FFWPU, how it should function.

The origin and growth strategy of FFWPU are quite distinctive. After the Holy Wedding of True Parents in 1960, three pairs of spiritual children were blessed. One year later, the 36 Couples Blessing was given, with 12 couples representing each of the three couples. The number of blessed families increased like the multiplication of cells, with the number increasing to 72 couples, 120 couples, and 430 couples. True Parents applied a strategy of binding three families into small groups and multiplied the blessed families. True Parents have described strategic church growth as a process similar to "multiplying new cells." [*Sermons*, 15-192]

The strategy of successful HTMs must follow the strategy of True Parents. The trinity home group is important in this sense. As if it were meant to serve as proof, the established FFWPU churches showed explosive growth through the cell church movement after 1980. The expansion providence of the trinity, which started from 1960 with dynamic and explosive power, led to the growth of FFWPU. Especially after the Seonghwa of True Father, True Mother, as the only begotten daughter of God, has been conducting the heavenly tribal messiah movement bound together centered on hyojeong. The hyojeong home group has started in the context of this historic trinity expansion policy.

True Parents have been conducting the home church providence since the 1970s. However, a home group form of "trinity" was first formed in June 1958. The home group, which is the word we currently use, began in September 2008 from FFWPU. In this sense, the term "home group" is another name for the dynamic cell group that originated from the family community culture, which is a characteristic of FFWPU.

FFWPU started in the form of the home group, or family gathering, led by True Parents. From the 1960s to the 1970s, fiery worship was held at each home and many brothers and sisters became members of the church from their experience in home groups. The church organization grew from three couples to 12, leading to the 36 Couples Blessing, then the 72, 120, and 430 Couples. It took the form of cell church growth, multiplying in a manner similar to cells. Through this process the members established strong trinity teams and a parental organization of faith. These organizations featured a developmental and explosive family structure, stronger and more influential than family blood ties of that time. The church shared a spiritual culture consisting of tears, affection, and love. Members experienced strong emotional exchanges among themselves, based on this root. They worshipped passionately and showed testimonies and the work of the Holy Spirit.

FFWPU is the home church that emerged from the healthiest and most passionate home group ever having appeared in the 20th century. The early church consisted of gatherings of three or more in homes, well-formed home groups, and it grew naturally. They were "evangelism home groups" that mainly aimed at multiplying the religion. Members who were well trained by their spiritual parents played the role of missionaries and pastors after a 40-day training session, and they became strong leaders and ministers.

In summary, family church at that time was the boot camp for the spiritual parents, each of whom was part of a trinity team to evangelize new members, grow them with tears and affection, guide them to become blessed families after a workshop, and send them off as missionaries. What are the keywords here? They are tears, affection, trinity, parents of faith, evangelism, growth, education of the heart, workshop participation, blessing, and training field leaders. What do these words mean to you? Would they not be the critical keys to the true growth and revival of FFWPU? Therefore, the heavenly tribal messiah movement must follow this road to be successful.

This is proven by the fact that more than 180,000 applications were filed for membership in FFWPU in 1966 after True Parents applied the trinity strategy directly and supervised the multiplication of blessed families starting in 1960. Through the home groups and HTM Leader School it is now time for everyone to do their best to live up to their faith, learning the process for restoring the essence of faith. Through this, we can accomplish the heavenly tribal messiah mission and bear the beautiful fruits of FFWPU through trinities, working with the only begotten daughter, True Mother.

1. The Relationship Between Home Groups, Home Church and the Hoondok Family Association

The home church movement started through the guidance of True Parents in 1976. However, the mission work of Unification Church was based on the home group, like a family, long before that. Home church came later, and it was named "hoondok family church" after True Parents announced hoondokhae in October 1997. Therefore, hoondok family church is the combination of hoondokhae and home church, and hoondok family church and home church are the same thing. According to the recently enacted Cheon Il Guk Constitution, hoondok family church is equal to hoondok family association.

Before Foundation Day in 2013, family church had a strong element of battlefield mode. This was because members studied True Father's words at home, and it originated from the *tongban gyeokpa* local breakthrough movement of the home church community whose goal was to spread the Blessing to every small community in Korea. However, after Foundation Day, it was necessary to make a change in the style of home church. This is because the hoondok family association needs to be renewed through experiencing the fullness of joy and happiness and starting a new life speaking to Heavenly Parent in the garden of Eden. If you think about the literal meaning of "Foundation Day," it means the origin of a new beginning. Here, it means the origin of Eden where people would stroll with Heavenly Parent, speak with God, and realize the dream of the ideal of creation. It is time to move to a healthy FFWPU that promotes natural growth rather than continue with this battlefield mode. A healthy hoondok family association is made up of healthy home group cells.

2. Types of Home Groups

① Home groups for evangelism

There can be various types of home groups, depending on their purpose and role, just as there are many types of small groups or clubs. The home group we are dealing with in this section is a strategic evangelism home group whose goal is to multiply the hoondok family association and make successful heavenly tribal messiahs.

The evangelism home group is the core home group that is activated by those who participate in the HTM Leader School and continue to conduct three-cycle report meetings for multiplication. These home groups are operated by merging the open home group and the closed home group. The open home group is one that anyone may attend, open to everybody—like the happy day invitation used for multiplying newcomers to the Family Federation. However, the three-cycle home group meeting follows the closed home group setup, because it accepts new people as members only after a certain amount of time and education. Nevertheless, home groups at the frontline of evangelism are open groups in the sense that they welcome new visitors.

② Home groups for fellowship, education, and hobbies

There are home groups for educating new members, members who will be key leaders in the future, members who will educate home groups and be in charge of educating members attending leadership school training sessions. There are also groups that gather to promote friendship and share hobbies. These home groups are purpose-driven and can have various names. They can be dismantled once their purpose is met, or they can be re-created. These home groups will be distinguished from the home groups that encompass both evangelism and worship, such as the three-cycle home group.

③ Master home group

A master home group is a high-ranking home group for the core members of a newly formed trinity who are the core members of a hoondok family association with a heavenly tribal messiah at its head. This type of home group conducts strategic meetings and makes plans along with the heavenly tribal messiah, who is the leader among the multiplied home groups. When it has expanded

[Figure 3-1] Home Group Relational Structure

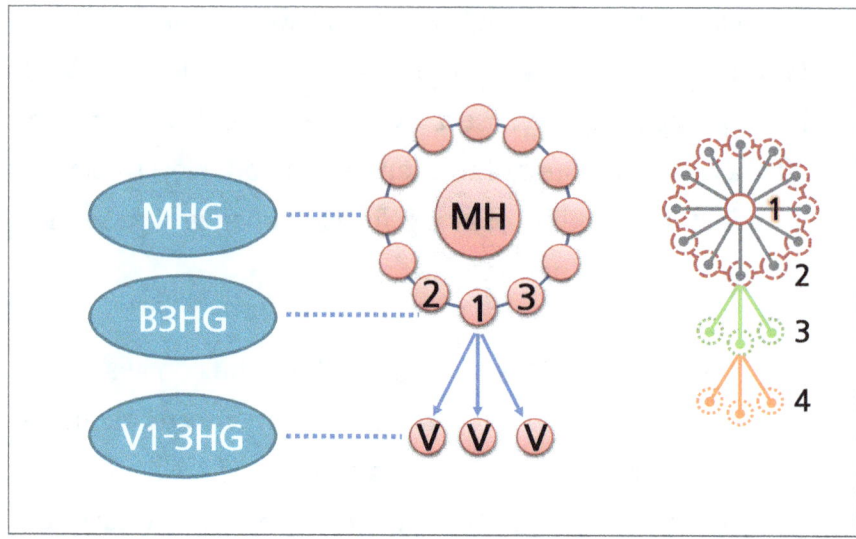

from a core trinity of three to a family group of more than 36 couples or completes the blessing of 430 couples, the core members gather and form home groups of three to 12 members. This is a master home group. When a group has grown from a trinity of three members to 12 members, that first trinity home group can be considered a master home group. If you take a look at the home group relationship structure shown below, a master home group is marked as MH and there is another group forming a trinity within the home group composed of 12 members. This is B3. This trinity meets new VIPs, spends time to evangelize them, and holds an open home group for them.

[Figure 3-2] Operational Types of Home Groups

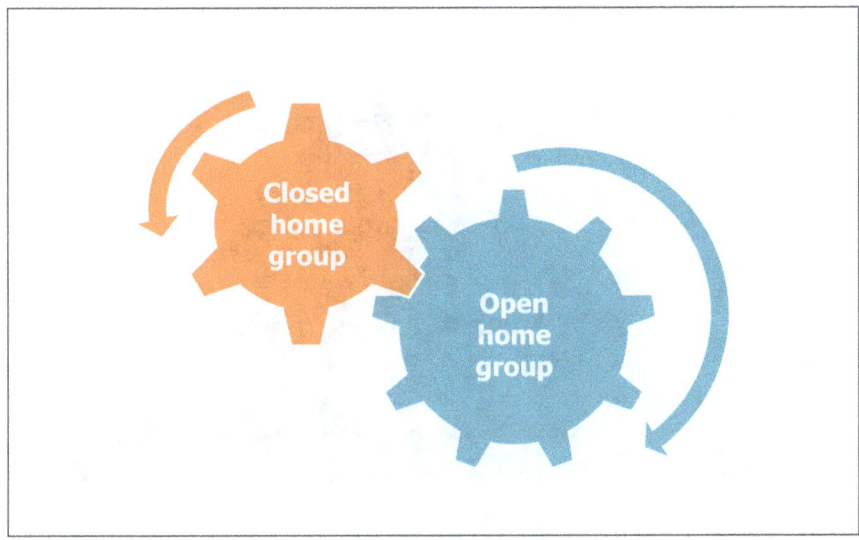

④ Open home groups and closed home groups in terms of function

An open home group is open to anyone and functions regardless of which participants are there. A closed home group is attended only by those who are invited. Strategies, human resources in the organization, and movement and closure of home groups are things that would be discussed in a closed home group. However, home groups that focus on and seek new members should offer natural and casual meetings that are comfortable for anyone to attend. At the same time, closed home groups and open home groups should be well connected. Through reporting, each should function while knowing what other groups are doing.

[Figure 3-3] The Structure of a Witnessing Home Group

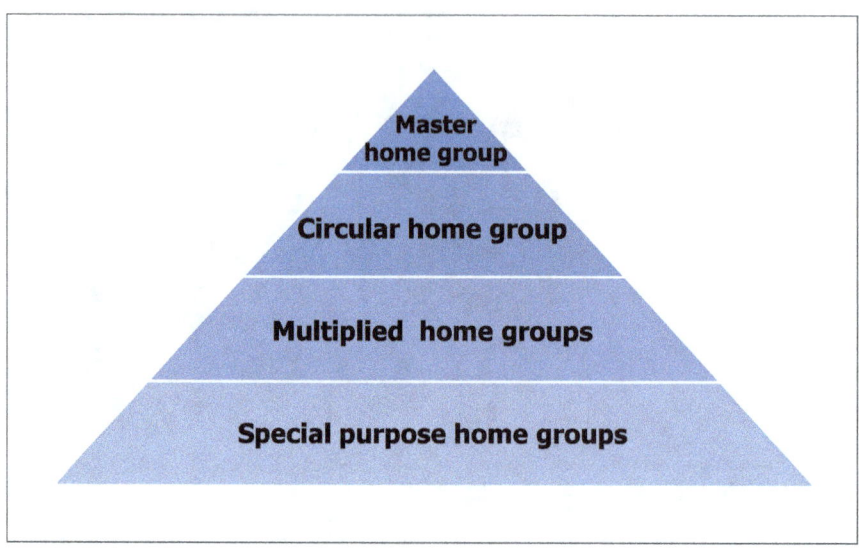

When a home group for evangelism becomes successful and begins to contain many home groups, the leaders who started the first home group become the group's master home group, which is a reporting home group. A master home group is a home group for planning and deciding strategies. This home group is a completely closed home group because only selected people can attend.

There are also home groups for special purposes, fellowship, and education. If we draw a pyramid structure of the home groups, there is a master home group composed of three persons at the top followed by a surrounding home group composed of twelve members. There are also many home groups under the circular home group that have been multiplied, and many home groups for specific purposes will be around or beneath the home groups. Please do not be confused about this and make the assumption that all home groups are for evangelism.

2. The Essence of the Home Group is the Trinity

A home group can be defined as a trinity. A trinity is a small group foundation community of members whose goal is to establish a healthy and beautiful hoondok family association. The ontological definition of hoondok family association is "a family community that reads the words of True Parents well, has the vision of Cheon Il Guk in its internal and external life, and realizes its mission and value." The home group is an operational force of trinity for the growth of Cheon Il Guk. The home group grows to be the hoondok family association, and the alliance of the hoondok family associations becomes the FFWPU. Therefore, the home group is a hoondok family association. A trinity of three persons or three families is the minimum unit of community that can be called a home group and serve as a Cheon Il Guk strategy team. A surprising fact is that True Parents used the trinity strategy long before they created the hoondok family association. Many of the families who participated in Blessing ceremonies were bound together as trinities of brother and sister families.

3. What are the Functional Values of Home Groups?

① Hyojeong family community

A home group should show clearly the consciousness of a "hyojeong family community." This is because a home group is a gathering of families centered on True Parents whose goal is to reveal the true value of hyojeong, and its members are connected by heartfelt bonds. A hyojeong family community, which is made up of chastity and love, is a family community gathered by our proud members.

② Evangelism and service

Evangelism and service comprise the values of home group and trinity life. The value of life is to embody evangelism and service, never forgetting about bringing salvation to the fallen world as we eat three meals per day. Members of a home group should show the values of evangelism and service through their lives. For example, every morning as a habit, we should think of whom we will serve, with whom we will make relationships, and whom we invite.

③ The core for producing hyojeong leaders.

The home group is "the core for producing hyojeong leaders." A heavenly tribal messiah is a Cheon Il Guk leader, so the home group, where Cheon Il Guk is rooted, should have a structure that is able to continuously produce leaders. This is made possible by connecting the home group and the HTM Leader School and providing more coaching leader experiences.

④ Mutual responsibility structure

The home group has "a mutual responsibility" team structure, in which members care for each other. Hyojeong families are rooted in the mind of hyojeong, so it is natural for them to sacrifice themselves for others and share their lives. If a team does not share mutual responsibility, the home group will be no different from other abundant small groups in the world. Caring is the creed of life given by True Parents.

⑤ Fostering new members

There are always members "to be fostered." The home group has the structure of a family, so it has a grandfather, a grandmother, a father, a mother, and siblings. Each member has a unique role, although it

[Figure 3-4] Home Group with the Values of the Trinity

may not be clearly seen. Therefore, a healthy home group always will have members to be raised. A healthy home group means that it has the power or momentum to grow and multiply. A home group that does not have any new members to educate and nurture may be at risk of shutting down. Therefore, a home group must have a structure suited to take care of new members.

If a home group does not have these five values, it needs treatment. In this case, the home group must utilize a coaching questionnaire, which can distinguish how to make it a healthy home group and head it toward healing, recovery, and growth together with a coach.

4. Multiplication is the Core Functional Definition of a Home Group

The home group is a cell organization that allows people to live in a beautiful and happy world beyond FFWPU. In the aspect of the Principle of Creation, a cell has multiplication DNA. This DNA is from Heavenly Parent. Therefore, a home group that does not multiply is the same as a dead group. In True Father's words,

> "You need to fulfill the mission of the second creator who will spread the Word of God. In other words, you need to be a propagator of the Word, a propagator of life, and a propagator of God's existence. You can serve God forever when you live as one and

have love as your center." [*Sermons*, 3-329]

Let's define the function of the home group to be an entity of propagation, of multiplication.

① The home group is the engine to build Cheon Il Guk.

The home group is the foundation of the hoondok family association and the driving force for acting as an organism. The driving force promotes only growth and multiplication. The engine promoting multiplication is the power that moves the entity, and it is not possible to make a healthy hoondok family association without it.

② The home group is a training camp to train true families.

The true family is achieved within the world in which we are living. Each member of the family needs to purify his or her own mind and body in order to achieve a true hoondok family association in this world which is saturated with wrong, self-centered values. The foundation is to achieve the true family of hyojeong. A home group is a place to practice it.

③ The home group is a training camp to experience a true family.

Wrong family values produce wrong family members. Families from all parts of the world will come to a home group, where people recognize and practice true family and experience what the true family means. Through home group communities, many people around the world will be able to experience a family that shares love and emotion.

④ The home group is the place where the heavenly tribal messiah will be established.

The heavenly tribal messiah has been empowered with the messiah mission, an amazing form that empowers blessed families with the authority and ministry of True Parents. Home groups are run by the blessed families raised by the heavenly tribal messiah leadership as new heavenly tribal messiahs. In other words, blessed families become the center of the mission and show leadership to foster new heavenly tribal messiah leaders.

⑤ The home group reproduces cells continuously.

Cheon Il Guk is the country of Heavenly Parent. The country is formed by the multiplication of Cheon Il Guk members. True Father has said that the structure of all organizations in the world should resemble the cells of the human body. The cells of the human body naturally reproduce and decay. This is based on the Principle of Creation. Therefore, Cheon Il Guk will multiply naturally like the cells of the human body.

> "If the leader of a family church spreads the good news to the first, second, and third generations, several thousand people soon will be working in the family church movement." [CSG, p. 956]

[Figure 3-5] The Functions of Home Groups

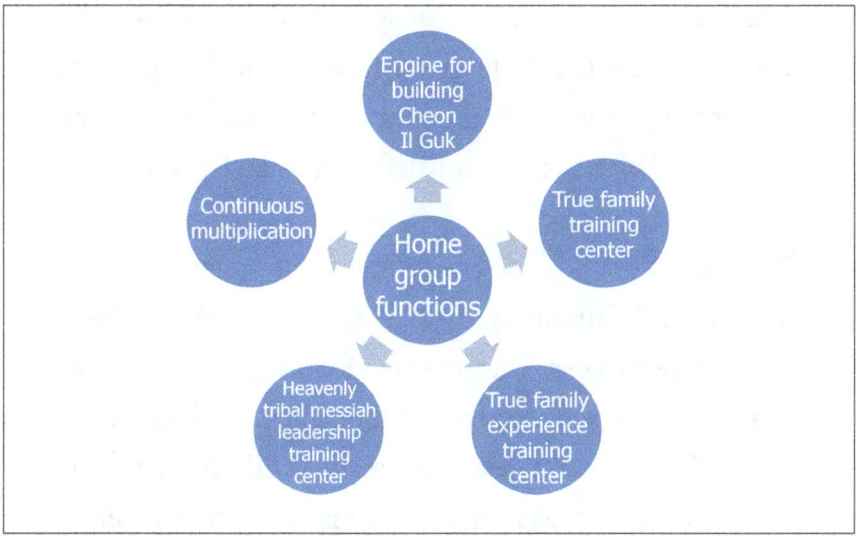

5. Meaning of Cheon Il Guk Expansion Through Home Group Activities

① All members will become heavenly tribal messiahs owing to continuous witnessing and growth.

The FFWPU church is characterized as a church praying "in my name." What does it mean? It is because we are already empowered by True Parents to carry out the heavenly tribal messiah mission. All members live as missionaries, not as laypersons. Above all things, to be a heavenly tribal messiah is the will of True Parents, so all blessed families need to be heavenly tribal messiahs.

The life of a blessed family is to conduct the home group report meetings for 16 weeks, pray, serve with heart, meet people to deliver True Parents' words, invite people, send members to the leader school for growth, and develop a three-member home group into a 12-member home group. As we work hard on this, all blessed families will become heavenly tribal messiah leaders.

② Achieve the vision of a foundation of 12, oriented by trinity.

The Cheon Il Guk ministry of True Parents is the multiplication of blessed true families. This structure follows the principle of creation. This vision can be traced back to the 12-tribal vision through Moses in the Old Testament. Jesus also served with the vision of 12 disciples. True Parents also carried out his vision for establishing 3-12-36-72-120 blessed families. This is the vision of God.

> "A family cannot stand alone. Families must organize trinities. This is the vertical standard. It is the number of heaven. The number of heaven is three. The number of the earth is four, which is manifested in north, south, east, and west, or spring, summer, fall, and winter. Multiplying three and four is the number 12, which also represents the 12 months. That is why there are the twelve tribes." [*Sermons*, 149-142]

What does it mean that no family should be alone in the Cheon Il Guk mission? It means that we should do "team ministry." It is the same as Heavenly Parent's being happy after having created human beings and everything on the earth instead of living alone. The Will of Heavenly Parent is for the team ministry to work together, not alone. FFWPU was able to grow to 180,000 members in 1966 because this strategy worked. Moreover, everybody must try hard to hold gatherings in order to revive the church. The smallest group that can support and take care of each other and understand and carry out a team ministry is three persons.

③ Becoming an evangelism-oriented church toward a community of heart

A church is a training ground for realizing Cheon Il Guk. However, how about the activities of current church members? According to church statistics, about 10 to 20 percent of members are active players playing on the field and more than 80 percent are spectators. Considering that the church is where all members achieve the three blessings and practice the great subject partners principle, it is urgent for the church to become a church filled with the culture of heart. If we can manifest the shimjeong culture, more than 80 percent of members will become active Cheon Il Guk players. These players naturally will live evangelism-oriented lives and act accordingly.

④ Vertical alignment—a vision of two wings

Cheon Il Guk is the expansion of the hoondok family association. However, it is not possible to grow the organization only with the hoondok family association. The hoondok family association fulfills the function of a small group, a part of a Family Federation center, which is a big group. A big group center has hundreds, thousands, or tens of thousands of members. Passionate worship and praise and a strong community spirit are the elements of revival. Therefore, the hoondok family association should receive varied types of support from the large group center. A large group center can make true fellowship and caring relationships among members only when all members are affiliated with home groups. Only when two wings (a large group center and small groups) flap together strongly can the flying bird (Family Federation) reach the desired goal.

At its beginning, Christianity was able to grow rapidly owing to the small family churches. However, according to researchers, after Constantine the Great recognized Christianity officially in 313 AD, people began to gather in large churches and family churches disappeared. Consequently, the church has been flying with only one wing. This led to the absence of missionaries. Christianity became a state religion, and believing in Christianity meant attending a big church. When a Christian nation conquered another country, the conquered country became a Christian nation naturally. It means that independent mission work became weakened and the church came into collusion with government and was subject to corruption.

In the early days, FFWPU had a vibrant culture of heart and small group gatherings. However, since the establishment of large congregations, the small groups have been weakened and the FFWPU has become a great, temple-oriented church. If we could grow to a large group church that is integrated with the hoondok family association, we could make a great revival as we move toward the settlement of Cheon Il Guk. The two-wing vision is very

[Figure 3-6] A Trinity Home Group Focused on True Parents' Words

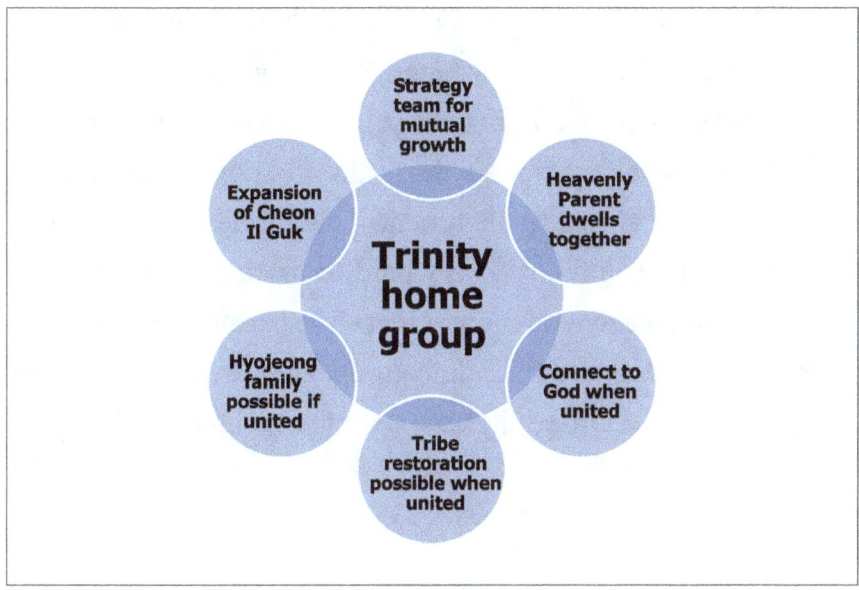

[Figure 3-7] The Meaning of Expanding Cheon Il Guk through Home Group Activities

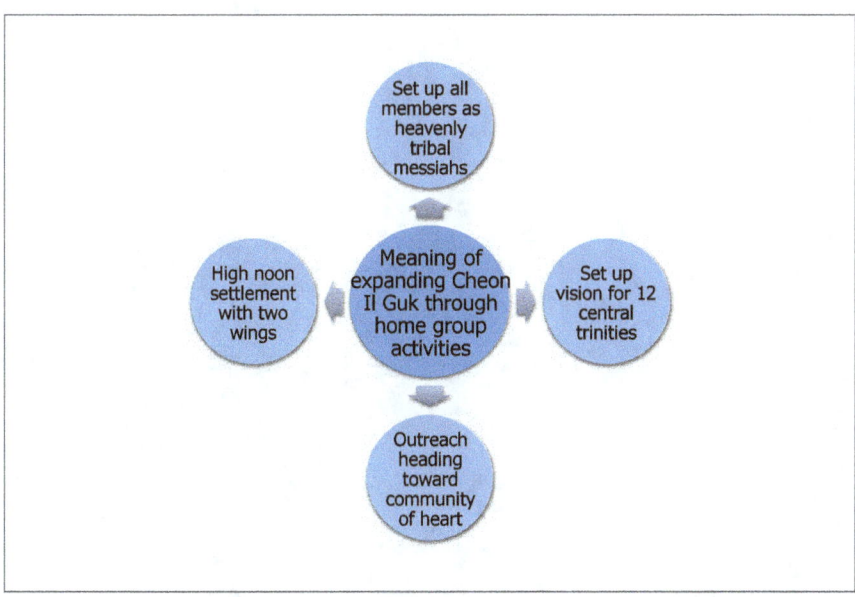

Chapter 3   HTM Organization Management through Multiplication of Home Groups • 279

important in this way.

One important thing is to protect the home groups from drifting away from the central teachings. If a home group is independent and not affiliated with a big group, it will become hard for the group to form proper right angles vertically and horizontally and it may fail to make a vertical alignment. This can lead to it becoming a problematic church. It is very hard to fix this problem unless the group is affiliated with a large group. The harmonious strong wings, the large group and the home group, are the elements of a bright Cheon Il Guk community with a vertical high noon alignment.

2

The Process of HTM Organization Management through Multiplication of Trinities

1. Establishing an HTM Coaching Management Organization

When the HTM organization is expanded, it will have a human organization composed of thousands or tens of thousands of people beyond 430 families initiated from three persons. Moreover, the organization is run and led by the leaders of Cheon Il Guk. What do we need to do to run such a large organization? It will not be enough with the experience of leading tens or hundreds of people. The HTM basically needs to be a leader of an organization that has hundreds, thousands, or tens of thousands of members. In order to achieve this, we need to apply the organization composition and the contents of management of conglomerates, which are managing big groups in the most advanced and exemplary manner. Here comes the coaching leadership.

The organization of Cheon Il Guk is different from that of the general social organization. It must have a true-love leadership that mutually cares and supports. It is different from the management organization, and it should be an organization of leaders, beyond a management organization. In other words, it should become a coaching leader organization that is led by hyojeong leaders, rather than managed by them. For this purpose, members learn how to be leaders specifically in Leader School III. The family nurturing structure, in which the invisible spring of love flows, must run within the home group. It should appear as a one-on-one nurturing structure centered on the trinity as parents and siblings raise a child in a family.

(1) Establishing a trinity-oriented one-on-one family nurturing coaching leader

We need to train and support those who have the spiritual gifts of serving and teaching others and the heart of loving souls among members who received coaching training according to the situations of HTM Leader School or hoondok family association. There must be at least one professional coach in a trinity home group, the three-, 12-, and 36-person structures, or 12-person hoondok family association. Even if the one person is not an expert, the person must receive training so they can nurture and coach newcomers on a one-on-one basis, like a mother. In this aspect, each spiritual parent needs to be a coach. This can be acquired in Leader School III. The coach serves as a guide to help members have the confidence of salvation and settle well in the home group and hoondok family association. Moreover, the coach takes responsibility for maturing members spiritually. When the coach does these kinds of jobs, people tend not to leave the hoondok family association. When a stranger attends a meeting, the person stays in the meeting and the coach helps the person to grow spiritually.

The principle of coaching was that a new member must be nurtured one-on-one or in a small group within the trinity. In the trinity there are invisible roles, such as grandfather, parents, and children. Therefore, you should not lead your home group hastily. It is a principle to work thoroughly, one-on-one through the trinity. In doing so, it is possible to give customized training and form rapport successfully, owing to confidentiality. Therefore, it is possible to consult and know the current struggles. Consequently, this can heal and treat the new member very well and increase the organization's growth. Because the first FFWPU established the spiritual parent structure and the trinity structure well, it was able to produce many good leaders, whom we can see now.

One-on-one caregivers let members know what kind of spiritual gifts they received from God through what is called the DISC assessment. The DISC assessment is based on psychological research, and it uncovers the behavior type of each person, helping people to draw their own profile in response to questions. A coach is assigned, according to the gifts identified by the assessment, and when the caregiver builds his hoondok family association or HTM Leader School in stages of 12 persons, 36 persons, 72 persons, and 120 persons, he may perform an outstanding ministry, often even better than other religious workers (including pastors, witnessers, staff).

They will be valuable workers joining the beautiful mission. They are the hands and feet of the heavenly tribal messiah, and they are the spiritual leaders of the tribe for the rest of their lives. When 120 one-on-one caregivers are established, they become the driving force of FFWPU and achieve a remarkable revival as professional ministers. As the previously studied three-cycle home group and 16-week report meeting program are also connected to a coaching style, there will be a continuous opportunity for the leadership of serving others.

(2) Establishing core coaching leaders for expanding the home group organization

One-on-one coaching care has limitations. However, one-on-one coaching care is the most powerful method because it can increase the spiritual maturity of a person in a customized way, according to the degree of faith of particular members. It is possible to do it at any time in a small hoondok family association (12 to 36 persons). However, it is very difficult when a hoondok family association grows to be more than a hundred people. Therefore, one-on-one coaching care should be set up within a home group, and the framework and the skill it embodies should be established in a healthy way with coaching techniques. Caregivers should be able to reach the professional level. Generally, it is recommended to have at least one professional coaching leader in each 12-person hoondok family association.

Additionally, we can have excellent organization management if the organization is established by well-structured home group reporting meetings (three-cycle) and other small groups. If home groups are made up of fewer than 12 people and they are expanding by forming a trinity relationship, making relationships, and receiving community training naturally, it will have a good management organization when it grows to over 430 people. This will be a successful system to become a large group. At the time of the initial home group report meeting, it already starts with three coaches centered on the heavenly tribal messiah, so the hoondok family association will make use of one to four coaches.

 Starting from a trinity of three persons, a trinity of three families (home group) expands to a hoondok family center of 12 persons.

(3) Establishing a core coaching leader for midsize groups

Several home groups become a hoondok family association meeting and their union makes a midsize home group. Then it will become a "village FFWPU" (*tong* and *ban*). These midsize groups should offer community training and service opportunities for education and training, including various leader school programs, and produce strong groups benefiting local organizations. Alternatively, a midsize group can be divided into districts. For example, it can be divided into 12 districts, with districts 1 to 6 grouped as Village 1 and districts 7 to 12 grouped as Village 2. Each village will have a leader. In other words, there will be a structure of training and educating within the village unit. Additionally, a mission declaration clarifying the mission and value of the village shall be created through the coaching training of core leaders of various groups, such as a blessing family group, a young adults group, a male evangelistic group, a female evangelistic group, etc., and the activities of the village shall agree with the vision of the village. The FFWPU of the village is composed of 12 or more coaching staff members. It is desirable that these coaches be recognized by the society and the nation through the training and education of Leader School III. In South Korea, more than 70 Korean and Japanese missionaries currently hold coaching certificates given by recognized institutions. It has been reported that a coaching certificate is more effective than experience in missionary activities in its potential to gather and nurture people.

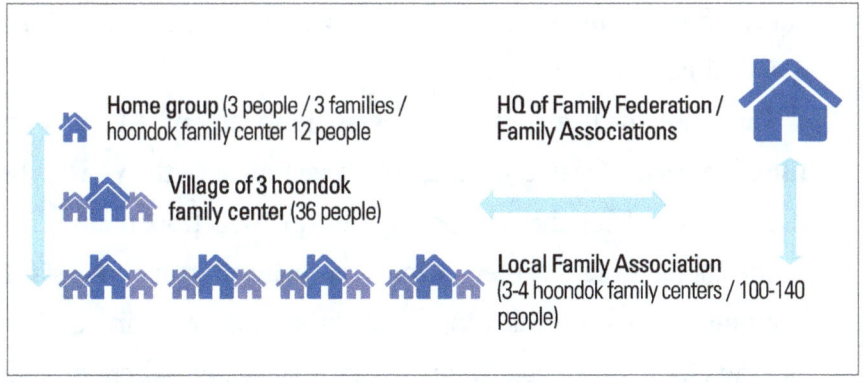

(4) Establishing HTM coaching leaders for large groups

Home groups grow into hoondok family associations. Hoondok family associations become FFWPU of districts and villages. When these districts are established, other regions or villages create districts and they join together to make a large group. It should be approved by the association.

For example, in case of a parish, FFWPU representing the villages of a region will be assembled to make up a parish. This organizational process is the process of becoming a large group, starting from home group pioneering. FFWPU chapters in villages are gathered to make a large group. The large group will be formed by a heavenly tribal messiah who has accomplished 430 families blessing, goes through an ongoing multiplication process of blessed families and leads other Blessing activities. When this occurs in each country, we will be able to see the process of the restoration of the country. This appears in the Words of True Parents. True Parents said, "The restoration of the country will be confirmed when 12 families are successful in completing the heavenly tribal messiah mission with 430 families."

Currently the heavenly tribal messiah movement is actively established in many Asian countries. However, most of the work is being done far away from the existing large groups, which are mainly located in the capital or city centers. Moreover, heavenly tribal messiahs are bringing victory and blessing small cities and towns in rural areas, not big cities. Therefore, there are many situations where people are

 District Family Association
(Village Family Association 430 people)

 HQ of Family Federation /
Family Associations

being blessed first and educated later. In this situation, the blessed families seriously require good organization and nurturing and education management structures. We must try hard to assign blessed families to trinities, bring them to a home group, assemble them to a hoondok family association, and create a parish by putting hoondok family associations together in a village. The coaching leader organization is essential to lead this process successfully.

The education of a coaching leader is accomplished by going through a process of experience and mastery while running the home group reporting meeting. In the 430-family heavenly tribal messiah organization, it is ideal to establish a coaching staff committee, which can do it right along with coaching staff. The coaching leader organization will be explained in detail during the third term of the HTM Leader School.

So far, we have reviewed the process of a blessed family multiplication system that starts from the trinity home group and grows to a large group. This process follows the way True Parents worked to initiate and grow the current FFWPU.

3

Organizational management relationship with HTM groups through large groups and home groups

When a large group already exists in a city, what will be the proper relationship between a midsize group growing through home groups and the existing large group?

"The relationship between the two groups is a vertical alignment. They have a two-wing relationship and a complementary relationship."

There are many ways to make heavenly tribal messiah work successful. However, regardless of the way, large groups and small groups should have a deep partnership at the organizational and management levels. High-noon vertical alignment is the most desirable way. The heavenly tribal messiahs and their organization, which have grown to a large group through home groups, should have a "vertical alignment" relationship with the affiliated existing large group, and establish a "two-wing" function. Therefore, there must be a system that defines and checks the relationship between the two organizations. In other words, there must be an internal regulation that helps a member who has become a successful heavenly tribal messiah and the existing large group to accept each other mutually and grow together. If there is no regulation, we may experience unmanageable incidents after the growth, and it can create an undesirable shadow. In order to prevent any improper outcomes, there should be a developmental and positive interaction among the large groups, the national headquarters, and the HTM organizations in the field.

1. What is the Vertical Alignment Relationship?—Identity

High-noon vertical alignment relationship means that the relationship between the horizontal position of existing large groups and the vertical position of the groups that have grown into HTM home groups should be the orderly figure of hyojeong, which is to be without any shadow under the light of True Parents, shining like the sun. This means "the function regarding the identity of the home group organization and the large group organization." The vision, mission value, and action plan of True Parents should be shown clearly in the heavenly tribal messiah organizations and should agree with the instructions and regulations of the head office. Existing large groups should support home groups with education programs, a martial arts studio, and a variety of support, which helps all blessed families become heavenly tribal messiahs. Moreover, the large group worship and meetings should be an opportunity to experience the spiritual power of God and the heart of hyojeong. To achieve this, we should operate a thorough and systematic reporting and management system and a coaching system that checks and develops it. It plays an important role in preventing the dissociation between the horizontal group and the vertical group due to the expansion of the former and avoiding the creation of a heresy group. We can achieve Cheon Il Guk when the horizontal and vertical groups expand continuously with the concept of high-noon vertical alignment.

2. What is the Two-Wing Relationship?—Functionality

A bird must flap two wings strongly to fly to the sky as it desires. The two wings stand for the large group and the group centered on the heavenly tribal messiahs. It indicates "the meaning of functionality" between two organizations. If a bird can move only one wing, the bird cannot reach its desired location and eventually will die. As such, in terms of functional activities, the head office and the heavenly tribal messiah group must be one body. In other words, the large group must fully support the growth and success of the home groups spiritually and physically as a training and management field.

We will need various educational and training programs, such as education for the principles and a life of faith, education to be HTMs, education for young children, students, youths and young adults, education prior to the Blessing, parental education, blessed family education, Cheon Il Guk membership training, home group education, hoondok family association education, HTM leadership training, Principle deepening education, True Parents' life, hyojeong education of heart, and leadership school field installation education. The collective prayer and jeongseong at a large group level will show incredible spiritual power.

Moreover, there is the function of worship. Members will experience a fiery external spirituality through large group meetings, report meetings, and a mega-large group report meeting. Hundreds, thousands, and tens of thousands can gather and experience jeongseong and spirituality. On the other hand, we can share the inner presence of God in the home group. As shown, the home group and the large group have a spiritually complementary relationship and people can experience Heavenly Parent.

The impact on society also will greatly expand. A member will experience something in a large group that is not experienced in a small group, and generate untiring spiritual power for the home group. The functional role is a relationship of two wings.

3. Development and Growth of the Home Group in the Large Group

So far, we have reviewed the multiplication, growth, and organization management at the home group and small group levels.

However, it is another matter to switch from a large group to home groups, when the large group already has a solid framework. This is because it is not easy to adjust people's thinking to match the awareness of the home group structure. Existing large groups must put in a lot of effort to make the home groups dynamic and multiplying. However, there are many differences between the contents of the large group's leadership operation, which is already established, and those of the small group's leadership operation. Essentially, there are three ways for a large group to run home groups.

They are "a church which has home groups," "a church converting to home groups" and "a home group church." "A church which has home groups" has many home groups with one large group, but not all strategies of the large group are directed at them, and the home groups have a district organization form or operation method, running on one of many strategies. "A church converting to home groups" means a large group heading to the point where all its operational strategies help and support the operation of the home groups. Lastly, "a home group church" is a midsize or large group that grew from home groups. This is oriented toward the home groups. The large group is organized for the home groups, and it exists to develop more home groups.

If a large group, regardless of how it came about, wants to lead the home groups and be successful, the relationship between the large group and the home groups must maintain a vertical alignment relationship and the two-wing form. If a large group wants to achieve the heavenly tribal messiah mission, it must create spiritual children who are ready to be heavenly tribal messiahs. All FFWPU large groups must engage in this, in one form or another. The HTM Leader School is an educational structure that is required to operate home groups in a large group or to create three spiritual children, three families, or twelve persons to be heavenly tribal messiahs. When a large group tries to establish home groups, it can produce more powerful heavenly tribal messiahs if it sets up an HTM Leader School in the large group. Moreover, it is recommended to have several home groups run the HTM Leader School jointly in the process of initiating the home groups. No matter which route you take, you will need a process to initiate home groups.

Chapter 4

Building a Foundation for the Success of a Trinity

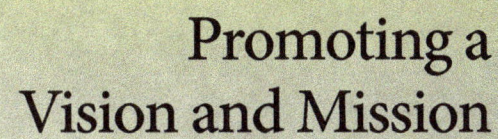

Promoting a Vision and Mission

There are some prerequisite processes to initiate a home group. It is necessary to imbue in all family members a strong intent to accomplish the mission True Father left us in his last prayer, together with an understanding of the heavenly tribal messiah mission. In other words, a motivation process is required.

"Belief forms behavior, behavior creates consequences, and consequences strengthen belief." For successful heavenly tribal messiah work, you need to assemble a team, rather than working alone. For this, a pastor or a leader of a large group needs to revolutionize the thinking of members through weekly meetings to present the relationship between home groups and heavenly tribal messiahs, case studies and success reports. Leaders of small or large groups should focus on fostering 12 hyojeong leaders, together with a trinity home group. Without this fundamental process, launching a home group is likely to fail. Important principles and focuses for the success of a home group are as follows:

Principles for home groups to be successful in HTM work

» The focus shall be on multiplication of home groups.
» Multiplication of home groups is possible only when a home group leader is thoroughly trained.
» All new members are regarded as potential hyojeong coaching leaders.
» All members must experience leadership training.
» Home group leaders together elect the leader of the large group.
» A member can start heavenly tribal messiah activities only when his hoondok family church has succeeded.
» To become a home group leader, this course must be completed.
» The hyojeong life of the only begotten son and only begotten daughter shall be shown in the work of the Holy Spirit.

To maintain a focus on the above principles, a process is required to teach them continuously to members, which is called the foundation work to elect a heavenly tribal messiah. A training course is needed to convey the understanding and context of the mission and to guide members in writing vision and mission statements after forming trinities.

2

Establishing a Vision and Mission

1. Vision Seminar, Vision Declaration and Launching Ceremony

Officially a large group conducts or hosts a home group or HTM vision-launching ceremony or a seminar. All members can perform activities to accomplish missions and values through the seminar or the ceremony, with their own goal and vision.

Members who start a trinity home group must have the time to enlighten each other in the course of preparing the home group's vision and mission statement together.

To form a coalition of homes through growth and multiplication of home groups, a pastor should keep giving sermons and hosting home group vision workshops. This foundation work to make the soil fertile before sowing is very important. For better foundation work, a vision declaration ceremony is recommended. There will be troubles if a pastor implements a home group in a large group without such procedures. In particular, a pastor implementing a home group without clear understanding of home groups and their visions or strategies could be one of the biggest causes of failure. Together with the foundation work needed to plant a tree called a home group, correct understanding of the tree is also required. What we have to do first for the work is take time to be a sympathetic community for hyojeong through evaluation and healing activities within the large group.

2. Establishing an HTM Growth Committee

To be a community that promotes home groups, we must establish an HTM growth committee within a large group, offer jeongseong, form trinities, and train hyojeong coaches. A coach is a person who draws out and develops people's capabilities, rather than issuing them instructions. It is obvious that a growing group will have to have a clear vision and goals.

According to a study on growing groups, it is important for all the members to have a strong consciousness of vision and mission. They should be able to explain the group's vision and mission in a three-minute presentation. This will ensure that they have a solid blueprint of the group's vision and mission. For this, it is recommended that all members learn the home group's mission statement in written format. Therefore, the establishment of an HTM growth committee is required, which will take the responsibility to coach, give feedback and follow up on the contents mentioned above.

3. Creating a Vision

A vision is a blueprint of the foreseeable future. It serves as a roadmap to advance toward future goals. A vision is a permanent instruction to accomplish a goal. If the vision is clear, people know where they are heading. A vision tells us who we are and where we are going. It is an answer to questions starting with who, when, where, how or to what degree. A vision helps us to gauge our progress in the mission.

If you have a goal but no vision, it will be like trying to reach your destination without a map. Vision is a process rather than a result, and a journey rather than a destination. Successful leaders of both large and small groups clearly present such visions to their members. However, the most important thing is "Vision is visible, and it is shown to the members by the leader." In other words, members can see vision through their leadership.

The vision of a home group is the same. Leaders of large groups should present the blueprint of a home group and HTM Leader School that can train members to be heavenly tribal messiahs in the future. The reason why a large group is not growing may be that no vision has been presented or that the core leaders of large or small groups do not provide a view of the vision. If members could not accomplish their mission, it may be because they had an unclear vision. Therefore, good Cheon Il Guk leaders will show clear vision to their members.

A synonym for vision is "dream." What is a dream? If a dream can be seen, it can be a vision. However, what distinguishes a dream from a vision is that the latter contains a strategy to accomplish the dream. In other words, a vision contains a ladder toward the dream. What is different between a goal and a vision is that a goal is meaningless once it is accomplished, while a vision allows us to see what comes next. A proper and clear vision can be spread among many people. A good vision benefits everyone. Therefore, a good vision can become Heavenly Parent's vision. For this, each large group and home group should prepare a mission statement and hold a vision declaration ceremony.

① Vision 2020

The short-term vision of the Family Federation is Vision 2020 for marching forward with True Mother, the only begotten daughter. Vision 2020 is the first step of the foundation vision of Cheon Il Guk, which started from Foundation Day in 2013. The vision is to celebrate the 100th birthday of True Father and restore the nation to realize True Parents' will. It is a vision we and the only begotten daughter, True Mother, must accomplish with the light and heart of hyojeong.

Our goal as the final vision is to establish Cheon Il Guk through completion of the four-position foundation, through the completion of the individual, the family and the realm of dominion, fulfilling the three great blessings and realizing the three objects purpose by becoming true parents, true teachers and true owners. The process to complete this is to create a trinity home group, expand it to a hoondok family church, and finally to complete the heavenly tribal messiah mission.

② Foundation Day vision

The Foundation Day vision refers to a vision of Eden where our ancestors originally were meant to enjoy a beautiful and happy life after the creation. Therefore, there must be some significant difference between the time before Foundation Day and the period after. After Foundation Day, we must have "innocence and purity" and achieve oneness in mind, oneness in body, oneness in thought and oneness in harmony with Heavenly Parent. Adam and Eve started their day in conversation with God and dreamed of their happy life in Eden as they walked through their day. Their vision was to accomplish three great blessings as the start of a beautiful and happy future. After Foundation Day, our blessed families should stand in the same position.

4. Visions and Values of the Home Group Trinity

A home group's vision also originates from the Foundation Day vision as the vision of Cheon Il Guk. After Foundation Day we seek to purify and cleanse our mind and body, aiming at absolute purity. We should live every day, every hour, every minute and every second living in oneness with Heavenly Parent. Through this process we can attain the completion of the first blessing. This vision of attaining oneness with God and uniting our mind and body centered on God leads us to fulfill the first blessing. In our home groups we offer jeongseong and hold report meetings to help us achieve this. The individuals or families who are part of the trinity home group must experience the heart of hyojeong. A true family is created by a man and a woman who have completed their individual perfection and who then receive the Blessing and fulfill the vision of the second blessing. The families that have completed the first and second blessings then work to achieve the third blessing and gain dominion by completing the heavenly tribal messiah mission. In order to move in this direction, the families of the Family Federation participated in the Foundation Day Blessing Ceremony. Now it is time to get started.

In other words, the vision of a home group is to accomplish the three great blessings, which are the original ideal of creation for human beings. During the process, the leadership of the heavenly tribal messiah must provide a vision for the home group. In the end, the course to achieve the vision and mission will be provided through hyojeong leadership.

5. Preparing a Mission Statement

Setting a goal and sharing a vision in a large group or a home group are very important. Particularly, creating a tree of vision together in the stage of home group formation and drawing a dream of the future are very effective in building a family community and a team. Under these circumstances, prepare a mission statement.

(1) What is a mission statement?

A mission statement includes an opinion about meaning or purpose of the existence of individuals, homes and home groups. The document is very important and plays the role of the "constitution" in decision making in a home or a home group. Mission statements for individuals, families, and home churches to achieve, are necessary in building true families, becoming heavenly tribal messiahs, and leading a hoondok family churches According to relevant studies, people who have a goal in written form have a higher probability of success.

Why is a mission statement so important for individuals, organizations and home groups? A mission statement makes people reflect on their life and mission. It helps people to examine their thinking and the feelings deep inside them. In addition, it can help people to clearly understand what is truly important to them. To achieve a long-term goal, people advance little by little every day. People's sense of value or purpose is engraved in their mind through a mission statement. People can advance every day to achieve their long-term goals. In other words, preparing our own mission statement means writing our own philosophy and beliefs on a paper.

Because of these reasons, it is very important to prepare a mission statement and live according to the mission statement we have prepared.

(2) What should be included in a home group's mission statement?

The purpose of a home group should be determined in accordance with the situation of the home group members, their witnessing goals and the society in which they live. A mission statement motivates the home group members and reflects their internal motivation. In addition, the statement should set out the core projects of the home group. More importantly, it should reflect a sense of value that applies to all the people in the organization. This sense of value can be expressed to people outside the group through behavior. A sense of value is expressed in words and then through practice. Therefore, the code of conduct followed by the home group leader and members is an illustration of the values contained in their mission statement.

Preparing a mission statement means answering a number of questions. A mission statement deals with questions like "What do I want to have?" "Why do I exist?" "What personality do I want to have?" and "What legacy do I want to leave for my community?" To prepare a home group's mission statement, approach the answers to these questions with the following considerations:

To ensure a good mission statement for a home group, the trinity members should discuss and prepare it together. "What qualities are necessary to create a healthy home group?" (This question relates to "have.") Then, "What should we do to achieve it?" (This question relates to "do.") Finally, questions like "What do I want to achieve through my home group?" and "What do I want to be?" relate to "be." Let's prepare a mission statement.

(3) Practice preparing a mission statement.

✔ **What you want to have ("have"): What results does a home group want to have?**

Considering "What must be included in a home group?" list the points that home group members consider important and want to have. "What they want to have" can be either tangible (e.g., a house) or intangible (e.g., a happy family). Either of them is fine. List as many as possible. If there are too many items, you can write them in a brainstorming style using sticky notes. Examples include a happy home, health, success, money and honor. From the items that you listed as important, choose the five that you consider most important (e.g., love, service, or home).

» ....
» ....
» ....
» ....
» ....
» ....

✔ **What you want to do ("do")—Contributions and accomplishments achieved by a home group**

Now let's think what you want to do in a home group. "What people want to do" refers to what people want to contribute or accomplish in a home group, according to the purpose of the home group or their sense of value. This can be also the answer to the question "Why does the home group exist?" For this, let's think more deeply. Think about the following questions and answer them. What excites you most when you think of your home group? An imaginative answer is very good because it expresses in the most exciting and passionate manner what your home group is seeking to do. Write down below.

» ....
» ....
» ....
» ....
» ....

✔ **What would you want to do if you were a heavenly tribal messiah in a successful home group?**

» ....
» ....
» ....
» ....
» ....

✔ What is the most valuable work in your home group?

» ....
» ....
» ....
» ....
» ....

✔ What kind of abilities do the people in your home group have (including developed and undeveloped abilities)?

» ....
» ....
» ....
» ....
» ....

✔ Is there any work you have attempted several times, because you felt you should complete it, although you failed it before for various reasons? If so, what is it?

» ....
» ....
» ....
» ....
» ....
» ....

✔ **What you want to be:** Let's imagine a successful home group and what makes you proud of it.

The behaviors, emotions and lifestyle of people may have a significant influence on other people. It is also true that many people surrounding us are also role models and examples for us. The following writing exercise can help us find what our home group regards as most valuable.

In a personal mission statement, people write down who is a positive role model in their life, how strong that person's influence is, and why it has influenced them. Similarly, in your home group's mission statement try to write down what kind of home group you want your home group to be. Considering what other people say about your home group and what your home group can do best, try to write down what your home group should be.

» ....
» ....
» ....
» ....
» ....

✔ **Write down what you want your home group to have.**

» ....
» ....
» ....

» ....
» ....

Now, try to make a brief sentence by combining items listed above. A mission statement, whether it is an individual, family or home group mission statement, can be updated and adjusted when necessary. If the family members who made the statement participate in the editing process and join in creating the content, the mission statement will be better and will be more familiar to them. Let's write a mission statement below.

✔ **Home Group Mission Statement**

» ....
» ....
» ....
» ....
» ....
» ....
» ....
» ....
» ....
» ....
» ....
» ....
» ....

(4) Example of a mission statement

The following mission statement was prepared by students who implemented a home group with me at Sun Moon University. I made the home group, called GLD (Global Leaders of Dream), with Chinese students, and, as a result, 12 blessed families were created while I was working at Sun Moon University. This home group's mission statement was prepared by myself and the students with whom I was working at the time.

> "We value principles and words—HAVE (owned by the home group).
> We will become leaders for the establishment of Cheon Il Guk and world peace—DO (what to do).
> We will foster 1,200 global leaders—BE (what to achieve)."

For your information, I will introduce a personal mission statement of Professor Yeong Hwan-gil.

- I will be a CIG hyojeong coaching leader for the pursuit of endless happiness of homes on the earth.
- I will be a psychological leader of 36 homes and nurture 1,200 hyojeong leaders.
- For them, I will create a special hyojeong coaching group consisting of 12 persons.
- I will keep expanding it to a cell group (home group).

- I will continue my training so that I will be able to create the best program to foster the growth of true families and organizations.
- In 2020, I will create a global Cheon Il Guk coaching network devoted to establishing true families and healthy organizations, with 12 dynamic model leaders.

(5) Preparation of a home group pledge

You can prepare a home group pledge when you complete a home group mission statement. Unlike a home group mission statement, a home group pledge is a written document including policies that people need to adhere to when running a successful home group. With frequent use of smart devices including smartphones, there are many difficulties happening in a home group report meeting. A pledge is necessary to secure time dedicated for communication with Heavenly Parent during a report meeting. A pledge specifies what home group members will comply with to effectively implement a home group. It would be better if home members prepare it together with discussion. It would be great if you read it in a home group report meeting. Examples are as followed:

- I am very punctual.
- I have a keen interest in others.
- I do not gossip about other people.
- I strictly keep the secrets of others.
- I have a meal with a VIP more than twice a week.

- I will be a home group leader for another home group within a year.
- I do not take my mobile phone to home group meetings.
- I will make 12 core leaders.

(6) Preparation of VIP cards

To be a mission-oriented home group, prepare a card containing the name of a target of the mission work. Write the VIP's name on the front and the names of other home group members' VIPs on the back, so you can read them aloud when you are offering jeongseong for purification. During home group sessions, put VIP cards on chairs and pray for them to participate in the next session. In addition, all members should always keep their VIP card with them at all times, including morning and evening, reading, praying, and even eating.

(7) Preparation of a daily progress report

A daily progress report is a report evaluating your work and outlining your plans for your daily work. This report is exchanged between members in a home group report meeting in order for them to advance toward new goals and development. The daily progress report includes self-assessment of your thoughts and activities on a daily basis. If you fill it out every day, you will automatically be following the instructions of True Parents requesting that all blessed families record an autobiography.

Daily Progress Report

- **Points for active practice:** 1 point (low), 2 points (normal), 3 points (high) . maximum possible is 105 points.
- **Please set your criteria for evaluating your practice of five elements**
  Example: for hoondok purification jeongseong . 3 points = 1 hour or more, 2 points = 30 minute or more, 1 point = 5 minutes or less; 3 points for three-cycle home groups meetings, 2 points for relationship home group meeting, 1 point for no meeting. At home group coaching sessions or report meetings, practice coaching with your trinity.

Family Federation
Date and time: _____(day) _____(mon) _____(year) . _____(day) _____(mon) _____(year)

Self- purification jeongseong						
Family trinity relationship						
Trinity VIP invitation						
Home group three-cycle multiplication						
Home group social service						

- **My total (** _____ **points)**

Report special experiences or feelings

Everyday feeling

Date	feeling

The important elements in the activities of a Cheon Il Guk organization are preparing good progress reports, submitting the reports, and acquiring feedback regarding your work. As part of the process, the responsible department will read the report carefully, provide good feedback, and keep following up. High-noon vertical alignment and the two-wings system are effective only when such an activity report system is clearly established in home groups and in medium and large groups. It is important to fill out your reports accurately and completely in order for the system to work well.

A growth system is needed in which you can make a SWOT analysis (Strengths, Weaknesses, Opportunities, Threats) of your situation periodically and report it in order to receive good feedback from above. Until now, there have been report systems, but there has not been a very clear system for feedback or follow-up. There are several types of reports. In this chapter we will deal only with the daily progress report and the home group report that record progress in individual growth and the development of relationships, moving toward the accomplishment of the three great blessings. The home group clinic survey is designed to determine how healthy your home group is. The daily progress report is used for self-assessment and organization of your daily life, similar to a daily journal. The report will be very valuable in helping you record your blessed family history, as True Parents have directed us to do.

This process gives home group members a chance to check their daily and weekly life to see if they are ready to become heavenly tribal messiahs themselves. Every week you should prepare your report and present it at the weekly home group report meeting.

The report contains five questions to assess the quality of your daily practice. You can assess your own progress by referring to the questions. Set your own assessment criteria, using scores from 1 to 3. The maximum score is 105, using a three point scale: 1 (low), 2 (moderate) and 3 (excellent). For example, if you are satisfied with more than one-hour reading, purification and jeongseong, you can input 3 points. If the duration is between 30 minutes and an hour, you can give 2 points. If the time is less than 5 minutes, it would be 1. You cannot input zero (0) or a negative value; assess yourself from a positive perspective only. Regarding the content of a home group, if you are participating in a three-cycle home group, you can have 3 points. If you are participating in a relational home group or fellowship home group, you can get 2 points. If you are not participating in any group, your score would be 1. Preparation of a daily practice report is a very important daily routine for heavenly tribal messiahs.

You should make this kind of daily reflection and assessment a priority in the routine of your heavenly tribal messiah life. You should take the opportunity to participate in coaching, based on the contents of the report, at your weekly report meetings whenever possible.

(8) Preparation of the home group report

A home group report is prepared after each home group meeting. The home group leader or secretary should write a brief report summarizing the work of all the group's members, have it signed by the home group leader, and submit it to the large group or heavenly tribal messiah who is next in line above the home group.

If you do not submit reports, it will be difficult for the large group or heavenly tribal messiah to know what kind of coaching, education or other support or assistance may be helpful for the development of your home group. It is important for each member to record their individual report each day, and report weekly at the group's report meeting so that they can be included in the group's weekly report.

① In general, the head of a home group prepares a home group weekly activity report, integrating the opinions of home group members.

② A report shall be prepared, using a form provided. It should be submitted within three days after the weekly report meeting of the home group.

③ Basically you should follow a new lesson from the 16-week program each week following the cycle (jeongseong, making relationships, invitation, multiplication). However, you can adjust the program according to the circumstances of your home group. For example, you may want to repeat the "day of jeongseong" program for four weeks, if you feel you need a stronger spiritual foundation. However, home group members should become accustomed to the cycle of jeongseong, making relationships, invitation, and multiplication, and learn to implement it for successful growth and multiplication of the home group.

④ An assessment of implementation of core elements is conducted by the home group leader with the home group members, after a home group meeting.
⑤ The comprehensive activity report records in a narrative manner specifically how core elements and relevant activities have been implemented. In addition, it provides a record of good programs, educational materials and good ideas that have been implemented previously.
⑥ Finally, the status of home group activities is reported to the relevant pastor. Then you receive and check the feedback before submitting a final report.

Home Group Weekly Activity Report

Affiliated large group / tribe		Name of home group	
Home group organization	Home group leader:		
	Assistant group leader:		

	Purification jeongseong	Doing purification jeongseong (for) witnessing, meeting VIPs	0	1	2	4
	Volunteer work	Doing volunteer work. (Doing service work at the center or in the community)	0	1	2	4
	Family community	Creating experiences for hyojeong family community. (Having constructive interaction with family members)	0	1	2	4
	Nurturing (group	Nurturing group members (Following the 16 week program in the manual)	0	1	2	4
	Leadership (group	Developing leadership for multiplication (Home group is being operated with cooperation between group members and leaders.)	0	1	2	4
Total score		* The home group evaluates itself, and each score should be a composite score for the whole group. 0. Not at all, 1. Preparing (jeongseong, discussion),	Total score			
Combined activity report		How well is the home group carrying out activities related to the core elements?				

Planned activity (witnessing, volunteer work, family community,	How can you do to improve core element(s) of home group activity?
Confirm progress report	**Have you reported about your activities to the leader of your large group or tribe? (yes / no)**

Chapter 5

The Trinity Home Group and HTM Leader School

Is It Good Enough Only with Home Groups?

So far, we have reviewed the meaning, formation process, and multiplication of the trinity home group.

This chapter will cover home groups and HTM Leader School. The term "HTM Leader School" appeared frequently in the first three chapters. This indicates that the home groups and the leader school are closely related.

What is the difference between a home group and other kinds of small groups? A home group is "a community of families centered on True Parents and on experiencing, practicing and multiplying a heart of hyojeong." A home group is a community that lives together and eats together as a family. That is, a home group shares the heart of hyojeong that is shared between parents and children. However, success as a heavenly tribal messiah requires more than home groups. Children who grow up in a family must advance into society. The family is the only basic community of a society.

A home group is like a family. In a family, children go to school

[Figure 5-1] The Relationship between Hyojeong Home Groups and HTM Leader School

after they have grown to a certain age. In the case of a home group family, this school is called HTM Leader School. This is the same as children who grow up to a certain age in a family and then gain more wisdom and knowledge and experience society at school. Currently FFWPU, which has many large groups, offers education programs and training centers for people to learn new things. The education and training of the HTM Leader School are different from these. They are focused on teaching specialized skills and material that will help people be successful heavenly tribal messiahs and inspire people to learn and practice them. The principles of practice are very important. Even though somebody has participated in many training sessions and lectures regarding principles, it is hard to apply them to life. The HTM Leader School, which offers a three-stage program, has been developed to complement this Divine Principle education, focusing on the practice of what we have learned, despite any difficulties we may encounter. The home group and the HTM Leader School are highly correlated in this way. The following quote explains the connection:

"Sometimes there is no one who can guide you and there is no one in charge. A lecturer teaching the Principle must teach people about this. After about a year, people know the Principle better and more deeply. They come to a wider and deeper understanding. People want to learn more about the Principle, but they cannot find anyone who can teach them. This tends to make people feel that the members around them are not taking responsibility. When one, two, and three experiences begin to accumulate, people start to become critical, with the result that we begin losing members." [Sermons, 29-191]

According to the speech above, the Hyojeong Leader School was established based on the hyojeong home group and on learning the Principle through experiential and empirical education. The program emphasizes experiencing and practicing the principles that have been learned. Henceforward, the hyojeong home group and the HTM Leader School will be called "home group" and "leader school," respectively.

Two Types of Leader School

There are two types of leader schools. One leader school is created and run naturally in a home group until it has 12 members. The description of the growth of a home group in the first three chapters of this book may make it seem as though the home group grows automatically by itself. However, in reality the home group must work closely with a leader school until 12 members of a hoondok family association have been found and brought into the group, much like the ongoing process of twisting straw together to make a strong rope. The structure is the same as a child who grows both at home and at school. What are the two types of leader school?

① **One type is a leader school operated by the home group itself.**
One type is the education programs offered by the home group itself. This is something like homeschooling. The lecturer for this leader school is affiliated with the home group's trinity, rather than with the local large group. A member or a coach who has received

training as a lecturer at the leader school of a large group runs this small leader school by himself in a trinity home group. This type of leader school usually is operated in a one-on-one coaching style.

This leader school is not hindered by the constraints of time, the lecture location, or the lecturer. The method is rapid and powerful because it is free to follow the home group plan or schedule. Although not a specialized large group lecturer, the lecturer is free to adapt his presentations to accommodate differences in understanding, communication, concentration, and spiritual aspects, resulting in programs suitable for the small group. Moreover, it is a powerful system that can link well the growth of new members' faith and progress toward the heavenly tribal messiah path through frequent communication with the home group.

This leader school is perfect for the rapidly expanding heavenly tribal messiah activities in Asia and Africa. It is impossible to communicate frequently with a large group leader school because the tribes are usually far away from existing large groups.

Therefore, a leader school formed on its own is faster and more mobile. Moreover, it can better cultivate talented people in the hoondok family association. When depending on the education programs of a large group, a long wait is often necessary before a new member can participate in training sessions. A local leader school attached to a home group is a perfect solution for this problem.

② The other type of leader school is one operated by a large group.

This kind of leader school is offered as part of the training program of a large group. A lecturer for the large group decides the time and space and gives courses within a limited timeframe. Alternatively, a large group may decide to increase its activities to match the multiplication of nearby home groups and create a leader school lecturer-training course. An existing specialized lecturer from a large group may also give leader school in-depth courses.

Perhaps the most successful model is for the large group to focus on lecturer training and in-depth courses, educating the senior members of the home group, who then can run the home group's own leader school, to avoid the complications of sending new members to take courses offered by the large group.

[Figure 5-2] Blueprint for Home Group Leader School

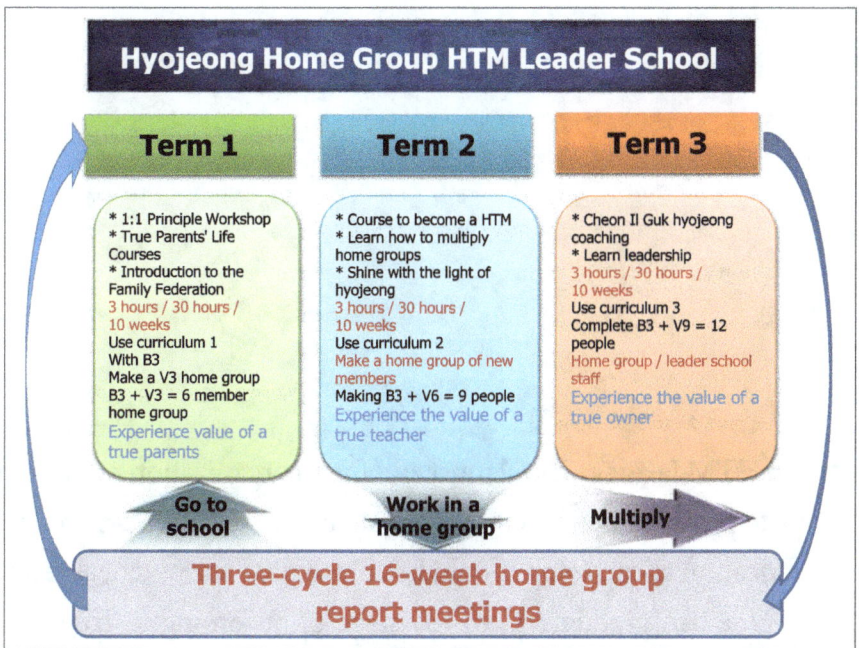

The Three-Step Value Realization Process of HTM Leader School

An HTM Leader School must aim for an organization management system that realizes the three great subject partners principle. The education at each step should be able to produce practical results.

One can graduate from the stage of becoming a "true parent" only by having a spiritual child. In the "true teacher" stage, one must continue to bring in spiritual children while learning the heavenly tribal messiah course regarding home group operation and multiplication. Finally, you will complete all three stages when you complete the "true owner" phase by building a 12-person hoondok family association. This is achieved through enhancing your hyojeong coaching leadership capability for leading members and heavenly tribal messiahs.

1. The First Step is the Process of Realizing the Value of a True Parent

The curriculum of an HTM Leader School is basically built upon the roots of three great subject partners principle. True Parents said that the three great subject partner ideals—which are the ideal of a true parent, the ideal of a true teacher, and the ideal of a true owner—must be the worldview of blessed families. The education and practice of HTM Leader School are designed to let people experience and share them. Primarily, a leader school is installed within a large group. Alternatively, a home group can create one as part of the process of growing to a midsize or large group.

To realize the value of a true parent, what do I need to have?

Parents can be parents only when they have a child. As physical parents can be parents after bearing a child, a heavenly tribal messiah must give birth to spiritual children as well as physical children. One can experience the road to becoming a true parent when one gives birth to a spiritual child and raises that person.

One can become a true parent by learning the principles and the life of True Parents in a leader school and multiplying that belief practically, thus experiencing and practicing the value of a true parent. When a child is born, parents must nurture the baby until the baby can stand properly on his own. The place of nurturing is the home group, and a new member grows by receiving love and spiritual elements, surrounded by the family in the home group. A new member spends about one or two weeks in a home group and then enters a leader school. The member learns and experiences the value of being a true parent. All members of a home group must help a new member, like a family, so that he can complete this basic course well. A new member who has completed the leader school comes back to the home group and repeats there what was learned at the leader school. One-on-one coaching style is ideal in this case. Moreover, existing members should help the new member successfully expand the home group through three-cycle report meetings and eventually make his or her own home group.

What are the contents of the first term of the leader school?

One learns the basic and major elements of the Divine Principle through one-on-one and group classes. Also, the member must learn about the life and achievements of True Parents. Particularly, the member must deeply understand the meaning of hyojeong, which the only begotten daughter, True Mother, is teaching about. Furthermore, the member must know the identity of FFWPU, to which the member belongs. In other words, the member learns the basic religious life of FFWPU and the value of the organization (e.g., purity movement and various organizations, including UPF and YSP). This can be taught over a period of 10 to 30 weeks or during a two- or three-day intensive course. Depending on the level, process, and environment, it could take longer. Trainees are encouraged and instructed to form their own trinity while they take this step. In order to make trinities, trainees are consistently helped by the home group working as an evangelism home group with three-cycle report meetings. When the member finds new members to make his own trinity and completes the training, the member experiences the value of becoming a true parent.

2. The Second Step is the Process of Realizing the Value of a True Teacher

In this process, a trainee learns the essential process of becoming a heavenly tribal messiah. Moreover, he experiences the growth process required to stand as a heavenly tribal messiah. One important point here is that one must learn how to run a small group and operate home group three-cycle report meetings well. This is because the large group operating leadership and the small-group operating leadership are different. In this process, new members are blessed and they are getting ready to be heavenly tribal messiahs. This second term is also a 10- to 30-week course. In this period, members make good family relationships in their home group with the heart of hyojeong and roots of affection. Moreover, they experience the process of bearing fruit by continuously inviting new members to a happy day or to home group functions. On a foundation of jeongseong, weekly meetings are held regularly, cycling through the three themes of making relationships, invitation and multiplication, with home group reporting every week.

Members experience and learn what it means to become a true

[Figure 5-3] The Three Stages of the Heavenly Tribal Messiah Leader School

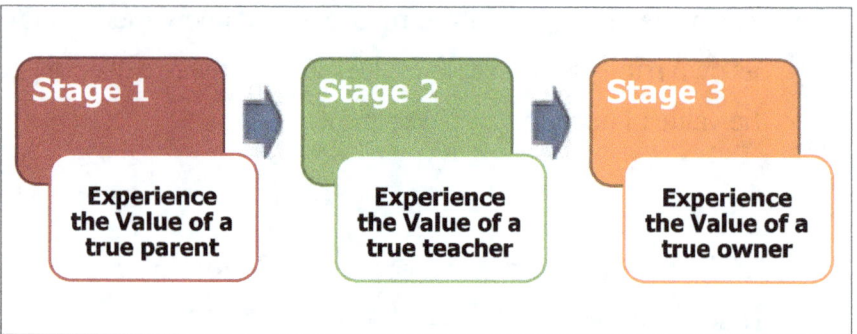

teacher by themselves going through this process. True teachers sincerely help the settlement of the 16-week evangelism home group in their own home group and help new members finish courses in the home group or leader school.

During this period as well, members of a home group are asked to create their own trinity to realize the value of a true parent. This includes the process of becoming a true parent and a true teacher who can give birth to children and raise them while exchanging the heart of hyojeong with other members of a home group.

This educational program is completely different from conventional lectures such as general Divine Principle lectures, evangelism, or education lectures. This is because a new member must expand his or her own home group up to three or nine members at least, while taking leader school courses 1 and 2, so existing members of the home group continuously put efforts into the expansion of the home group. An evangelism home group must bear the fruit of evangelism while continuing the three-cycle report meetings because it is evangelism-oriented. To do this, all members of the home group need to have strong, high-quality leadership abilities. After completing these courses, members receive training to enhance their capabilities to be true owners.

3. The Third Step is the Process of Realizing the Value of a True Owner

Understanding the value of a true owner involves the process of cultivating hyojeong coaching leadership, in order to nurture and coach the culture of hyojeong as a healthy Cheon Il Guk citizen. You need to stand in the position of true owner by expanding your Cheon Il Guk leadership capability.

These value realization processes also should value other tribes as well as one's own tribe. True Parents said that when we recover the Cain tribe we will automatically recover the Cain tribe. [*Cheon Seong Gyeong*, 9.2.1:6]

They said that this has to be based on the home church.

In particular, the tribal messiah must embrace both the Cain tribe and the Abel tribe. The home church should embrace Cain and the tribe church should embrace Cain's tribe.

True Parents said that the mission of the tribal messiah is completed when he combines the two clans of Cain and Abel. [*Cheon Seong Gyeong*, 9.2.2:2]

In other words, they said that tribal restoration can be completed

[Figure 5-4] The 3-3-3 Strategy Leading to a Four-Position Foundation

VALUES
Three Great Subject Partners Principle
1. Ideology of true parents
2. Ideology of a true teacher
3. Ideology of a true owner

VISION
Three great blessings
1. Individual perfection
2. Perfection of the family
3. Perfection of dominion

3-3-3 Strategy

MISSION
Trinity
- Trinity
- Three-cycle
- Cain-Abel B3/V3

easily if we invest our entire lives and all our assets to restore 120 persons who represent the Cain tribe. This passage has strategic meaning to becoming a heavenly tribal messiah, and it means we need to make a tribe church of 120 Cain-type persons a top priority. [*CSG*, 9.2.2:3]

What is hyojeong coaching leadership we learn from the three-term course?

There are various types of leadership ability that must be learned. In the third term of leader school, trainees learn hyojeong coaching leadership. Why? "Leadership of caring for others," which cares for and serves others, is the leadership ability most required for Cheon

Il Guk leadership. This helps us to recognize that Heavenly Parent lives within us, and it helps us to work with others. Hyojeong coaching leadership helps develop active interaction between the feelings in the human heart with hyojeong. Particularly, it pursues "the leadership overflowing with hyojeong." Hyojeong coaching leadership ability, which makes someone realize that he or she exists for others and helps others to succeed, is essential to achieve this. The capability is also a process of learning awareness of the body through the Word. Coaching is to empty myself and help others realize their true heart, through object figures.

This course can be between 10 and 30 weeks, but it can be longer. It may be longer than 30 weeks when the trinity is not yet formed or if make-up classes are required due to absence. The key point is that each trainee must form his or her trinity (a home group) within the Leader III course. In other words, a trainee must fully recruit 12 persons before the end of the Leader III course and make a home-group that succeeds in developing a hoondok family association. It is because the seed of a heavenly tribal messiah who can lead a hoondok family association by expanding a home group must be created at the end of this period. When a trainee completes this course successfully, he stands in the position of a true owner who can continuously multiply the hoondok family association and guide blessed families. HTM Leader School is one of the ways, and it reinforces the process of achieving the 3·3·3 strategy, referring to the three blessings, the three great subject partners principle, and the trinity. While we conduct the 3·3·3 strategy, the four-position foundation—the objective of our lives—will be formed as a result.

The large group throws a big party for the members who successfully complete this course and presents them with certificates recognizing them as Hyojeong Cheon Il Guk coaches, hoondok family association presidents, and the beginning heavenly tribal messiahs.

A Brief Summary of the HTM Leader School

Leader School I is:

A basic course to give basic understanding and beliefs for achieving the three blessings and multiplying trinities to realize the three great subject partners principle. To achieve these goals, trainees learn the life and achievements of True Parents and the religious life of FFWPU. A trainee must make a home group by giving birth to three spiritual children in order to realize the value of a true parent.

Leader School II is:

Prepare a substantial foundation for multiplication to be a messiah and multiply the trinity. This is the center of the home group three-cycle report meeting. A participant forms a second trinity (now six persons) and enhances the capability to continue home group reporting and multiplication for completing the three blessings. This is the process of experiencing and realizing the value of a true teacher.

Leader School III is:

In order to multiply home groups successfully, a trainee becomes a hyojeong coaching leader. Three or four home groups will be formed and connected while going through Leader Schools I, II and III. By the end, 12 persons become one and carry out home group reporting to form a hoondok family association that functions passionately. They are core members and they will become hyojeong coaching leaders, running home groups and working as staff and lecturers at Leader Schools I, II and III. This is the process of realizing the value of a true owner. A master home group begins a process of continuous multiplication centered on the newly formed hoondok family association.

These contents are called the 3·3·3 strategy for heavenly tribal messiah success. In the external action strategy, 3 stands for the forming trinity, conducting three-cycle home group report meetings, and creating three new members for each leader school term. In the internal principle aspect, 3 stands for the three blessing visions, realization of the three great subject partners principle, and the success of the trinity multiplication mission.

Appendix

Appendix 1 Implementing Happy Day

1. What is Happy Day?

Happy day is an intensive witnessing approach program over four to seven weeks in which new VIPs to resolve concerns or misunderstandings about the church without any awkwardness. The focus of this program is for you to introduce yourself to the newly invited neighbors and guests, let them know about True Parents and greatly inspire them spiritually so that they take interest in the church. These days, spirituality, happiness and health have been attracting a lot of interest. This program is designed to get a favorable response from VIPs by tackling these issues at church centering on the Word.

Happy day is an invitation program. The pre-happy day, to which you can easily invite anyone, is the step before having them participate in a home group, Leader School I or Divine Principle workshop.

They first have to attend the pre-happy day four times. This workshop is rooted in purification jeongseong. Everyone in the outside world is pursuing happiness, but one of the main reasons why they are unhappy is that they cannot manage their own mind. We analyze this based on the structure of the mind found in the Divine Principle. The goal is to have people cleanse themselves (purification) of the ego within themselves and realize that there is a divinity within them.

In the content presented on the fourth happy day, we leave guests curious about the principled interpretation and understanding of the Word so that they come to the next Divine Principle lecture. Happy day is the intensive stage before that. It focuses only on the participant's current issues and on having them do purification jeongseong so that they can have deep experiences. There are two types of happy day: one that is held in the church or center and another that is held in a coffee shop, restaurant or other place outside the church.

2. Preparation and Execution

Happy day is the first official encounter that the VIP has with members before they attend a home group. This consists of four or seven weeks or four or seven workshops. The happy day introduced below is done at a chosen church or public place.

(1) Schedule for Evening Meeting

It is possible to adjust it for mornings as well.
- 19:00 to 19:10: Registration and fellowship
- 19:15 to 19:30: Greetings and praise songs
- 19:30 to 20:00: Lecture
- 20:00 to 20:30: Group discussion
- 20:30 to 20:50: Announcement for sharing food
- 20:50 to 21:00: Praise song, closing prayer

(2) Table Set-Up

1 home group leader, 2 table volunteers, 3-4 people from the trinity cooperate together.
- During the first week, pick a name for your table and present it.
- It is good to have round tables.
- You may consider having separate tables for brothers and sisters to facilitate smooth conversation.

(3) Four-Week Lecture Topics

- Week 1: Who are you? — Finding your original mind/heart
- Week 2: Offer jeongseong for purification
 —Forgiveness, Gratitude, Love
- Week 3 : Raising up the influential power of the sacred
 — Becoming one

◇ Week 4 : Forgiveness, Gratitude, Love, and Oneness graduation ceremony
—Continue

The above four topics are even more effective when carried out one on one. In the case when several home groups gather to do a happy day together, it is necessary to do it in a bigger place, make it more exciting and promote even deeper relations.

A short workshop is held to briefly introduce the Divine Principle, Family Federation and True Parents through topics such as "Where does happiness come from?" "God and human beings," "Satan and human beings," "The spirit and body of human beings," "Family Federation," "True Parents" and "Blessed family life."

(4) Workshop Feedback

◇ After the workshop, feedback on the lecture and location is carried out for about 30 to 40 minutes.
◇ The workshop leader guides the discussion to talk about the process and outcome and then to prepare for what is next.

(5) Graduation Banquet

◇ The graduation ceremony takes place after completing all four weeks, and a graduation certificate is given out.
◇ There should be plenty of food at the banquet prepared with love and devotion, and there should be a festive atmosphere.

▼ Happy Day, a program for new members

◇ After the graduation, guests should be guided to register for the two-day Divine Principle workshop and Leader School I and sign on for a home group.

◇ Starting from weeks 2 and 3, the programs (home group, Leader School I, Divine Principle workshop) offered after should be introduced and application forms collected.

(6) Conducting Happy Day

✔ **Team Structure**
The director leads the entire program (centering on the trinity).
Assistant: Responsible for and manages the volunteering
Lecturer: A prepared staff or member leader can do this.

Workshop leader: one or two persons per table

Table volunteer: One or two persons serve each designated table.

Accounting: in charge of creating a budget and administration for happy day.

(7) Team Member Training and Jeongseong

◇ Thorough team training is important for the success of the happy day.
◇ The team member training should be carried out at least once before the start of the happy day.
◇ Fasting, prayer and sincere jeongseong, as decided by the trinity, are necessary for success.

(8) Things to Prepare Beforehand

◇ Prayer must be prepared. Jeongseong for purification is mandatory.
◇ Structure the team.
◇ Decide on the date.
◇ Choose the place.
◇ Advertise happy day, and raise awareness and participation among all members.
◇ Prepare a textbook or testimony book, necessary materials, application forms.
◇ Always have two persons prepared to give testimonies on their experience and how they changed through purification jeongseong.

Appendix 2 DISC Assessment: Getting to Know Each

[Figure 6-1] DISC Assessment Table

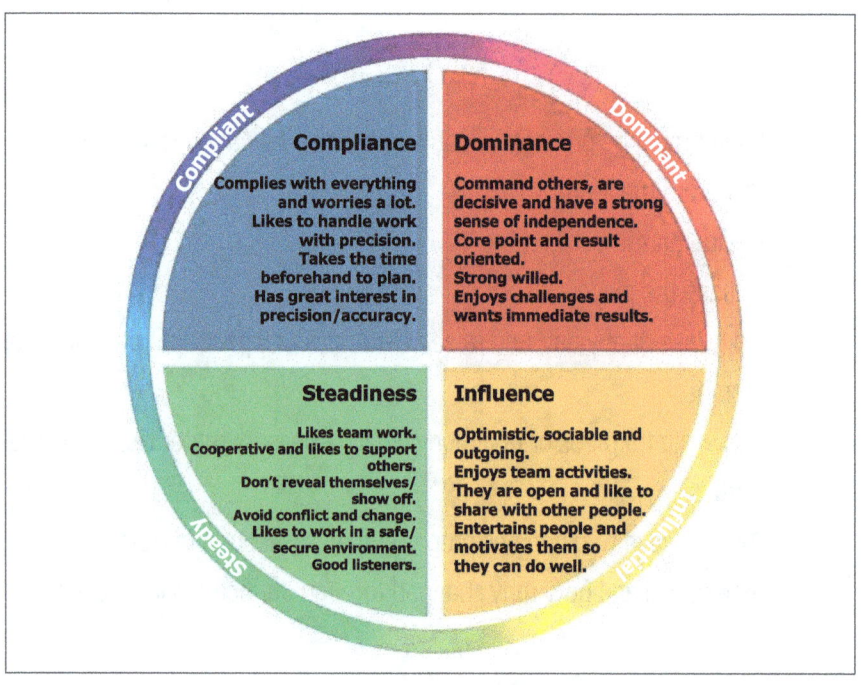

Other—A Tool for Healthy Home Groups

Starting a DISC Assessment

◇ Give out the assessment paper below.
◇ Score the parts that most resemble you, from 4 to 1. You shouldn't overlap or skip scoring.
◇ Compile the points and write down the total.
◇ "I" is D, "II" is I, "III" is , and "IV" is C.
◇ Put the total points for each on "Drawing a Graph with Points"
◇ If there is a part that is greater than 36 points, draw and connect dotted lines on the graph.
◇ Record the score in order. The biggest score comes in front.
◇ It is significant if you get 36 points or more.
◇ Once you find out, write down your type in the blank "My type is _____." (e.g., DIS or SID)
◇ Take the score you got and look for your future behavior type in the 40-behavior-type file.
◇ Take the results and discuss it
◇ Carry out the DISC assessment in the home group to enhance healthy relations.

DISC Action-Type Evaluation

	D		I		S		C	
My personality is...	Commanding and dominating		Social and I express emotions well		Easygoing and slow		Serious, careful and sensible	
I like environments surrounded by	Individual achievement and compensation. Goal oriented		Likes people		Drawings, letters and my things		Order and functional organization	
My personality type has a tendency to...	Focus on the result		Focus on people		Focus on the process and team		Focus on details	
My attitude towards others...	straightforward		Kind and pleasant		Trustworthy and have self-control		Cold and objective	
When I listen to others...	Sometimes lack patience.		Not focused on surroundings		Gladly listens to surroundings		Focus on the truth and analyze.	
I like talking to other people about...	My accomplishments		Myself and other people		Family and friends		Events and information structure	
I have the tendency to...to others	Give commands to others		Have influence over others		condone		Evaluate with values and order	
If I were in a football team, my position would be...	Frontline attacker		Attacking style defender	50	Offensive attacker		Last defender	
To me, time is...	Always busy		Spend a lot of time on relationships	40 36 30 20	Time is important but I don't feel pressure/burden		Know the importance of time and uses time well	
If I were to make a road sign...	Reckless driving! Calls out to death.		Yield to the smiling mom and bright dad	10	If you yield even just a little, even narrow roads become wider		You and me keep the order Hello country, prosperity of the country/ prosperous nation	

My voice on a normal basis…	Emotional, commanding, powerful, quick and high-pitched		Emotional, passionate, thin/ fine and high-pitched		Little emotion, thick and low-pitched		Cold, emotions suppressed, thin and low-pitched	
My gestures are usually…	Strong and nimble		Open and kind		Stiff and slow		Calculated and careful	
I like…style of clothing	formal		Cool Casual		Practical and comfortable		Simple, informal and clean	
My overall attitude can be said to be…	authoritative		Charming social, outgoing		Accepting and open		Evaluative or don't speak much	
My life pace is…	Fast		Enthusiastic		Secure		Controlled/ regulated	
Total points	I		II		III		IV	

Drawing up a Graph with Your Score

1. "I" is the total for D, "II" is the total for I, "III" is the total for S, and "IV" is the total for C.
Mark the number in each space on the graph.
For example, if you have 39 points for "I," simply put a dot at the 39 mark on the D line on the graph.

2. Circle the dots that are higher than 36. This is your main personality type.

50 I am (   ) type.

My behavior type is (   ).

※ Refer to the profile below

DISC 40-Behavior-Type Profile

	Behavior type		Behavior type		Behavior type
D	Supervisor/director type	I/S	Encourager type	S/C/D	Strategist type
D/I	Result-oriented type	I/S/D	Dedicated/devoted type	S/C/I	Peace mediator type
D/I/S	Relationship-centered Leader type	I/S/C	Coach type	C	Logical Thinking type
D/I/C	Chief justice type	I/C	Interpersonal negotiator type	C/D	Architect/planner type
D/S	Achiever type	I/C/D	Business negotiator type	C/D/I	Producer type
D/S/I	Work-centered Leader type	I/C/S	Mediator type	C/D/S	Contemplative/thoughtful type
D/S/C	Professional type	S	Team player type	C/I	Critic type
D/C	Pioneer type	S/D	Professional achiever type	C/I/D	Author/writer type
D/C/I	Public lecturer type	S/D/I	Designer type	C/I/S	Mediator type
D/C/S	Meister type	S/D/C	Detective type	C/S	Principle-centered
I	Mood maker type	S/I	Advisor type	C/S/D	Crisis-solver type
I/D	Persuader type	S/I/D	Peaceful leader type	C/S/I	Professor type

I/D/S	Politician type	S/I/C	Counselor type	D/I/S/C	Supervisor type
I/D/C	Leader type	S/C	Manager type		

Practice Class for Promoting Healthy Relations Within the Home Group

Through the DISC assessment, you now know about your own personality, your behavior type and the characteristics of all the members of the home group. This is very helpful for healthy relations within the home group. Healthy relations and harmonious/peaceful communication allows for strong/powerful teamwork. Now you will have the opportunity to improve your relationships by getting to know about yourself and others by answering the questions below. It can be even more significant if you do this as an extension of building relationships in the home group reporting meeting. It can bring greater results if members have done this test before receiving coaching.

① What did you learn through this process?

② What is the top characteristic that represents you?

③ What is the strength of your behavior?

④ What is the weakness of your behavior?

⑤ Write down all the behavior types of your home group members. Offer purification jeongseong for them.

⑥ What are some of the thoughts and behaviors you have that you are most afraid will affect/inconvenience the home group?

⑦ What can you do to make a great contribution to the home group?

⑧ Who is the most difficult person to deal with? Write down their name. How will you treat them in order to become an excellent trinity or heavenly tribal messiah?

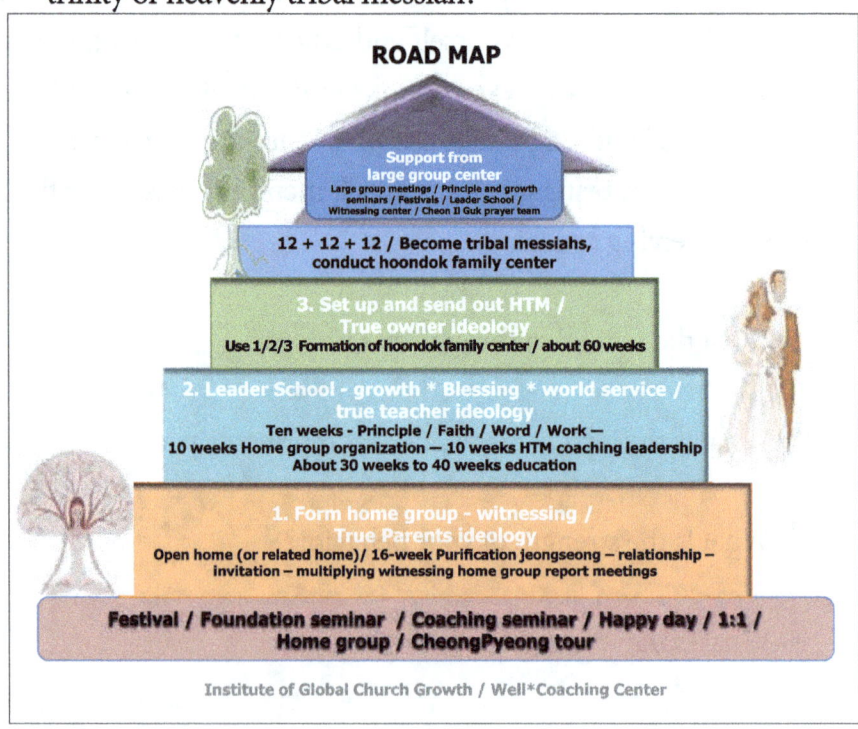

Home Group Multiplication (Family Church)

3. HTM – Set up leaders / True Owner
1/2/3 Ministry / Pioneering

Goal: Completion of the 3rd Blessing – Completion of Dominion – Birth of a Home Group (12) – Advance to Role of HTM Coaching Leader
1. Participate in home group report meetings and attend Leader School / form trinity
2. 30-week training – 10 Divine Principle / 10 Home Group / 10 HTM Coaching Leader
3. Do 16-week home four-cycle group report meeting program (Jeongseong – Relationships – Invitation – Multiplication)
4. Training for qualifications: Divine Principle, shimjeong, home group leader, jeongseong

HTM Leader School (16 weeks x 3 = 48 weeks)

2. Leader School – Jeongseong blessing / true teacher
10 weeks – HTM Coaching Leader
10 weeks – Experience of home group organization and multiplication
10 weeks – Divine Principle / Faith / True Parents' Words

Goal: Completion of the 2nd blessing – victory of jeongseong and Blessing – composition of a home group (3-12) – growth as a HTM Coaching Leader
1. Formation of true love relationships (participate in home group report meeting and attend Leader School / form trinity
2. 30-week training – 10 Divine Principle / 10 understanding home group / 10 HTM Coaching Leader
3. Do 16-week home four-cycle group report meeting program (Jeongseong – Relationships – Invitation – Multiplication)
4. 30 weeks Divine Principle lecturer training, shimjeong training, home group leader training, hoondok purification jeongseong training

Happy Day (7 weeks) / two-day seminar

Form 1 home group / initiate a home group report meeting / true parent
4. Multiplication
3. Invitation (1:1 / Team)
2. Make a Relationship (Trinity)
1. Hoondok purification jeongseong / Blessing seminar

Goal: Complete 1 Blessing – Spiritual experience with God through purification
1. Individual – Cleanse myself and liberate Heavenly Parent – Hoondok purification jeongseong
2. purification jeongseong
3. Form a trinity for coaching home group and Blessing (formation of B3)
4. Do 16-week home four-cycle group report meeting program (Jeongseong – Relationships – Invitation – Multiplication)
5. Continuous invitations for open home group, home group report meetings, Blessing seminars

Blessing seminars / Sosa sthome udy club / foundation seminars / one on one / Happy Day / groups / CheongPyeong tours

Appendix 3 Blueprint for HTM Leader School

[Figure 6-6] DISC Assessment Table

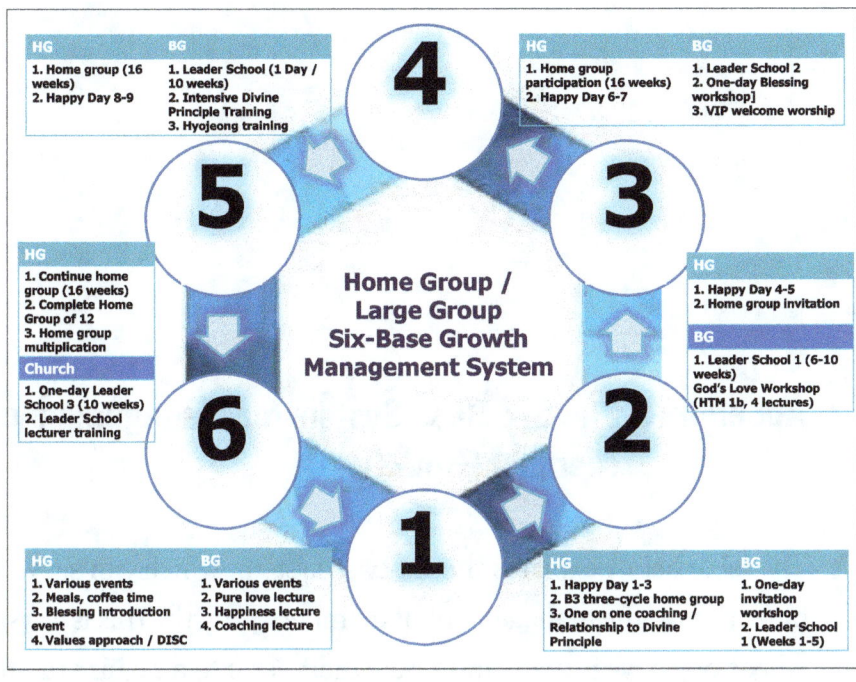

Appendix 4 Roadmap for Multiplying a Home Group into a Hoondok Family Center

Appendix 5 The Six-Base System for Management of Member Growth

The table below explains the six-base system, which can serve as a blueprint for the management of members' growth. This is a system whose objective is maturing a new member into a regular member

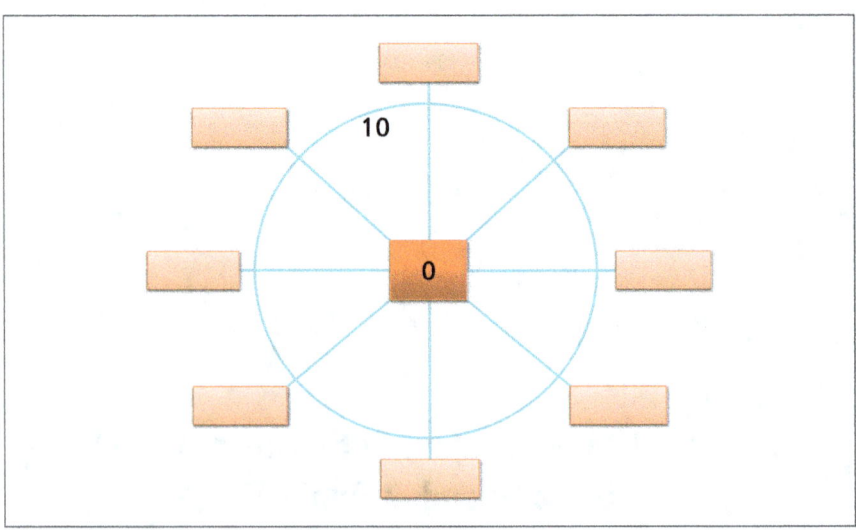

as defined by the International Headquarters. The International Headquarters created four stages through which a new member can go to become a regular member.

The six-base system, however, goes beyond this, and is aimed at maturing a new member into a core member who ultimately completes his or her heavenly tribal messiah activities. The blueprint shows a side-by-side comparison of what a home group and its tribal group need to do in hopes of helping them with their mission of high-noon settlement.

Appendix 6 Heavenly Tribal Messiah Practice Balance Coaching

Out of the five items in the progress report, the coach can pick one item in which he wants to see improvement.

The coach then discusses it with the member, and creates an index with eight items. It ranges from 0 to 10.

0. What are the eight core items that can help to solve this issue? (Fill in eight blanks.)

1. This is a balance picture aimed at solving the issue. What do you feel while looking at this picture?

2. How do you want it to become? What score do you want? / explain how you would like your success to look.

3. Please describe the current situation in detail.

4. What do you have to do in order to turn your picture into a reality?

5. What are some of the things that interfere with your work? / How can you eliminate them?

6. Please summarize the discussion so far. / Summarize it in one sentence.

7. How are you feeling now? What can I do to help you more?

Appendix 7 Education Testimony Report

1. Testimonials from Korea's HTM Leader School

(1) Song Jong-ik, the minister at the District 2 Bundang Church

During the 20-week HTM leadership course, I was able to witness the direction and the path we have to pursue. There are many members who want to march forward for Vision2020 but are unable to find the right objectives and methods and the courage to make it all happen. Thanks to this course, I was able to understand that transforming myself and witnessing to VIPs require consistent genuine love and devotion, not short-term and exhausting efforts. Some useful methods are the DISC Assessment and Well*Coaching. I feel that these are the tools that are essential in the field. I wish they had given us these precious tools in the past.

(2) Kang Tae-moon, the minister at the District 2 Sungnam Church

I have always wanted to receive a heavenly tribal messiah education. I decided to participate in one such session with church members as soon as I was installed in my current position. The one-year course (20 weeks) has made me confident about heavenly tribal messiah activities. It taught me to become united with other members and set a clear objective as the head of my home group. I was able to attain a coaching certificate with which I believe I can play the role of heavenly tribal messiah and help members find the solutions to their problems.

The Family Federation has gained a lot of strength through becoming one with the outside coaches. It may be small for now, but I am sure that all of our efforts for heavenly tribal messiah activities will bear fruits one day. This is an essential education.

(3) Kim Jong-young, the minister at the District 2 Ilshin Church

The successful growth of a church depends on the efforts of mid-level ministers. Churches can become successful if the four-base system is utilized by talented mid-level ministers. Then how can we raise talented mid-level ministers? I believe that a good way is through the HTM Leader School. The HTM Leader School gives its members the ability to carry out their heavenly tribal messiah activities. They are raised to become home group leaders, develop the ability to use the four-cycle system, and provide coaching and healing to their members. That is why the HTM Leader School, which trains ministers, is an important educational course that has to be implemented. It only seems to yield its results slowly because it focuses on the internal ability. Just as trees with deep roots bear fruits plentifully, the effect of this education will be great.

(4) Song Jeong-sub, the head of the District 4 Jeonnam District

I chose Professor Gil Young-hwan's course because I wanted to take the teachings of True Parents and turn them into reality. I believe that it was a very good choice to select the minister training program. Some of the ministers said they wanted to continue receiving this education. I felt that people wanted to do more but were unable to do so not because they didn't want to, but because they simply didn't have the means. I realized that the gathering of happy people naturally leads to witnessing and growth.

(5) Moon Sang-pil, the head of the District 4 Ocean District (currently the president of CARP Korea)

New understandings and new standards are required for a new age. The new standard for ministers after Foundation Day tells us that we need to have burning desire and clear awareness. I gained hope that coaching, which is one step higher than counseling, can be implemented within our ministries to help us grow.

2. Testimonials from Japan's HTM Leader School.

(1) Kim Du-hyeong, the head of Fukuyama District, East Hiroshima Region, Japan

Since March 2014, all of our members have been trying to train their hearts and conscience through something called "purification jeongseong." The progress was slow, but the evidence of it working has started to show.

The members were guided to nurture their conscience, the original mind, through holding hoondokhae sessions, and received the answers to their questions through praying to Heavenly Parent. From September of last year, the members who are 70 years or older have conducted prayer and devotion sessions from 10:00 in the morning to 4:00 in the afternoon, from Monday through Saturday every week. Regular members filled out wish papers, put them in the wish box, and offered prayers and devotions for 12 days. After the 12th day, they filled out result reports and put them in the report box. Regular members could wish for anything, from something very personal to something public. They could feel while writing their reports that their prayers and devotions were indeed having an effect on fulfilling their wishes. Those who actually prayed also received a lot of benefits.

On April 6, 2015, the head of the Family Education Department gave a lecture called "Husband Restoration Lecture" in which he explained "purification jeongseong" from the perspective of indemnity restoration. The lecture provided a clear explanation about the things that are happening in our family and our movement. The lecturer also explained that it is by Heavenly Parent's guidance when we utter the words "gratitude" and "love" (Thank you. I love you.) because we, as the central figures in the providence, have come to experience these feelings in order to restore our ancestors' sins vertically. Many of the wives and other participants gained a deep understanding of this fact, and they testified to this truth.

① On coaching

I have been implementing coaching in my ministry from March 2014. In January of this year (2015), the Education Center was changed to a Coaching Center, and both guests and members were provided with coaching-style guidance. From March, the participants of the leader school have been practicing coaching. We used the Question Manual to divide the group into "coach" and "coached" to hone our coaching skills.

② On home group activities

In March 2014, we began our home group study gatherings. However, it wasn't until the home group training given by Professor Gil Young-hwan on August 23 and 24, 2014, when he created new trinities, that we began our "home group witnessing." In our home group meeting, we are holding free happy day (gatherings with snacks) and happy day (containing hoondokhae and lectures). We are inviting VIPs to these events. From September of last year (2014), we have been holding weekly HTM Leader School workshops.

Thanks to these activities, Mrs. Sato Yuko received an award from the Family Federation, representing Japan's District 11. Her home group has held five happy days in the form of new lecture events. A total of 20 new guests came to these events, six of whom received Divine Principle education in the coaching center. Other guests are receiving one-on-one Divine Principle lectures.

③ On one-on-one lectures

In March 2014, we put together a one-on-one Divine Principle lecture plan for CIG members and new guests. Some of the missionaries who visit houses door to door also use this plan, and they sometimes give a one-on-one lecture right on the spot. When the guests agree to hearing a one-on-one lecture, the missionary enters the house and gives a "visiting lecture." There are already 50 guests who have received this lecture. The staff members at the coaching center (education center) are offering the guests not only DVD lectures, but also one-on-one lectures.

④ Large-group support

In January 2015, thanks to strengthened support for the home group (church coaching center), we allocated staff members at the education center to the "Department of Loyalty and Filial Piety" and members of the education department to the "Home Group Support Department." The Department of Loyalty and Filial Piety supports home groups and filial and loyal members to take responsibility for finding and educating guests and the Home Group Support Department keeps track of guests brought in by witnessing activities, providing coaching sessions for group members, as well as providing external support for Cheon Il Guk home group members.

(2) Kim Won-sik, the head of the Osaka Church for Korean Residents (the current secretary general of the Japanese Association for Peace and Unification)

The heavenly tribal messiah leader school took place three years after Foundation Day which was established by Heavenly Parent and True Parents. Now I have a firm commitment that each of us has to accomplish victory in our heavenly tribal messiah activities in order to repay Heavenly Parent and True Parents for their glory and encouragement until the upcoming 2020. I believe that this is what True Mother wants from us. I asked myself often about how to accomplish this objective, but I could not receive a clear answer. Then I received an answer last year.

In need of a leader to guide us, we invited Professor Gil Young-hwan. His burning passion was conveyed to us through his HTM Leader School and the coaching leadership classes.

My colleagues online and I tried to do this a few times, but it was difficult for the home leader to fulfill his duties because the home group activities conflicted with regional witnessing activities. That is why we decided to divide the activities into economy and witnessing. Our test run from April 3–7, 2015, yielded the following results.

First, we always believed that it is the regional director's role to stand in front of an audience and give a talk. However, when a home leader stood in front of an audience, he was nervous and had a hard time speaking coherently. I think more time and thought should be given to preparation.

Second, the home leader was not aware that he stands in the position of Abel, a person who is in charge of witnessing. Through being taught what a home leader should do, he was able to develop a sense of calling.

Third, it was hard enough for the home leader to convey messages to the home members, but he needed a firm determination to conduct more activities.

Fourth, I resolved to put into practice the things I learned during the gathering. The home leaders said that they learned a lot through this occasion, more than those listed above.

Only 12 of the 40 home leaders took part in this event, due to their schedule. We tried our best to study and train and to create an opportunity for us to put these things into practice. However, some home leaders wished the HTM Leader School also would be offered on weekends because they are too busy on weekdays. I will put the things I learned into practice first, and organize the home leaders' schedule and hold another leader school in the near future.

The reason I focused as much as this is because I felt that home leaders should offer purification jeongseong, fill out wish papers and promise papers, and put them into actual practice when interacting with their home group members. I also lead my home group members to make records of everything, and train themselves to write reflections as we share the teachings of hoondokhae, and in their activities of building relationships, inviting, and multiplying.

Our church organization currently is trying to create a two-stage system. We are laying the foundation for it. In addition, we hope that this training promotes heavenly tribal messiah activities and church growth and becomes a source of power for Heavenly Parent and True Parents. I want to continue to receive the guidance of Professor Gil and focus on raising leaders.

(3) Yoko Tsugawa from Osaka Dongpo Church

Thanks to what I've learned in the HTM Leader School, I was able to go beyond just thinking abstractly about establishing Cheon Il Guk and Vision2020 and take tangible and necessary actions. In the past, I was always filled with desire and hopes but never able to put them into action. I experienced a tremendous shift transition in my view of the world ideologically while writing a wish paper for the detailed actions of establishing the three great blessings based on the three great subject partners principle. Writing this wish paper helped me change my value system.

The hoondok purification jeongseong taught me clearly what I should do while living my faith with my mind and body united. I understood that the old way of thinking and force of habit were what made it difficult for me to realize the three great subject partners principle in order to gain victory in heavenly tribal messiah activities. Things were difficult for me, but I was able to take actions one by one, and now I can actually see the vision.

Being able to clearly see the vision enabled me to begin my home group activities. At first, it was difficult to ignore my past training, and what was supposed to be coaching often became teaching. One effective way of fixing this bad habit was to write a "heart diary." The DISC assessment and putting what I learned into practice helped me greatly in creating a healthy home group relationship. I wanted to learn more about this and make improvements.

A change of value brings a change in point of view. A change in perspective changes the heart, and the changed heart brings changed actions. A change in action yields righteous results, and these results helped me as a signpost that guided me toward being a heavenly tribal messiah. I am not yet perfect, but I will work hard toward attaining it. Thank you.

(4) Nagasawa Katsunori, head of the mission department at Yahata Church

Since Mr. Kawabata became our minister in April 2013, we have invited Professor Gil Young-hwan once every other month for over a year, receiving more than 120 hours of heavenly tribal messiah workshop (home group workshop). The workshops were about how to conduct home group activities based on hoondok purification jeongseong, practice, and trinity, and how to train people as coaches.

Up until that point, there was a 20 percent chance of a newly witnessed person completing their education and becoming a member. There are some reasons for this, but I thought that the hoondok purification jeongseong, home group activities, and coaching methods are necessary to increase this number to close to 100 percent and reduce the time it will take to achieve the victory of Blessing.

In this process, we created new trinities and formed purification jeongseong prayer teams. The trinities then regularly offered hoondok purification jeongseong, regularly had home group gatherings, and created a loving and trusting relationship with each of the witnessing candidates.

Before, we had almost no meetings with our area or home group activities. Now, however, three groups are pursuing heavenly tribal messiahship through home group activities. Although they are yet to be successful, their methods are systematized and their activities regular. Now with three districts that are gathering regularly, their activities are on the right track.

In addition, the Cheon Il Guk coaching style of ministry has helped the people of responsibility and staff members to fulfill their missions as the people of the Mother Nation three years in a row. The number of members that returning to church are increasing second-generation activities and witnessing activities are vitalizing and many people have received the Blessing for single persons or for already married couples. I believe that all of this is attributable to the efforts invested by all members in taking the HTM Leader

School centering on the minister.

(5) Sasaki Junko's testimony of Sennan Church's purification jeongseong

On the day of my father's anniversary, I discovered that I had a lump under my chin. My father died due to lymph gland cancer. I was worried that I might die of the same disease, so I went to hospitals and received different check-ups. I was not surprised that I had gotten a disease, since spiritual battles are always raging. Each time this happened, I went to a big bathhouse together with my church sisters, thanks to the church leader who organized the trip. I was so grateful for the hot bath and uttered, "Thank you, church leader. Thank you, God." In the bathhouse, my gratitude became deeper and I was able to purify myself.

"I am sorry. Please forgive me. Thank You. I love You. I will unite." When I said these words, tears began to fall. I could imagine the spiritual suffering my father must had had to endure while on earth. I also could realize that True Parents have been winning such spiritual battles through the ways of Divine Principle and true love.

"I am sorry that I have fallen ill at such a time. Had I not found True Parents and received the Blessing, I would have died much earlier. Thank You for allowing me to live so long. I am very happy. Thank you." This was my confession. I continued to say these words in the bathhouse. "God, True Parents, thank You. I love You." I repeated these words with tears falling down my cheeks. The lump under my chin began to decrease in size and became softer and softer. After 40 days, it completely disappeared. God, True Parents, thank You. I offer my sincere gratitude to Heavenly Parent, who has allowed me this miracle of hoondok mind and body purification jeongseong.

(6) Choi Dae-shik, the minister at the East Okayama church

True Father had directed me to go to Unification Theological Seminary in 2001, while I was serving as a minister in Japan. That is where I met Professor Gil Young-hwan, who also was studying at UTS. The concept of home group was not born yet. Instead, we were organizing "cell groups," which are the root of today's home group. We created a cell group called "Gathering of Love," and this group lasted for two years.

I talked with the regional director, Mr. Sano, and invited Professor Gil to Okayama seven times to teach us about home group and coaching. The members of my church participated with great interest, and the number of home groups soared to 26 at that time. Many amazing things happened when the members began to offer purification jeongseong. Many wives who were beaten often by their husband offered the purification jeongseong and saw improvements in their relationship.

Members who previously left the church but came back through home group activities are making large donations and receiving the Blessing. They are helping the world providence greatly. Their changes are especially attributable to Professor Gil's coaching classes. The church members in the East Okayama church are afraid of their family members, relatives and friends. They were able to overcome the fear through home group and coaching, and began to understand that an explosive increase in witnessing is possible through coaching. The church leader has been visiting each member's house and explaining about purification jeongseong in order to advance heavenly tribal messiah activities to the next level. This year, we will continue to work toward establishing the HTM Leader School.

3. Asia Pacific Region's Report on Heavenly Tribal Messiah Activities through Home Groups

(1) Yong Chung-sik, regional director of the Asia Pacific Region

The explosive growth of home groups and leader school is the reason for the success of heavenly tribal messiah activities in Asia. Six strategic nations already have seen their heavenly tribal messiah activities grow, and we are now training the blessed members to create and manage home groups. Cambodia and Thailand, especially, have experienced an increased number of regular members in places where the home group system is firmly established. The term "home group" is essentially another name for trinity, the core mission strategy devised by True Parents. The expansion of trinities helped spread the Family Federation around the globe.

As the person in charge of the Asia Pacific Region, I am working to realize the continued expansion of trinities, our mission strategy. This will mean the expansion of home groups. The members of these groups then will be educated and trained to complete their own heavenly tribal messiah activities. Twelve persons who have completed their heavenly tribal messiah activities have turned all the 430 families in their tribe into regular members, and their models of success will be repeated in other countries. Everyone in the Asia Pacific Region will work hard and use the home group system and leader school, which have been developed for more than 10 years, to realize True Mother's wish of Vision 2020.

(2) Yutaka Yamada, the national leader of Malaysia

Heaven has blessed us with the application of home group and leader school to the Unification Movement in Malaysia. The Blessing is especially precious for our blessed families. One good thing about home groups is that they provide a place for members to create heartistic relationships. Of course, they see each other during Sunday services. However, Sunday gatherings often do not lead to deeper heartistic relationships.

Home groups create a place where the members in a trinity, or just three families, can get together to talk about their feelings, their everyday challenges, and the ways to work together.

The life of a home group does not end with the assignment of three families. Its 16-week program helps the members develop heartistically. This program is very easy to follow, yet spiritually rich. The members can feel the joy and happiness that they felt when they first joined the church. That is why it is very good for building heartistic relationships between members.

Second, home groups provide a platform for witnessing. The members of a home group can gather at any place, either their home or a coffee shop. A home group is filled with joy, so it's not difficult to invite someone, and a new person can be assimilated into the group easily. If church is like school, a home group can be compared to home. Instead of sending your witnessing candidates straight to the church, you can invite them to your home first and help them grow a little before they can go to the school, meaning church. This helps the candidates to grow spiritually upon the foundation made through the home group.

Home groups gather once a week, not because they were told to do so by the church but because the members themselves want to. Some people even say that they can't wait until the next home group gathering. A home group is a meaningful instrument in witnessing activities. A home group can start with just three persons, with the aim to increase its membership in the future. Based on True Parents' teachings, the home group system gives immense joy to the members. I firmly believe that this is the most fundamental and correct path toward the creation of Cheon Il Guk. It is still in an early stage, but we are already seeing good results. We have high hopes for this system. We will do our utmost to establish the substantial Cheon Il Guk.

(3) Hajime Saito, Cheon Il Guk Special Emissary to Cambodia

I received a great inspiration regarding the management of hoondok families. Professor Gil Young-hwan from Sun Moon University visited the Asia region and helped us implement the home group system. Since then, we have been showing many positive results. Given its communist history, Cambodia still has the past habit of creating groups of five persons. All we had to do was use these small groups and infuse them with our home group trinity materials.

Guiding the already blessed 430 family members is very important. This is possible through raising 43 leaders and guiding them to take care of 10 families each. This also means that 43 lecturers are required as well. To raise 43 lecturers, we need 12 leaders who can play a central role. To raise 12 leaders, we need three top-level leaders, meaning a trinity. True Father talked often about trinities during his early years of ministry. The three top-level leaders form a trinity, and this trinity continues to reproduce until it has reached 430 families. We don't need to look any further than True Mother's *Cheon Seong Gyeong, Pyeong Hwa Gyeong, Chambumo Gyeong*; they contain all the information we need to raise leaders. Educating "outside" leaders through Asian Leadership Conferences is merely an expansion of what True Parents used to do. This means that success is guaranteed if you follow the footsteps of True Parents, and the exact method of how to do this is already written down in *Cheon Seong Gyeong, Pyeong Hwa Gyeong, and Chambumo Gyeong*.

The heavenly tribal messiah activities that are experiencing an explosive growth in Cambodia also started here. Everyone is amazed how fast home groups based on trinities are expanding. I wish that, in the near future, the world will see many successful heavenly tribal messiah activities through the multiplication of home groups.

(4) Reflection on Philippines Workshop

◇ I learned a lot about home groups. All the participants were reminded of the importance of home groups. I will make a commitment to form a home group and achieve the three great blessings. I will follow the simple steps of the home group in order to achieve the positions of true parent, true teacher, and true owner. I will strengthen my home group and multiply it. Thank you!

◇ I am good at making relationships with other blessed members. This lecture has helped me understand that we need a proper method of managing the process. The members who are working at the forefront need more than just theories. They need a way to actually practice those theories. That is why a framework for practice is imperative. Theory is one thing and the reality is another. I will do my very best to help the people who are managing that practice stage through the trinity and the home group.

◇ Today's lecture was amazing. I am very thankful for the lecture-because I was able to apply it to practice immediately. I have understood the value of the trinity that can lead to a home group and 430 families. My original mind is awakened, and I want to become the source of light in the darkness that spreads this message. I will begin the revolution with myself, centering on the vision and mission given to me by Heavenly Parent and True Parents. I want to fulfill my portion of responsibility through purifying myself and creating a true family. This lecture has given me the means to become one of the true sons and daughters of Heaven, and for this I am very grateful.

◇ This workshop was immensely helpful in helping me to realize the importance of awakening my inner strength. I feel that now I can talk to Heavenly Parent every day, and it has given me the potential to become the heavenly tribal messiah of my tribe.

◇ I realized that Professor Gil is doing a perfect job in giving his lectures to the families in Philippines. He shows clearly why the power of the trinity is an integral part of heavenly tribal messiah activities. The formation of trinities is a revelation that has been given to us by True Parents.

◇ I have wasted a great deal of my life because I did not know the essence of my destiny. What I had to do more than anything was know what it is that I desire, what I need, and how I can achieve it. Listening to the lectures helped me feel more confident and made me realize what I have to do.

Bibliography

Covey, Steven. *Seven Habits of Leadership Success, Korean edition.* Seoul: Kim Yeong Publishing, 2017. Cominsky, Joel. How to Be a Great Cell-Group Coach, Korean edition. Seoul: NCD, 2000.

Editorial committee for the Collected Sermons of Sun Myung Moon, Ed. *Collected Sermons of the Rev.* Sun Myung Moon, vol. 3. Seoul: Sung Hwa Publishing, 1957.

Editorial committee. *Sermons, vol.* 5. Seoul: Sung Hwa, 1958.

Editorial committee. *Sermons, vol.* 8. Seoul: Sung Hwa, 1959.

Editorial committee. *Sermons, vol.* 11. Seoul: Sung Hwa, 1960.

Editorial committee. *Sermons, vol.* 12. Seoul: Sung Hwa, 1962.

Editorial committee. *Sermons, vol.* 15. Seoul: Sung Hwa, 1965.

Editorial committee. *Sermons, vol.* 17. Seoul: Sung Hwa, 1966.

Editorial committee. *Sermons, vol.* 18. Seoul: Sung Hwa, 1967.

Editorial committee. *Sermons, vol.* 19. Seoul: Sung Hwa, 1967.

Editorial committee. *Sermons, vol.* 25. Seoul: Sung Hwa, 1969.
Editorial committee. *Sermons, vol.* 29. Seoul: Sung Hwa, 1970.
Editorial committee. *Sermons, vol.* 30. Seoul: Sung Hwa, 1970.
Editorial committee. *Sermons, vol.* 33. Seoul: Sung Hwa, 1970.
Editorial committee. *Sermons, vol.* 36. Seoul: Sung Hwa, 1970.
Editorial committee. *Sermons, vol.* 40. Seoul: Sung Hwa, 1971.
Editorial committee. *Sermons, vol.* 42. Seoul: Sung Hwa, 1971.
Editorial committee. *Sermons, vol.* 43. Seoul: Sung Hwa, 1971.
Editorial committee. *Sermons, vol.* 44. Seoul: Sung Hwa, 1971.
Editorial committee. *Sermons, vol.* 45. Seoul: Sung Hwa, 1971.
Editorial committee. *Sermons, vol.* 73. Seoul: Sung Hwa, 1974.
Editorial committee. *Sermons, vol.* 76. Seoul: Sung Hwa, 1975.
Editorial committee. *Sermons, vol.* 91. Seoul: Sung Hwa, 1977.
Editorial committee. *Sermons, vol.* 102. Seoul: Sung Hwa, 1979.
Editorial committee. *Sermons, vol.* 107. Seoul: Sung Hwa, 1980.
Editorial committee. *Sermons, vol.* 112. Seoul: Sung Hwa, 1981.
Editorial committee. *Sermons, vol.* 113. Seoul: Sung Hwa, 1981.
Editorial committee. *Sermons, vol.* 115. Seoul: Sung Hwa, 1981.
Editorial committee. *Sermons, vol.* 149. Seoul: Sung Hwa, 1986.
Editorial committee. *Sermons, vol.* 168. Seoul: Sung Hwa, 1987.
Editorial committee. *Sermons, vol.* 185. Seoul: Sung Hwa, 1989.
Editorial committee. *Sermons, vol.* 216. Seoul: Sung Hwa, 1991.
Editorial committee. *Sermons, vol.* 254. Seoul: Sung Hwa, 1994.
Editorial committee. *Sermons, vol.* 262. Seoul: Sung Hwa, 1994.
Editorial committee. *Sermons, vol.* 292. Seoul: Sung Hwa, 1998.
Editorial committee. *Sermons, vol.* 293. Seoul: Sung Hwa, 1998.

Editorial committee. *Sermons*, vol. 295. Seoul: Sung Hwa, 1998.

Family Federation for World Peace and Unification, ed. *True Parents' Life Course*, vol. 3. Seoul: Sung Hwa Publishing, 2001.

Family Federation for World Peace and Unification, ed. *The Holy Scriptures of Cheon Il Guk: Cheon Seong Gyeong*. Seoul: Sung Hwa Publishing, 2014.

Gil Yeong-hwan. *Growth in the Family Federation*. Chungnam: Sun Moon University Press, 2002.

Gil Yeong-hwan. *HTM Leader School*. Chungnam: Sun Moon University Press, 2016.

Gil Yeong-hwan, et al. *Introduction to Coaching*. Seoul: Shin Jeong Publishing, 2003.

Gil Yeong-hwan. *Introduction to Unification Mission Work*. Chungnam: Sun Moon University Press, 2003.

Gil Yeong-hwan. "*HTM Leader School*," *Tongil Segye*, vol. 33. Seoul: Sung Hwa Publishing, 2016.

Neighbor, Ralph. *Where Do We Go from Here: A Guidebook for the Cell Church, Korean edition*. Seoul: NCD, 2000.

Warren, Rick. *The Purpose Driven Church, Korean edition*. Seoul: Timothy Book, 2008

Unification Thought Institute. *Unification Thought Summary*. Chungnam: Sun Moon University Press, 2007.

A GLOSSARY OF KEY TERMS

home church :
A style of community ministry that was emphasized in the Unification movement in the 1980s. Each blessed family had the mission to create a model home and family and seek to love and care for 360 families living nearby. Providentially the home church movement had the goal of restoring from Satan the authority of the eldest son.

tribal messiah mission :
The tribal messiah mission was the family ministry that followed home church. Starting in 1991, blessed families were called to return to their home towns and minister to their extended families and others in their home towns. Tribal messiahs worked to bless 160 couples to the Blessing. The tribal messiah age led to the restoration of the authority of parents.

family church / hoondok family church :
The age of hoondok family church was declared in 2005. From this time forward each blessed family was called to establish a hoondok family church, establish

a strong tradition of hoondokhae in their families, and put into practice what they learned through hoondokhae in ministering to their extended families and neighbors. Through hoondok family church the authority of the king was restored.

heavenly tribal messiah mission :
The role of heavenly tribal messiahs was first introduced in March 2012, and True Father emphasized it again in his final prayer. Working in their hometowns or another mission area, heavenly tribal messiahs can shorten the time required for the complete restoration of their lineage from a vertical period of seven generations to as little as one generation, by liberating and blessing 430 vertical generations of their ancestors, and gathering and blessing a horizontal tribe of 430 families, with three generations of their families working together.

home group :
A small group of people, often organized around a few families, who gather regularly as a community of faith, to pray, study, fellowship and minister together. In heavenly tribal messiah activities, a home group sometimes serves as a local pioneer church center.

small group :
see "home group"

midsize group :
A community of faith formed by combining a number of small groups which are in the same vicinity, to work together and support each other, by organizing education programs or community events, for example.

large group :
A larger local church or center which provides opportunities for weekly worship, workshops, and other support services. Parts of the congregation might separate off into small groups and create new pioneer centers.

jeongseong :

An act of devotion, service or care offered to mobilize spiritual support and protection as part of a life of faith. Jeongseong can include prayer, bowing conditions, fasting, taking special care of people, cleaning the church, cooking a special meal, writing letters, and many other types of offering of heart.

"To offer jeongseong means to do your utmost internally and externally. You must offer everything, combining your words, your attitude, your mind and thoughts, all your actions, everything in the internal and external realities of your life." [CSG 11.1.2.1]

hyojeong :

A heart of filial devotion, love given by children in response to the love they have received from their parents, and the exchange of heart between humankind and Heavenly Parent, who also stand in a parent–child relationship. A heart of hyojeong is the starting point of a world that expresses the ideal of creation.

hoondokhae :

Hoondokhae is a meeting where people gather to read, discuss and understand the teachings of True Parents. It is also a time for offering jeongseong of the mind and the body. By engaging in hoondok reading with the whole mind and body, we participate in "hoondok mind-body purification jeongseong."

Cheon Il Guk :

Cheon Il Guk is the shortened name for "Cheonju Pyeonghwa Tongil Guk," which is the "Cosmic Nation of Peace and Unity." Cheon Il Guk is the kingdom of heaven on earth, which we build by practicing what we have learned about love and living for the sake of others.

Seonghwa :

In the Unification movement, the transition from life in the world of air to life in the world of love is call *Seonghwa* (成和: completion and harmony) The end of life in the world of air is nothing to be feared, but is a time of ascending nobly to heaven. When we gather for a Seonghwa Service after somebody has ascended, we celebrate their life up until now, and rejoice for their coming life.

BonHyang Won :
True Father's final resting place above Cheon Jeong Gung is called *BonHyang Won*, which means "garden of the original homeland."

weonjeon / Paju Weonjeon :
Weonjeon is the word used to describe a memorial garden where Unificationists have been laid to rest. The Paju Weonjeon is a special weonjeon in Paju, Korea, for members of the True Family and early church members.

supporters :
Already married couples who received the Blessing through Heavenly Tribal Messiah activities, or other active supporters of FFWPU and/or related providential organizations.

registered members :
Members who attend worship services or donate at least once every six months.

associate members :
Members who donate (tithe if possible) and attend at least two worship services every three months.

regular members :
Members who tithe twice and attend at least six worship services every three months.

Editors
Wonju McDevitt (Head Editor, Chief of Staff, Dr. Hak Ja Han Moon's Secretariat)
Yun Young-ho (Secretary General, FFWPUI HQ)
Yong Jin-hun (Director, FFWPUI HQ Heavenly Tribal Messiah Academy)

Writers
Gil Young-hwan (Publishing Committee Chair, Sun Moon University)
Jo Han-sik (Sun Moon University)

Heavenly Tribal Messiah Collection 4 Management Care
Managing and Caring for Your Heavenly Tribe

Published June 21, 2018

First edition © 2018
Layout by Sung Hwa Publishing Co., Korea
Published by Heavenly Tribal Messiah Academy
Printed by HSA-Books, New York, NY   June 2019

www.ingramcontent.com/pod-product-compliance
Lightning Source LLC
Chambersburg PA
CBHW050611300426
44112CB00012B/1455